The Use and Abuse of Literature

The Use
and Abuse
of Literature

MARJORIE GARBER

Pantheon Books, New York

Pantheon Books and colophon are registered trademarks of Random House, Inc.

Grateful acknowledgment is made to the following for permission to reprint previously
published material: Alfred A. Knopf: Excerpts from "The Man on the Dump" from
The Collected Poems of Wallace Stevens, copyright © 1942 by Wallace Stevens and
renewed 1970 by Holly Stevens. Reprinted by permission of Alfred A. Knopf,
a division of Random House, Inc. • Anne Bernays: Letter to the editor, printed in
The New York Times, March 7, 2008. Reprinted by permission of the author. •
Houghton Mifflin Harcourt Publishing Company: Excerpt from "Burnt Norton" from
Four Quartets by T. S. Eliot, copyright © 1936 by Harcourt, Inc. and renewed 1964 by
T. S. Eliot. Reprinted by permission of Houghton Mifflin Harcourt Publishing
Company. • Random House, Inc.: Excerpts from "In Memory of W. B. Yeats"
from *Collected Poems of W. H. Auden*, copyright © 1940 and renewed 1968
by W. H. Auden. Reprinted by permission of Random House, Inc.

Library of Congress Cataloging-in-Publication Data

Garber, Marjorie
The use and abuse of literature / Marjorie Garber.
p.   cm.
Includes index.
ISBN 978-0-375-42434-2
1. Literature—Philosophy. 2. Literature—Appreciation. I. Title.
PN45.G312 2011   801—dc22   2010035417

www.pantheonbooks.com

Jacket design by Brian Barth

Printed in the United States of America

First Edition

2 4 6 8 9 7 5 3 1

FOR JANE GALLOP

Contents

Acknowledgments

This is a book about my lifelong engagement with literature and language, about the way I have come to think and live through literature, and about how literature thinks and lives through human beings.

The genesis of the project came in a conversation with my editor, Erroll McDonald, and my agent, Beth Vesel. To them I am enormously grateful, as always, for their commitment to the vital centrality of reading, writing, and thinking about literature and culture, and for their extraordinary faith in me.

I owe a particular debt of gratitude to Sol Kim Bentley, whose editorial eye and unerring sense of literary form and style was joined with a generosity of time and spirit as she read, with care, through the final text. Alexander Raymond, Sanders Bernstein, Eliza Hornig, and Daniel Wenger worked with imagination and energy to help find documents and check sources. Sara Bartel was of great assistance in helping me to balance teaching, scholarship, and administration during the time it took to assemble the materials for this book, and then to write it.

The book is dedicated to Jane Gallop, a wonderful close reader. To her I am indebted for gifts of friendship and of writing and reading that I can never adequately repay. William Germano has been, throughout the writing process, an invaluable ally and friend. Finally, I thank Joanna Lipper, who has given me a vision of the future that extends, like literature, far beyond what the eye can see.

The Use and Abuse of Literature

Introduction

At the beginning of the twenty-first century, the National Endowment for the Arts reported a disturbing drop in the number of Americans who read "literary" works. Drawing upon responses to the 2002 Census survey, which had asked more than seventeen thousand adults whether they had read any novels, short stories, poetry, or plays in their leisure time, the NEA noted that 45 percent said they had read some fiction, 12 percent had read some poetry, and only 4 percent had read a play. These findings, published in *Reading at Risk: A Survey of Literary Reading in America,* showed an alarming decline of reading in all age groups across the country, and especially among eighteen- to twenty-four-year-olds. The chairman of the NEA termed the results an indication of a "national crisis," one that reflected "a general collapse in advanced literacy," and a loss that "impoverishes both cultural and civic life."[1]

Among the report's "10 key findings" were that under half of the adult American population now reads literature; that although women read more than men ("Only slightly more than one-third of adult American males now read literature"), reading rates were declining for both men and women; that reading among persons at every level of education, including college graduates and postgraduates, had declined over the past twenty years; and that "literary reading strongly correlates other forms of active civic participation," including volunteer and charity work, cultural involvement with museums and the performing arts, and attendance at sporting events. It was less surprising to find that competition with other modes of information, like the Internet, video games, and portable digital devices, had a negative effect upon the number of adults who regularly read.[2] Race and ethnicity seemed not to be crucial factors: the rates of decline included whites, African Americans, and Hispanics. "Listening" to literature counted as a kind of reading for this survey, although watching films did not: women are more likely to listen to novels or poetry than men, whites more likely to listen to book readings, African Americans most likely to listen to poetry readings. Here the report suggests that "in part" the reason may be "the popularity of dub and slam poetry readings in the U.S."[3]

The idea that fiction/nonfiction should be the determining category for "literary/nonliterary" is spelled out in a brief section called "Literature vs. Books," in which "literature" is explicitly defined as including "popular genres such as mysteries, as well as contemporary and classic literary fiction. No distinctions were drawn on the quality of literary works."[4] So a work of "literature" for the purposes of respondents to this survey could be a Harlequin romance or a Sidney Sheldon novel but not Gibbon's *The Decline and Fall of the Roman Empire,* or Machiavelli's *The Prince,* or David McCullough's biography of Harry Truman. I can understand why the survey wanted to make some kind of distinction, and I agree with the democratic decision not to judge works on their putative "quality" (which, in any case, a longer historical view would show is likely to change over time). But the decision to exclude "nonfiction," or what an older tradition once dubbed "intellectual prose," does seem to undercut a little the message that "anyone who loves literature or values the cultural, intellectual, and political importance of active and engaged literacy in American society will respond to this report with grave concern."[5]

There was a time when the word *literature* meant an acquaintance with "letters" or books—the confident possession, that is, of humane learning and literary culture. "He had probably more than common literature," wrote Dr. Johnson about the poet John Milton. "His literature was unquestionably great. He read all the languages which are considered either as learned or polite"[6] Although Milton *wrote* great literature, that is not what Johnson's sentence says. It says that he *had* literature, which is to say learning, a familiarity with and understanding of words and texts. The nineteenth-century novelist Maria Edgeworth uses *literature* in a similar way, describing "A woman of considerable information and literature."[7] This sense of the word is now generally obsolete, and would, as is the fate of such obsolescences, undoubtedly be regarded as an error if used in the same way today. For example, if I were to write that J. M. Coetzee "had great literature," any copy editor would immediately "correct" my phrase to say that Coetzee *wrote* great literature. The new meaning, the only meaning current in departments and programs of literature, is this:

> Literary productions as a whole; the body of writings produced in a particular country or period, or in the world in general. Now also in a more restricted sense, applied to writing which has claim to consideration on the ground of beauty of form or emotional effect. (*Oxford English Dictionary* 3a.)

It's worth noting that the first instance of this use of the term given in the historical dictionary of the English language is comparatively recent—1812—hundreds of years after Chaucer and Shakespeare (and, of course, thousands of years after the Greek and Latin "classics"). Thus, over the centuries in England, the U.S., and indeed in France, "literature" has changed from a personal attribute or characteristic (something one *has*) to an institution and a product (something one *writes* or *knows*).

Concurrent with this development was the emergence of a personage called a "man of letters," whose profession was the production of literary work, whether or not he—or, latterly, she—actually earned a living by writing. Here is Sir Walter Scott, one of the most financially successful of nineteenth-century novelists: "I determined that literature should be my staff, but not my crutch, and that the profits of my literary labour . . . should not . . . become necessary to my ordinary expenses."[8] For Scott, literature was a product of "labour" and produced "profits" of a pecuniary as well as of a more rarefied kind. Despite his disclaimer, he speaks here as a professional man.

At the same time that a specifically high-cultural sense of literature was coming into currency, what we might call the general case of *literature* as meaning any body of writing on a given subject ("the scientific literature") was developing, again concurrent with the establishment of academic and technical disciplines, each of which was supported and buttressed by specialist publications that came to be called a "literature." And below that, if we might speak for a moment in terms of cultural hierarchy, was the most general case of all, the equation of *literature* with all printed matter. It's instructive to see the sequence of examples offered by the *OED* for what it still calls a colloquial usage:

1895   "In canvassing, in posters, and in the distribution of what, by a profane perversion of language, is called 'literature.'"

1900   "A more judicious distribution of posters, and what is termed 'literature.'"

1938   "It is some literature from the Travel Bureau."

1962   "Full details and literature from: Yugoslav National Tourist Office."

1973   "I talked my throat dry, gave away sheaves of persuasive literature."

Where, at the end of the nineteenth century, this use of the term was deemed profane and perverse, and thus encased in scare quotes, by the late twentieth century (the citation is from a 1973 crime novel by Dick Francis), the word *literature* no longer needed parsing or protecting and was routinely used to describe flyers, brochures, and other disposable printed stuff.

So the meanings of *literature* as a term have, perhaps paradoxically, moved both "up" and "down" in recent years. On the one hand, it now seems to denote a particular reading, writing, and publishing practice associated with middle to high culture, with the notion of a literary canon, and with English majors; on the other hand, it has been co-opted— or universalized—so that it means just about anything professional— or research-based—written in words.

In the pages that follow I will attempt not only to argue for but also to invoke and demonstrate the "uses" of reading and of literature, not as an instrument of moral or cultural control, nor yet as an infusion of "pleasure," but rather as a *way of thinking*. That is why, in my view, it is high time to take back the term *literature*. To do so will mean explaining why reading—not skimming for information or for the plot (or for the sexy, titillating "good parts" of a novel or a political exposé)—is really hard to do; and why the very uselessness of literature is its most profound and valuable attribute. The result of such a radical reorientation of our understanding of what it means to read, and to read literature, and to read in a "literary" way, would be enormous. A better understanding of these questions is the only way to return literature to the center, rather than the periphery, of personal, educational, and professional life.

Literature Then and Now

The word *literary* does not appear in Samuel Johnson's *A Dictionary of the English Language* (1755). Though based on the substantive *literature*, which—as we've seen—itself originally meant "humane learning," *literary* evolved, from the eighteenth century to the present, as something between a compliment and an epithet. Like other, similar concepts and terms, this one changed as its context changed. From the qualitative categories of "literary merit," "literary reputation," and "literary education" (all eighteenth-century usages) to the social and economic realms of "literary dinner," "literary lunch," "literary circle," "literary agent," and "literary executor" (all hallmarks of twentieth- and twenty-first-century culture), the uses and fortunes of *literary* have fluctuated and either evolved or devolved depending upon one's view. When fewer persons were literate in the most basic sense, that is, able to read, a person of literature or literary training was a prized, if undercompensated, member of society (Oliver Goldsmith: "A man of literary merit is sure of being caressed by the great, though seldom enriched").[9]

The nineteenth century made celebrities of some of its writers. Dickens and Wilde toured triumphantly in America, while "Longfellow . . . largely paid the poet's penalty of being made the lion of all the drawing rooms."[10] (A characteristic modern version of this "lionization" is a handbook called *Sleeping with Literary Lions*—which, despite its title, is not a hookup service but a guide to U.S. bed-and-breakfasts located near literary landmarks.) Today novelists and poets are read and praised, but by a smaller subsection of the population, since they now compete with films, television, the Internet, and other modes of cultural leisure.

"America's favorite book," according to a Harris poll that sampled just over 2,500 people, is, unsurprisingly, the Bible. As the proponents of the Butler Act in the famous Scopes trial controversy about evolution learned, not everyone will agree about what the Bible is, but let us put that question aside for a moment. The second favorite for men is *The Lord of the Rings;* the second favorite for women, *Gone with the Wind*. Others in the top ten include J. K. Rowling's Harry Potter books, Stephen King's *The Stand,* Ayn Rand's *Atlas Shrugged,* Dan Brown's *The Da Vinci Code,* Harper Lee's *To Kill a Mockingbird,* and J. D. Salinger's *The Catcher in the Rye.*[11]

Even with a tiny sample, this is a dispiriting list, suggesting that after high school (where *To Kill a Mockingbird* and *The Catcher in the Rye* remain on required reading lists), what used to be known as "canonical literature" is nowhere in sight.

But what is the use of literature? Does it make us happier, more ethical, more articulate? Better citizens, better companions and lovers? Better businesspersons, better doctors and lawyers? More well-rounded individuals? Does it make us more human? Or simply human? Is what is being sought a kind of literary Rolodex, a personal *Bartlett's Familiar Quotations* of apt literary references ("To be or not to be?" "Only connect"; "Do I dare to eat a peach?")—phrases that can be trotted out on suitable occasions, at the dinner table, or on the golf course? Such literary taglines or touchstones were once a kind of cultural code of mutual recognition among educated people—but their place has long been taken by references from film, video, TV, rock music, advertising, or other modes of popular culture. Is literature something that everyone should study in the same way that we should study other basic cultural facts about the world we live in, like the history of art or the history of music, studying them all in one fell swoop, in survey courses or general introductions or appreciations?

Why read literature? Why listen to it on audiotapes or at poetry slams or at the theater? Why buy it? And even if you enjoy reading literature, why *study* it?

What do we mean by *literature* today, when the term is used by medical and technical professionals to mean "instructional brochures" and by social scientists to mean "a survey of academic research"? "Please send me the latest literature on your new headache drug" or "your most recent software" or "your latest cell phone." "Enclosed you will find a review of the literature on gender discrimination in higher education." Indeed, the relationship between *literature* and *litter*, though not etymologically correct, seems seductively close. (This homology, in fact, occurred to Jacques Lacan, who attributed it to James Joyce.)[12] Literature is, all too often, pieces of paper we should consult for expertise but often simply toss in a drawer or in the trash.

To overschematize a little for the sake of argument, let us say that there are two poles in the debate over the "use" or "value" of literature. One pole is utilitarian or instrumental: the idea that literature is good for you because it produces beneficial societal effects: better citizens, for example, or more ethically attuned reasoners. The other pole might be characterized as ecstatic, affective, or mystical: the idea that literature is a pleasurable jolt to the system, a source of powerful feeling that—rather like Judge Potter Stewart's famous pronouncement about pornography—is unmistakable even if undefinable. (For Stewart's "I know it when I see it," we could substitute "I know it when I read it / hear it.") Emily Dickinson's "If I feel physically as if the top of my head were taken off, I know that is poetry" is perhaps the best-known expression of this view. It's worth quoting the longer passage from which this sentence is excerpted, since it makes the point even more vividly:

> If I read a book and it makes my whole body so cold no fire can ever warm me, I know that is poetry. If I feel physically as if the top of my head were taken off, I know that is poetry. These are the only ways I know it. Is there any other way?[13]

The poet A. E. Housman offered a similar somatic test:

> Experience has taught me, when I am shaving of a morning, to keep watch over my thoughts, because, if a line of poetry strays into my memory, my skin bristles so that the razor ceases to act."[14]

For Housman, a noted classical scholar who prized the intellect, poetry was nonetheless "more physical than intellectual." Other symptoms he reported included "a shiver down the spine," "a constriction in the throat and a precipitation of water to the eyes," and a sensation in the pit of the stomach that he likened to a phrase from Keats, when "everything . . . goes through me like a spear." Although these symptoms may sound painful, Housman clearly associates them with a singular kind of pleasure.

So, once again: "feels good" or "is good for you." Both of these desiderata, we might think, are covered by Horace's *Ars Poetica*, with its celebrated advice that poetry should be *"dulce et utile,"* its aims to delight and to instruct.

A latter-day "Ars Poetica"—one too often dismissed these days— is the popular poem by Archibald MacLeish, with its two famous and quotable pronouncements:

> A poem should be equal to:
> Not true.

And

A poem should not mean
But be.

These precepts, so perfectly attuned to close reading and New Critical thinking, also embody a sentiment elegantly summarized by Keats when he wrote, "We hate poetry that has a palpable design upon us—and if we do not agree, seems to put its hand into its breeches pocket."[15] Yet some of the best literature, whether poetry or prose, has been polemical, political, and/or religious (not always in an orthodox way; think of Blake, whose Jerusalem hymn is, ironically, sung in churches all over Britain). Some of the novels of Dickens (the Brontës, Woolf, Conrad, Lawrence, Cervantes, Flaubert) have had palpable designs for political, social, or moral change, as have the great epics, from those by Homer and Virgil to those by Milton and Joyce. This palpable design of epic is the glorification of nationalism and empire; Wordsworth's personal epic, *The Prelude,* acknowledges the boldness of using such a public genre for chronicling "the growth of a poet's mind." But MacLeish's poem is a poem about poems. Paradoxically, this witty, sensuous verse about what poetry should not do—it should not "mean," it should not be taken as true— has been read both as a truism and as an explanation of a poem's proper "meaning."

Before we leave the questions of whether and how literature can be good for you, we should perhaps note that in the matter of whether works of fiction should model—or inculcate—virtue and morality, "good for you" and "bad for you" have the same status. Both are judgmental and moral. These effects may be claimed or discerned by preachers or censors or even by the courts. But they are incidental and accidental by-products of literature, not literary qualities. In *The Art of Fiction,* Henry James queried the whole category of the morality of the novel: "Will you not define your terms and explain how (a novel being a picture) a picture can be either moral or immoral? You wish to paint a moral picture or carve a moral statue; will you not tell us how you would set about it? We are discussing the Art of Fiction; questions of art are questions (in the widest sense) of execution; questions of morality are quite another affair . . .

The only condition that I can think of attaching to the composition of the novel is . . . that it be interesting."[16]

There have always been schools of thought about literature and its value, or lack of value, from Plato's suspicions of poetry to Aristotle's codification of its terms and rules. (The fact that Plato's chosen form was the dialogue, and Aristotle's, the category, sorts oddly with their views, since Plato is arguably writing "literature," just as Aristotle is writing "criticism.") Horace's *Ars Poetica* claimed literature as an art or craft— just what Plato said it was not—and proposed genial, workmanlike procedures for the aspiring poet. Pope and others followed in this tradition, establishing what are sometimes thought of as classical rules, only to be disrupted by the return of admiration for the mad or inspired poet, a taste often associated with Romanticism. There were vatic, inspired, and mad poets before the Romantic period, and classical poets during it; like all pairs of opposites, these are as much alike as they are different. It is the claim of their difference, the insistence on the overthrow of the imprisoning past at the same time that the past is inevitably repeated, that produces the dialectical push and pull of literary history—and often generates some of the best kinds of literary criticism. But it is hard to imagine today the claims for the *importance* of literature that were still being debated in the middle of the twentieth century. What happened to the primacy of literature, once regarded as the indispensable lingua franca for educated men and women?

Matthew Arnold considered a knowledge of literature to be beneficial not only to the critical thinking and moral health of the individual but also to a program of social advancement. In his work as an inspector of schools, he saw English education as a way of "civilizing the next generation of the lower classes, who, as things are going, will have most of the political power of the country in their hands."[17] It's important to note from today's vantage point that Arnold—who was named professor of poetry at Oxford during the period when he also served as a government schools inspector—understood literature to be a key aspect of social improvement, both for the individual and for the general culture. In his view, poetry and criticism were not merely pleasant diversions but, rather, undertakings as serious and valuable as moneymaking or scientific advancement. The way to secure the future of England—then a Victorian powerhouse of industry and empire—and the future of the laboring classes, was through literary education, a kind of education heretofore regarded as the privilege of the privileged.

Today that sense has pretty much disappeared, replaced by expertise in science and in information technology, on the one hand, and by visual literacy on the other. By *visual,* what is now meant is moving images (films, videos, television, MTV, advertising) as well as paintings and photographs. Quotable quotes are far more likely to be cited from films, television, or advertisements than from literature. "Just do it." "Go ahead, make my day." "I'll be back." Even politicians, who once studiously quoted poets and philosophers, now choose slogans and citations from popular culture. "Mission accomplished." "Bring 'em on." So the idea that knowledge of and easy familiarity with literature is either a social accomplishment or a cultural or professional asset must seem quaint. Yet the wordplay involved in coining terms for modern popular culture—especially in visual rebuses like INXS, Ludacris, or Xzibit—is not completely dissimilar to the kind of visual cleverness in, for example, the hieroglyphic poems of George Herbert in the seventeenth century.

After a spurt of enthusiasm among scholars in adjacent fields like history, anthropology, and philosophy—the so-called linguistic turn of the 1970s and 1980s—literature, literary theory, and literary studies have fallen behind in both academic cachet and intellectual influence. More to the point—for the key questions here do not concern scholars so much as they do readers and the general public—literature is often undervalued or misunderstood as something that needs to be applied to the experiences of life. Practical concerns with careers and financial security have dominated the choices made by ambitious and worried young people who want to make sure education fits them for the lives they think they want to lead. Careers in economics, banking, technology, or law do not include literature, except as an add-on or elective. Nor is the typical

English major necessarily the way to encounter literature in an active, inquiring way. Even when literature is read, taught, and studied, it is often interrogated for wisdom or moral lessons. The clumsy formulations I grew up with—what is the moral of the story? what is the hero's or heroine's tragic flaw?—still influence and flatten the questions people often ask about literary works, as if there were one answer, and a right answer, at that. The genius of literary study comes in asking questions, not in finding answers.

On the one side, hard science and social science, including technology; on the other side, contemporary visual and musical culture, framed by moving images, file swapping, and the Internet. Between these two poles, one of which implicitly defines literature as a potentially useful social enhancement for success in financial and practical life, the other one of which leaves literature behind in favor of livelier, more supposedly "interactive" cultural forms, literature has been devalued—sometimes for reasons that seem, on the surface, benevolent, and sometimes by those who profess to love it best.

In his essay collection *Promises, Promises,* psychoanalyst Adam Phillips refers with a sense of nostalgia to "what was once called Literature."

> Coming, as they say, from what was then called Literature as a student in the early 1970s, to psychoanalysis in the late 1970s, has made me wonder what I thought psychoanalysis could do for me—or what I wanted psychoanalysis to do for me—that Literature could not. And, of course, what I might have been using Literature for that made psychoanalysis the next best thing—or rather, the other best thing.[18]

And again,

> Anyone who loves what was once called Literature can teach it, write it, and of course, read it. But people who love psychoanalysis can teach it, write it, read it, *and* practise it. Because there is a real sense—a pragmatic sense—in which we can practise what Freud writes, we can wonder, by the same token, what it would be to prac-

tise Henry James or Shakespeare, and what the effect on our reading is when we are finding out how to do something.[19]

It wouldn't be unjust to call this set of constraints and wishes a kind of love letter, one that—from the author of a book on monogamy—represents a desire for both surprise and fulfillment. In seeking literature, Phillips found psychoanalysis. But having found psychoanalysis, he still fantasizes about his first love, literature. Phillips wants literature to have something like a use, what he calls a practice. But what if we were to understand literature as its own practice?

Central to this book is the question of how we can understand the importance of "what was once called Literature," and how we can distinguish it from other distinct, though valuable, human enterprises like morality, politics, and aesthetics. My purpose and my goal are to explain the specificity of literature and literary reading.

On the Importance of Unanswerable Questions

Philip Sidney wrote a *Defence of Poesie* in 1595. Percy Shelley wrote a *Defence of Poetry* in 1821. Why, we might ask, does literature have to defend itself?

In part, it's Plato's fault. His famous exiling of poets from a well-ordered republic, on the grounds that they offered *doxa*, or opinion, rather than *logos*, or reason/discourse, instantiated an unhappy split between what we now call art and what we now call science. For Plato, the classic Greek poets—Homer and the tragic dramatists—whose work had formed the basis of a Greek education (*paideia*) depicted in their work all manner of deleterious behavior: murder, incest, cruelty, cowardice, treachery, strong passions out of control. Poetry thus weakened moral character and potentially influenced both actor/performer and audience. Since *poetry* in this period meant oral poetry, whether epic or dramatic—not the reading and study of written texts—the possibility of such emotional effects, rather than a rational assessment and distance, was, he thought, strong. If a schoolchild memorized Homer on the wrath of Achilles, what he learned was wrath, not poetry.

From the perspective of a modern educational system, where poetry is far less central than it was to the ancient Greeks, Plato's insistence on the dangers of poetry and poets may seem either quaint or excessive. But that is because we have so diminished the importance of literature (and music and art) over the years.

Both in *Republic*, where he describes what he regards as an ideal education for guardians and citizens of Athens, and elsewhere in his dialogues, Plato emphasizes the role of poetry and music on the one hand, and physical training on the other, as the key elements for training the soul and the body. In his own academy, Plato taught a different kind of learning, one based upon dialectics and philosophical reasoning, with the claim that literature should serve a moral and social function and should teach cultural elements like goodness, grace, reason, and respect for law.

This instrumental view of literature (Plato's poetry includes epic, tragedy, and other modes of imaginative writing), which demands that it do some good in the world, is, I will argue, part of the difficulty that literary study has wrestled with from its beginnings to the present. What is often called "the ancient quarrel between philosophy and poetry," the idea (voiced from the side of philosophy since Plato) that literature needs to make us better people, is now partnered with and augmented by a more modern set of questions about why we should read and study literature in a world increasingly global, economic, technological, and visual. Are the blandishments of the rhapsodes and sophists, the interpreters and orators, still dangerous? Still seductive? Does literature threaten society, or does it help to build society's values and institutions? Or are these the wrong questions and the wrong justifications for literature and its readers?

Sidney's *Defence of Poesie* famously declared that "the poet nothing affirmeth and therefore never lieth." The truths told by poetry are figurative, not literal.

What child is there that, coming to a play, and seeing Thebes written in great letters on an old door, doth believe that it is Thebes? If then a man can arrive at that child's age, to know that the poet's persons and doings are but pictures what should be, and not stories what have been, they will never give the lie to things not affirmatively, but allegorically and figuratively written.[20]

In this, he thought, the poet differed from the philosopher and the historian, who argued their cases by precept and example rather than by story and figure. "The philosopher teacheth, but he teacheth obscurely, so as the learned only can understand him; that is to say, he teacheth them that are already taught. But the poet is the food for the tenderest stomaches; the poet is indeed the right popular philosopher."[21]

Almost four centuries later, the issue of whether poetry (by which Sidney meant all imaginative literature) should affirm its truths in the world was still very much on the agenda.

In 1961 the French literary review *Tel Quel* asked critic and literary theorist Roland Barthes to answer a questionnaire about literature. The questions and responses were published by Barthes under the title "Literature Today." Here is an extract from his salient commentary in those more political, and yet somehow more innocent, years: "it is not literature that is going to free the world," Barthes wrote, "Yet, in this 'reduced' state in which history places us today, there are several ways of creating literature: there is a choice, and consequently the writer has if not a morality at least a responsibility."

We can make literature into an *assertive* value—either in repletion, by reconciling it with society's conservative values, or in tension, by making it the instrument of a struggle for liberation; conversely, we can grant literature an essentially *interrogative* value; . . . the writer can then at one and the same time profoundly commit his work to the world, to the world's questions, yet suspend the commitment precisely where doctrines, political parties, groups, and cultures prompt him to an answer . . .

This interrogation is not: *what is the meaning of the world?* nor even perhaps: *does the world have a meaning?* but only: *here is the world: is there meaning in it?* Literature is then truth, but the truth of literature is at once its very importance to answer the world's questions and its power to ask real questions, total questions, whose answer is not somehow presupposed in the very form of the question: an enterprise which no philosophy, perhaps, has brought off and which would then belong, truly, to literature.[22]

Notice that Barthes stresses the role of questions, rather than answers. This is a point that needs to be emphasized in trying to explain the specificity of literature in comparison with other modes of writing, thinking, and research.

The Use of "Use"

So what is the use of a discussion about the use of literature? Inevitably, it will depend on the context. Do we mean by this question the social utility of literature in the practical world? Or the cultural value of qualities sometimes called *aesthetic* or *philosophical,* as they seem to be derived from reading literary works? Are we trying to assess why a college student should major in literature, or even in the humanities, rather than in something more pragmatic, more lucrative, more amenable to the generation of data, or more directly applicable to the improvement of society? Or are we asking whether there is still, or was ever, anything persuasive in the poet Shelley's statement that poets are the unacknowledged legislators of the world? Is literature useful because it is beautiful or moving (both of these are claims that have been made by some commentators and dismissed by others as impressionistic and unprovable)? Is it useful because it puts commonly shared ideas into words.

Is a discussion of literature either a blind or a category mistake when what is really under critique is the role of literary criticism, especially literary theory, in the wake of the culture wars of the 1980s? It is conventional, though perhaps neither inevitable nor exhaustive, to divide the realms of literary study into literary criticism, literary theory, and literary history, broad rubrics under which a variety of approaches, from post-structuralism to biography, could be subsumed. But for some readers, and some thinkers, this will miss the point, because even so broad a division omits the actual composition of literary works. What is the use of writing literature? And what is the difference between creative writing and literature? Or even, for that matter, between critical writing (what used to be called intellectual prose) and literature? If Bacon's *Essays* and Johnson's *Rambler* and Coleridge's *Biographia Literaria* and Woolf's *A Room of One's Own* are literature, what about the book reviews and essays and feature articles in today's newspapers and magazines? Do they need to stand the test of time?

What is at stake, anyhow, in classifying something as *literature,* or as *literary,* at a time when that adjective seems itself somewhat contestatory, re-posing the very problem it would seem to resolve: is the *literary* a marker of quality, of intent, of genre, of context, or of readership and reception? What about post-facto designations of works as literary, although they were very differently received when they first appeared? Examples in this realm would include Renaissance drama, early ballads, popular novels of the nineteenth century, and the graphic novel (aka comic book) of the twentieth. Or might we decide that most, if not all, discussions of use are *inevitably* post facto? Is the need to explore the use of literature a manifest indication of the increasingly minor place that literature—and literary study—occupies in a visual, aural, musical, and technological era?

It was Immanuel Kant who set the philosophical terms for the modern discussion of the use of art. In his *Critique of Judgment* (1790), Kant said, in a phrase that would be cited and echoed many times, that the beautiful object exhibited "purposiveness without purpose." In other words, a work of art (whether it was a painting, a garden, or a poem) was created on purpose but not *for* a particular purpose. The artwork was (in a positive sense) useless, and the apprehension of beauty was a disinterested activity, one not motivated by a desire to achieve an effect or result. "All interest," Kant wrote, "ruins a judgment of taste and deprives it of its impartiality, especially if, instead of making the purposiveness precede the feeling of pleasure as the interest of reason does, that interest bases the purposiveness on the feeling of pleasure."[23]

Later critics have debated Kant's central point. The literary theorist Barbara Herrnstein Smith has argued that, far from being "useless" in Kant's sense, the work of art has a function—an economic "use value."[24] Some vestiges of the extreme position Smith describes here can be seen, for example, in the periodic surfacing of complaints about commercial art and advertising, "found" art, and a sentimental branch of amateurism that regards book contracts and lecture fees as suspect while exalting the idea of literary prizes (from the Booker Prize to the Tony Awards) as disinterested rewards for excellence. For writers and literary critics in the years that followed Kant's *Critique,* though, the question of use was posed not so much in terms of the literary object itself but, rather, in relation to what literature could do, and should do, in the world.

To Matthew Arnold, literature was a path to moral improvement and spiritual growth, and a potential gateway for workers, as well as for the educated and the privileged, to accede to social, economic, and cultural power. In his essay "The Function of Criticism at the Present Time," first delivered as a lecture at Oxford in 1864, Arnold defined criticism as "a disinterested endeavour to learn and propagate the best that is known and thought in the world," and maintained that "to get anywhere near this standard, every critic should try to possess one great literature, at least, besides his own."[25]

Arnold's theory of critical disinterestedness, clearly indebted to Kant (and reinforced later by T. S. Eliot), has been challenged—and sometimes simply dismissed—by later critics concerned with the "situatedness" of literature and criticism and with what Stanley Fish called "interpretive communities." Arnold's idea that a critic should, and could, "know the best that is known and thought in the world" presumes both a wide and capacious reading and a somewhat restricted world. And his belief that a generally accepted canon of what he called "touchstones" from classical literature could be used as a measure of the greatness of modern poets has been often taken, or mistaken, as a naive notion about universal standards of value. Arnold did not hesitate to evaluate authors and works: Homer, Dante, Shakespeare, and Milton are classics. Chaucer and Burns "come short of the high seriousness of the great classics." Dryden and Pope are classics of prose but not of poetry; it is Thomas Gray who is the "poetical classic" of their period. Not every critic will agree with these views. But Arnold's method was designedly comparative, aimed at avoiding the personal when it comes to judging the poetry of times so near that a critic's feelings are likely to be not only personal but "personal with passion." Thus he thought that "using the poetry of the great classics as a sort of touchstone" might "correct" an overly personal assessment, or at least put it in a broader context.[26]

Arnold was forthright about suggesting the function of *criticism*. But what was the use of *poetry*? Again, he was not reluctant to say what he thought.

> More and more mankind will discover that we have to turn to poetry to interpret life for us, to console us, to sustain us. Without poetry, our science will appear incomplete; and most of what now passes with us for religion and philosophy will be replaced by poetry.[27]

It is because of these lofty ideals that Arnold proceeded, in his essay "The Study of Poetry," to articulate a plan for identifying "the best poetry," the "really excellent." His comparative—and, to a certain extent, transnational and transhistorical—project was conceived as a way of getting beyond the historical and the personal toward "the best, the truly classic, in poetry." This goal may strike some twenty-first-century readers as misguided or impossible, but it is premised on the notion that poetry and literature *count*—that a great deal is at stake.

> We are often told that an era is opening in which we are to see multitudes of a common sort of readers, and masses of a common sort of literature; that such readers do not want and could not relish anything better than such literature, and that to provide it is becoming a vast and profitable industry. Even if good literature entirely lost currency with the world, it would still be abundantly worth while

to continue to enjoy it by oneself. But it never will lose currency with the world, in spite of monetary appearances; it never will lose supremacy. Currency and supremacy are insured to it, not indeed by the world's deliberate and conscious choice, but by something far deeper—by the instinct of self-preservation in humanity.[28]

I think it would be wrong to think of this spirited peroration as utilitarian. Arnold's "end . . . of supreme importance" is enjoyment; he thinks of that as coterminous with the instinct of self-preservation, not as the evolutionary by-product of that instinct. If anything is subliminal or instinctual here, it is poetry, which is why he could say that "the strongest part of our religion today is its unconscious poetry."[29]

Matthew Arnold's essay on "The Function of Criticism" was written in 1864, "The Study of Poetry" in 1880. It's intriguing to compare the ideas of the earnest though determinedly polemical Arnold to the more deliberately provocative statements of adherents to what became known as "art for art's sake" in the same years.

These writers—novelists, poets, and critics—were not only temperamentally attracted to in-your-face confrontation; they also felt themselves to be pushing back against a suffocating, and insufferable, tide of utilitarian moralism. Conservative critics insisted that art must be conducive to virtue; liberal critics, that art must "do good," must be enlisted in the cause of social justice. In response to such apologists, moralists, and crusaders, whatever their political or religious doctrines, "aesthetes," delighting in the paradox, claimed that the true use of art was to be useless.

The originator of the phrase *l'art pour l'art* (often translated as "art for art's sake") in the nineteenth century was the novelist Théophile Gautier. The phrase was used first in English by two figures associated with the Aesthetic Movement, Walter Pater and Algernon Charles Swinburne. The essence of art for art's sake was captured in J. M. Whistler's oft-quoted remark that "art should be independent of all clap-trap—should stand alone . . . and appeal to the artistic sense of eye and ear, without confounding this with emotions entirely foreign to it, as devotion, pity, love, patriotism, and the like."[30]

"Nothing is really beautiful unless it is useless," Gautier asserted in the preface to *Mademoiselle de Maupin* (1836), and Oscar Wilde adapted this as "All art is quite useless" in his preface to *The Picture of Dorian Gray* (1891). In his preface, Gautier wrote feelingly about "moral journalists" and the "fine sermons which have replaced literary criticism in the public prints" and addressed himself directly, and at length, to "utilitarian critics" and the vexed question of "use."

> When an author tossed some or other book, novel or poetry, on to their desk—these gentlemen lay back nonchalantly in their armchairs, balanced them on their back legs, and, rocking to and fro with a knowing look, a superior air, they said:
>
> "What is the use of this book? How can one apply it to moralization and to the well-being of the largest and poorest class? What! Not a word about the needs of society, nothing civilizing and progressive! How, instead of making the great synthesis of humanity, and following, through the events of history, the phases of regenerating and providential inspiration, how can one produce poems and novels which lead nowhere, and do not advance the present generation along the path to the future? How can one be concerned with style and rhyme in the presence of such grave matters? What do we care, ourselves, about style, and rhyme, and form?"

The "very faithful imitation of the utilitarian style," as he happily admitted, was Gautier's own, and he was therefore able to offer, immediately, his scathing reply: "a book does not make jellied soup; a novel is not a pair of seamless boots; a sonnet, a syringe with a continuous spurt; a drama is not a railways, though all of these things are essentially civilizing, and they advance humanity along the path of progress."[31]

> A novel has two uses: one is material, the other spiritual, if you can use that expression about a novel. The material use is, for a start, the several thousand francs which go into the author's pocket . . . The spiritual use of novels is that, while people read them, they sleep,

and don't read useful, virtuous and progressive periodicals, or other similar indigestible and stupefying drugs.[32]

And what of beauty, music, and painting? In a strictly utilitarian sense, none of these entities is useful, since "nothing useful is indispensable for life," and "nothing is really beautiful unless it is useless." Contrariwise, "everything useful is ugly, for it expresses a need, and the needs of man are ignoble and disgusting, like his poor weak nature. The most useful room in the house is the lavatory."[33]

When Oscar Wilde came to adapt and adopt these sentiments almost half a century later, he focused on the persona of the artist as maker:

We can forgive a man for making a useful thing as long as he does not admire it. The only excuse for making a useless thing is that one admires it intensely.
      All art is quite useless.[34]

Wilde's art, and his artfully crafted aesthetic persona, did, of course, achieve the material rewards sardonically noted by Gautier, and at the end of his life, after the reversal of fortune brought about by his trial and conviction, the writing and publication of *The Ballad of Reading Gaol* might fairly be considered spiritual, whether or not it was useful (the poem, when published, sold extremely well). "Catastrophes in life bring about catastrophes in Art," Wilde told one friend, and to another he described *The Ballad* as "the cry of Marsyas and not the song of Apollo. I have probed the depths of most of the experiences in life, and I have come to the conclusion that we are meant to suffer. There are moments when it takes you like a tiger, by the throat, and it was only when I was in the depths of suffering that I wrote my poem."[35] As Richard Ellmann noted, *The Ballad* had for Wilde an explicit and specific use: "The length of the poem was necessary, he said, to shake confidence in the penal system; he knew that it must fall between poetry and propaganda, but he was prepared to face some artistic imperfection for the sake of changing what was intolerable."[36]

As a young man at Oxford, Wilde had been the student of John Ruskin and Walter Pater, and he was impressed by both the moral view of art held by Ruskin and by the aestheticism and conscious "decadence" of Pater. Pater became Wilde's tutor and made editorial suggestions about *The Picture of Dorian Gray*. Ruskin took him—and other students—on a road-building expedition and gave credence to Wilde's view that art had a role to play in the improvement of society. Ellmann, tracing the beginnings of Wilde's career, saw Ruskin and Pater as "heralds beckoning him in opposite directions" and noted quietly that "he outgrew them both."[37]

We might note here that all of these writers—Arnold, Gautier, Ruskin, Pater, and Wilde—were both artists and critics. Arnold wrote poetry ("Dover Beach," "The Scholar-Gypsy," "Empedocles on Etna"), Ruskin and Pater, works of elegant essayistic prose (Ruskin's *The Stones of Venice*, Pater's *The Renaissance*). When they offered strongly held views about the use of poetry, literature, or criticism, they gestured at once toward the activities of reading, writing, and study. The question of use (or uselessness) here does not translate into the question of whether or not there was value in *being an artist*—though this was clearly on the mind of each—but rather on the value of *literature*. Even the word *value*, though, carries a certain connotation of use, whether measured by merit, social utility, instrumentality, or evaluation.

Another kind of use was on the minds of Marxist writers and critics. Karl Marx himself had been an exceptionally literary economist, often demonstrating his theoretical arguments by means of extended references to works from Shakespeare's plays to *Robinson Crusoe*. Despite some early attempts to remand literature to the category of superstructure rather than base, influential and foundational moves were made by critics like Lukács and the members of the Frankfurt School, as well as by writers like Bertolt Brecht, to bring to the forefront instances of both use and abuse.

Some genres, such as realist fiction and drama, were more readily seen as agents of social change than others, such as lyric poetry or pastoral (even though these had been effective instruments of cultural critique in the past). But works of art were the products of social labor. Thus, Theodor Adorno contended, "That artworks are offered for sale at the market—just as pots and statuettes once were—is not their misuse but rather the simple consequence of their participation in the relations of production."[38] As for the idea of art for art's sake, Adorno saw it as an unwitting strategy for "the neutralization of art": "What is ideological in the principle of *l'art pour l'art* does not have its locus in the energetic antithesis of art to the empirical world but rather in the abstractness and facile character of this antithesis."[39]

Whatever the conscious claims of art (or literature) with respect to purposelessness, its unconscious function was always a motivation, always a kind of use. Here it might also be of interest to recall what Adorno and Max Horkheimer had to say about use and uselessness in their essay "The Culture Industry" in *Dialectic of Enlightenment*.

> The use which men in this antagonistic society promise themselves from the work of art is itself, to a great extent, that very existence of the useless which is abolished by complete inclusion under use. The work of art, by completely assimilating itself to need, deceitfully deprives men of precisely that liberation from the principle of utility which it should inaugurate. What might be called use value in the reception of cultural commodities is replaced by exchange value; in place of enjoyment there are gallery-visiting and factual knowledge: the prestige seeker replaces the connoisseur.[40]

Uselessness itself becomes a commodity, and a sign of leisure, culture, and social standing.

Raymond Williams, who deftly traced the history of *literature* as a term, noted that even as it changed from the old sense of "literacy" toward our modern understanding of the word, literature was "a reading rather than a writing" and "a category of use and condition rather than of production."[41] Williams suggested that the emergence of *literature* in a modern sense was a class-based event that established "the reading public" as a bourgeois accomplishment. It was at about this time that the general term in older use, *poetry* or *poesy*, was supplemented or replaced by *literature*. Criticism and the development of a concept of taste and discrimination became linked to "the use or (conspicuous) consumption of works, rather than on their production."[42] Subsequent categories of value, like *imaginative literature* (distinguished from intellectual prose, discursive or factual writing) were also responses to "a new social order: that of capitalism, and especially industrial capitalism." Distinctions began to be made within categories as well as between them: not all writing was classed as literature, and ("ironically," Williams thought) where the idea of literature had developed simultaneously with the dissemination of printed books as a mark of the new reading class, now popular writing and "mass culture" were to be distinguished from "literature." Ideas of "national literature" and of a literary "tradition" were part of this new "recognition of 'literature' as a specializing social and historical category."[43]

Williams's account of Marxism and literature was itself written from within a historical, social, and national context, as he readily acknowledged. But these categories of national, social, historical, political, ideological, and other motivating frameworks shaped the debate about "use" from other twentieth-century perspectives as well.

For much of the nineteenth century and well into the twentieth, then, the debate about the usefulness of literature was focused on social issues: moral instruction, ethical concerns, and societal and political advancement. Whether the governing ideology was liberalism, conservatism, aestheticism, Marxism, or Western democracy, the arguments for use were deployed in the service of a certain vision of a humane society. From the 1990s onward, various forces converged to completely change the nature of the question. Perhaps most significant was the advent of the Internet, with its 24/7 news cycle and its globalized, democratized mode of user participation. Every reader could be a critic, publishing reviews on sites like Amazon.com. Every poem, every quotation, and every misquotation could now be searched instead of researched. Vast quantities of literature were available online, including facsimiles of rare books once only found in libraries, museums, or monasteries.

A shift in attitudes toward the role of undergraduate education was also under way. A student's college years were seen increasingly as preparation for life, by which was often meant training in fields that led directly to jobs and careers. Words like *assessment, impact,* and *outcome,* all borrowed from the social sciences, became central in discussions of higher education, whether those discussions took place in the public media or in government circles.

Assessment is certainly one of the integral components of criticism, whether it takes the form of a review, a critical article, a book, or a decision whether or not to publish (or reprint). But the rise of this vocabulary and the accompanying bureaucratic—often computerized— processes measuring outcomes and impact of qualitative fields using quantitative methodology has arguably raised the stakes for use in ways that are inappropriate for literature and the arts. This shift has been further compounded by the economic crisis and the insistence on justifying investment and resources in the humanities using the same set of problematic keywords.

The outcome of a work of literature might occasionally be an obscenity trial and the consequent expansion of understanding about free speech, or stream of consciousness, or artistic integrity—or even, in a few rare cases, the fomenting of a revolution. In a more ordinary material sense, perhaps the outcome of a literary work would be publication or production, with or without a suitable monetary reward. But these are not the primary meanings of words like *assessment* and *outcome* when they are deployed in the context of an institutional review. As we have already noted, poems and novels do not have answers that are immutably true; they do not themselves constitute a realm of knowledge production. Instead, they raise questions, they provoke thought, they produce ideas and generate arguments, they give rise to more poems and more novels. The impact of a poem might be answered with Emily Dickinson's phrase about feeling that the top of her head has been taken off, but this is not a reliably replicable result. And yet scientists and social scientists will often join poets, writers, critics, and general readers in saying that literature and the arts are what they are saving the world *for.*

Concurrent with the national debate about standards and assessment is the question of rhetoric and its power to sway and to persuade. Traditionally, aspiring politicians were encouraged to study literature, oratory, and rhetoric, in the same way that aspiring generals studied famous battles: to know the history, the terrain, and the moves. From Winston Churchill to John F. Kennedy to Martin Luther King, Jr., the great orators of our time have been inspired by the reading of literature—inspired not only in the cadences and references of their own speeches and books but also by the way "words in their best order" made for logic, tautness of formulation, and powerful, effective figures of speech. But modern eloquence is often met with a sense of distrust, criticized as elite and not representative of the average American. It is symptomatic of the current popular ambivalence about the arts of language that Barack Obama's rhetoric became a flashpoint for both the left and the right.[44] For some listeners, his facility with language was itself suspect, while others, stirred by his words, felt visceral pleasure and deep emotional engagement.

The reemergence in the late twentieth century of politicians and world leaders who are also accomplished and honored writers, like Václav Havel, attests to the possibility of a creative synthesis between writing and politics. In a similar way, the public and political use of a work of classic literature, like the printing and distribution of a million free copies of *Don Quixote* by Venezuelan president Hugo Chávez to mark the four hundredth anniversary of Cervantes's novel, suggests the pleasures and the dangers of the literary in a world that, like Quixote's, often seems both out of sync and out of joint.[45]

The Art of Making Nothing Happen

The uses of literature themselves grow and change as cultures and technologies grow and change. *How* we read changes, too—witness the development of the e-book, and the electronic reader. Here is another paradox: although literature is properly useless, the experience of reading it produces essential, and irreplaceable, cultural effects.

W. H. Auden famously declared, "Poetry makes nothing happen."

But he did so in the context of a memorial poem for another poet, W. B. Yeats, who was deeply concerned with social and political issues—just like Auden himself.

Revisiting Auden's great poem evokes the despairing political climate of Europe on the eve of World War II ("Intellectual disgrace / Stares from every human face") while it also raises the issue of the impossibility and undesirability of seeking a single message or meaning for poetry.

> By mourning tongues
> The death of the poet was kept from his poems.
> . . .
> Now he is scattered among a hundred cities
> And wholly given over to unfamiliar affections . . .
> The words of a dead man
> Are modified in the guts of the living.
> . . .
> For poetry makes nothing happen: it survives . . .
> A way of happening, a mouth.

We do literature a real disservice if we reduce it to knowledge or to use, to a problem to be solved. If literature solves problems, it does so by its own inexhaustibility, and by its ultimate refusal to be applied or used, even for moral good. This refusal, indeed, is literature's most moral act. At a time when meanings are manifold, disparate, and always changing, the rich possibility of interpretation—the happy resistance of the text to ever be fully known and mastered—is one of the most exhilarating products of human culture.

ONE

Use and Abuse

In his *Defence of Poesie,* Sir Philip Sidney responded to the claim that Plato had banished poets from his ideal republic by asserting that Plato banished "the abuse, not the thing."[1] The poets he sought to discredit were those who "filled the world with wrong opinions of the gods, making light tales of that unspotted essence," and Plato "therefore would not have the youth depraved with such opinions." But, Sidney observed, the poets did not create those wrong opinions; they merely gave them expression. Plato disapproved not of poetry but of the abuse of poetic gifts. "So as Plato, banishing the abuse, not the thing, not banishing it, but giving due honour unto it, shall be our patron and not our adversary."

Yet it was the power of poetry, not the "depraved . . . opinions," which was apparently seductive. (Sidney made sure to remind his readers that the ancient poets "had not the light of Christ.")[2] It is because poetry is powerful that its abuse has any effect. Thus, the arguments against poetry that Sidney set out to refute (it lies; it wastes time; it is "the nurse of abuse, infecting us with many pestilential desires"; Plato "banished" poets) are, it is not surprising to see, identical to its main attractions. I do not mean this cynically, nor in a negative light. If "lies"=fiction; "wastes time"=leisure and entertainment; "pestilential desires"=allure and seductiveness; and "banishment"=transgression and risk, we have at hand all the ingredients for a contemporary best seller.

The phrase *use and abuse* has a chiming resonance that authors and publishers have found difficult to resist. Among the many dozens of works that employ these words in their titles, we might consider:

The Use and Abuse of Africa in Brazil
The Use and Abuse of Arsenic in the Treatment of Skin-Disease
The Use and Abuse of Art
The Use and Abuse of Books
The Use and Abuse of Expert Testimony
The Use and Abuse of Female Sexual Imagery in the Book of Hosea
The Use and Abuse of Force in Making an Arrest
The Use and Abuse of History
The Use and Abuse of Money
The Use and Abuse of Power
The Use and Abuse of the Public Range
The Use and Abuse of Reading
The Use and Abuse of Sea Water
The Use and Abuse of Smoking
The Use and Abuse of Social Science
The Use and Abuse of Spectacles
The Use and Abuse of Statistics
The Use and Abuse of the Sublime
The Use and Abuse of Sunday
The Use and Abuse of Television
The Use and Abuse of Tobacco
The Use and Abuse of Zoological Names by Physicians

This is, needless to say, only a partial selection. One of the earliest texts to bear the title was Erasmus's treatise from 1525, *Lingua, The Use and Abuse of the Tongue*. One of the most recent is Margaret MacMillan's *Dangerous Games: The Uses and Abuses of History* (2009).

The parent title here is Nietzsche's *Vom Nutzen und Nachteil der Historie für das Leben* (1874), variously translated as *The Use and Abuse of History for Life; On the Advantage and Disadvantage of History for Life; On the Utility and Liability of History for Life;* and many other elegant—and less than elegant—variations. It has been suggested that Nietzsche's title is indebted to that of Leon Battista Alberti, whose *De commodis litterarum atque incommodis* (1428)—translated as *The Use and Abuse of Books* or *On the Advantages and Disadvantages of Letters*—might have been called to Nietzsche's attention by his friend and fellow scholar Jacob Burckhardt. If that is the case, then the trail loops back to literature as a first-order troublemaker rather than depending upon the model case of history.

My purpose is to give some sense of the powerful rhetorical logic of *use and abuse* as the way of framing an argument—and, not completely coincidentally, to indicate some ways in which the pro/con tension depends upon the conjunction *and* as its fulcrum.

In fact, as we have already begun to see, *use* and *abuse* are versions of the same. The point may be clearest in titles that seem to be about addiction (tobacco, smoking, alcohol), but it is of more intellectual and theoretical interest when the element used or abused is an idea, a concept, or a way of thinking, like an academic discipline. No use without abuse; no abuse without use. The phrase as a container, and as a logic, sets the stage for the kind of debate and dialectic that will ensue.

Let's look briefly at three symptomatic works that employ *use and abuse* in their titles and that speak directly to literature as an experience in the world, and to reading and criticism as a profession. As you'll see, my three examples are rather disparate: the first is a treatise by an Italian Renaissance humanist, the second a lecture by a twentieth-century judge best known for his role in the Nuremberg trials, and the third an account of the uses and abuses of literary criticism by a British literary critic. The latter two are thus versions of the celebratory oration or the after-dinner speech, urbane, self-deprecating, learned, and droll, while the first is a passionate—and dispassionate—account of the low regard in which literary scholars are held, their low pay, sickly complexions, and general social disfavor.

The Use and Abuse of Scholarship

As we have already noted, Alberti's *De commodis litterarum atque incommodis* (ca.1428–mid-1430s) is a probable source for Nietzsche's later essay on history, and the title of the modern English translation, *The Use and Abuse of Books*, is a manifest homage to the current fame of Nietzsche's work. By *books* or *letters*, Alberti meant the study of literature and an education based on reading and writing, according to the humanist program.

In fifteenth-century Italy, to study books meant also to copy them, laboriously. Before the advent of printing, copying, memorization, and quotation were essential tools of the scholar. The tone of *De commodis*— aptly described by Anthony Grafton as "mordant"[3]—is a familiar mix of irony, self-abnegation, pride, and cautious optimism, easy (like that of Machiavelli) to mistake as merely ironic or merely satirical. The humanist scholar of this period was a striver, required to balance long and arduous study—often without dictionaries or other tools—with the necessities of patronage and diplomacy, and without a clear path to wealth or even to financial independence.

Bearing this historical context in mind, I invite the modern reader to do something distinctly unscholarly: that is, to consider some passages from the text as if they were written today, for a contemporary audience:

> I have often heard distinguished scholars say things about scholarship [wrote Alberti], that could really make anyone give up the desire to engage in it. Among other points, for there were many and varied arguments, they were open about the fact that they themselves, though at one time they had chosen to study books, would, if they could start over, gladly take up any other kind of life. I was far from believing that they were sincere, these men who had never spent any period of their lives not engaged in the study of texts, and not only did I believe that they spoke quite differently from what they felt, but I actually blamed them a little bit for it. I thought it wrong for learned men to discourage younger students and also wrong for highly intelligent men to continue on a course if they did not really believe in it. I diligently interrogated many men of learning and discovered that in fact almost all were of the same mind, namely estranged from the very study of books to which they had devoted their lives.[4]

And again:

> No art, however minor, demands less than total dedication if you want to excel in it. What we know to be true of all other arts is most especially true of reading and writing; there is no freedom from striving at any age. We see those who dedicate themselves to study poring over books, as the expression goes, from an early age, and left

alone by everybody; we see them worn out and exhausted by anxious worrying—about the rod, the teachers, the struggle to learn—and by their constant assiduous reading. They often look anemic and lethargic for their age. In the next period, youth, when we are told that we can expect to see joy and happiness in boys' faces, look at their pallor, their melancholy, how in every aspect of their physical bearing, as they come out of their daily imprisonment in schools and libraries, they seem repressed and almost crushed. Poor creatures, how exhausted, how listless, they are, thanks to long hours of wearisome reading, lack of sleep, too much mental effort, too many deep concerns. Anyone with a bit of humanity in him tends to pity their relentless toil or angrily condemn their folly, especially if they have hopes of being eventually rewarded by fortune. And rightly so, for outside of knowledge itself, no success (as measured by fortune's goods) is going to come their way. They are very mistaken if they waste their labor and ambition on this particular pursuit, while a life led along other lines could, with no more labor and striving, probably raise them to the highest pinnacle of financial and social success.[5]

As for wealth, public recognition, and pleasure, forget it. "From these prizes," Alberti explained, "scholars are excluded." He set out in the remainder of his treatise to "make this perfectly clear" by "show[ing] first how much they get to enjoy themselves, second what fortunes fall in their laps, and finally, what honors are likely to be showered upon them."[6]

It is almost irresistible to continue to quote Alberti in this vein. I will provide one more extended (and delectable) example to illustrate both the tone and the odd "contemporaneity" of this little book written over five hundred years ago. Scholars, Alberti said, are criticized if they travel, or even if they take time out for other simple enjoyments:

. . . who does not see at weddings, concerts, singing groups, or young people's games how scholars are looked on with scorn and even hatred? Everybody thinks it becoming in a young man to play the lyre, to dance, and generally to practice the pleasing arts, and people consider these appropriate activities for the young. Those who are even moderately skilled in such arts are generally welcomed and are popular. If they are credited with some such ability, they are invited and asked to join in. But not the young scholars, *they* are pushed away and excluded. If they show their wan faces at such occasions, people consider them either ridiculous or burdensome, and if they try to participate, how they are laughed at and what disparaging remarks they get to hear! Who doesn't look down on a singing or dancing scholar?[7]

I wonder if members of the Shakespeare Association of America had this warning in view when they set in place, many years ago, the social event known as the Malone Society Dance.[8]

Alberti's treatise is full of such monitory, and minatory, advice. "For serious students all pleasures are a bad idea and harmful."[9] "[T]he odors of food and wine, and those of Venus, cause the senses to empty the mind and fill it with shadows, to spatter the intellect with dirt, to dull the powers of perception and to occupy the seat of memory with doubts and suspicions and with various amatory images that thoroughly perturb the spirit."[10]

Furthermore, once one is embarked on this path—let's call it graduate school—it becomes difficult to change course. "Once having started, you will be afraid to turn to lighter things and abandon serious study without some immense good reason. You will be forced to choose which burden you can bear with less harm to your pride, the frank admission that your mind is not good enough for scholarly work or the implication that your spirit and character are too craven to stand up under the strain."[11] Remember that this is advice to aspiring scholars in the fifteenth century—not today. Alberti is particularly adept in the use of personification, speaking in the voice of the books that might be used or abused: "When you wish to buy some clothes, isn't it true that your library will say to you: 'You owe *me* that money, I forbid . . .' If you wish to pursue the hunt, or music, or the martial arts or sports, won't the books say: 'You are stealing this energy from *us*, we will not bring you fame or reputation!'"[12]

So much for pleasure. What about wealth? Scholarship is expensive and low-paid. Consider "those forms of ostentation associated with the achievement of the doctorate." These include big sums "for clothes and university gowns, for a celebratory feast, even for remodeling the house and embellishing it."[13] The very spirit of humanistic learning is inimical to the goal of wealth. "No one who is not degenerate chooses to put elegant learning second to moneymaking. No one who is not deeply corrupted will think of making learning a form of commerce for his own enrichment."[14] Again, let me remind you that he is talking about Italy in the fifteenth century. Alberti's time seems to have been a heyday for the public intellectual as pundit: "It is very well known that the man who wishes to make money from academic knowledge cannot begin to sell anything until he has proved himself to have some extraordinary level of knowledge. Hence we see them showing off whatever brilliance and learning they possess in speeches, disputations and debates, at schools and [universities] and public occasions." For if they "get people to think that they are considered learned by the public," this will, they believe, "lead more readily than actual merit to the earning of money. So they want to be called doctor and see men admire their gold clasp . . ."[15]

A life of learning, it seems, is likely to be nasty, brutish, and short. It is not until the advanced age of forty that "these covetous men can possibly earn money," and how many can be expected to live beyond forty? (*The Use and Abuse of Books* was written when its author was in his twenties.) "If few among those who lead an easy life do so, surely you will find many fewer quattrogenarian scholars."[16] If this marks a difference between Alberti's time and ours, so does another of his criteria for worldly success: the ability to gain wealth by marriage. The scholar cannot compete with the athlete or with the "nicely groomed and polished lover." He should avoid marrying either a poor woman or a young one, since "youth is an age unfavorable to scholars and offers them little security."[17] If a scholar insists on marrying, he should choose "some little elderly widow." (Here, in case we should mistake his tone, Alberti interjected an aside to the reader: "If I seem to be joking in this discourse about matrimonial matters, just call to mind the wives of learned men you know, consider their ages and dowries, to say nothing of their faithfulness.")[18] Book learning, in short, "is not the slightest use for gaining wealth, but just the opposite, a great financial drain."[19]

All this was, for Alberti, a prolegomenon. He wanted to address the honors due to those who "learn from books to understand the noble arts."[20] But he found that the populace always gives the highest honors to gold and wealth. Learning has been "put up for sale as if on the auction block."[21] He himself could have gained wealth "had I transferred my activity from books to business."[22] But the truth about the use, as opposed to the abuse, of books does not finally come from the scholar. Instead, it comes from the books, reanimated and in full voice. The final pages of Alberti's treatise are ventriloquized, projected into, and through the very entities that stand to suffer either use or abuse. This "is what the books themselves (if they could speak) would demand of you."

> Do you hope for wealth, while you learn from us not to fear poverty? Or have you somehow overlooked the fact that nothing belonging to us is for sale? . . . Do you want power, honors, glory, and status? . . . Can you have missed . . . the fact that virtue is all around you when you are with us, that we love no greed, no arrogance, no passion, no spiritual flightiness . . . ? . . . With us, you will expend more moderate labor and show a more exacting kind of virtue . . . Learning and the arts give you this glorious thing: that you are free to aspire to wisdom . . . If you focus your energies . . . in the direction of the goals we have described, you will find that study is full of pleasure, a good way to obtain praise, suited to win you glory, and to bear the fruit of posterity and immortality.

Learn from us. With us. Nothing belonging to us is for sale. The animated and personified voice of "the books themselves (if they could speak)" is uncannily anticipatory of another and later discussion of use and abuse, Karl Marx's evocation of the voice of the commodity in the section of *Capital* called "The Fetishism of Commodities and the Secret Thereof":

> Could commodities themselves speak, they would say: Our use value may be a thing that interests men. It is no part of us as objects. What, however, does belong to us as objects, is our value. Our natural intercourse as commodities proves it. In the eyes of each other, we are nothing but exchange-values.[23]

Alberti's books do not see themselves as commodities—or, to demystify the speaker, Alberti did not envisage his talking books as having an exchange value. "If a man wishes to cultivate his mind," the books declare, "he will inevitably come to despise, hate, and abhor those filthy things called pleasures and those enemies of virtue known as luxury and riches, as well as all the other plagues that infest our life and our spirit, such as honors, elevated stature, and grandeur."[24] And "Let it be no secret to you . . . that we are more inclined to have our lovers poor than rich."[25]

It's not easy to say whether this idealistic fantasy about literary studies is due more to the era when Alberti was writing or to the youth of the author. But it is clear that it is a condition contrary to fact.

When Friedrich Nietzsche came to write his own, equally caustic estimation of the pitfalls of historical scholarship, its use and abuse, he, too, would use the device of literary projection onto a (normally) nonspeaking object/subject, in this case "the animal," distinguished from mankind in that it lives unhistorically, without memory, anticipation, or context.

> Observe the herd as it grazes past you: it cannot distinguish yesterday from today, leaps about, eats, sleeps, digests, leaps some more, and carries on like this from morning to night and from day to day, tethered by the short leash of its pleasures and displeasures to the stake of the moment . . . The human being might ask the animal: "Why do you just look at me like that instead of telling me about your happiness?" The animal wanted to answer, "Because I always immediately forget what I wanted to say"—but it had already forgotten this answer and said nothing, so that the human being was left to wonder.[26]

Books, commodities, animals. What do they have in common? Within these respective arguments, each is a counter in a discourse about a discipline in crisis, a discipline at a turning point: literary studies, economics, history. In each case, personification, prosopopoeia, plays the role of aphorism and oracle. Each states the case for the abuse of use.

Nietzsche thinks too much consciousness of history prevents action and engagement in the world. Alberti thinks too much engagement in the world prevents reading and writing. Neither is hostile to fame, but both are keenly aware of the dangers of seeking it.

Marx sees that the commodity articulates false consciousness, erasing or occluding human labor. But there are commonalities in their approaches. Here is Nietzsche on what's wrong with scholarship:

> Believe me: when human beings are forced to work in the factory of scholarship and become useful before they are mature, then in a short time scholarship itself is just as ruined as the slaves who are exploited in this factory from an early age. I regret that it is already necessary to make use of the jargon of slave owners and employers in order to describe such conditions, which in principle should be conceived free of utility and free from the necessities of life.
>
> . . . just look at the scholars, the exhausted hens . . . they can only cackle more than ever because they are laying eggs more frequently. To be sure, the eggs have kept getting smaller (although the books have only gotten bigger). The final and natural consequence of this is that universally favored "popularization" (along with "feminization" and "infantization") of scholarship; that is, the infamous tailoring of the cloak of scholarship to the body of the "mixed public" . . . Goethe saw in this an abuse, and he demanded that scholarship have an impact on the outside world only by means of an *enhanced praxis*.[27]

What is the praxis of literature? Is it creative writing, the production of poems, plays, novels, and fictions, or does its praxis extend to literary criticism—and if so, who are the intended readers? Nietzsche's scornful reference to the "mixed public" and to "popularization" foreshadows today's focus on "the public humanities" and on accessibility, from book clubs to PBS specials. Nietzsche divides history into three kinds: monumental history (the study of great men and great works, which "deceives by analogies"[28]), antiquarian history (the study of facts and "the habitual, which foster[s] the past"), and critical history (the study of oppression, which "judges and condemns"[29]). We might draw an analogy, however inexact, with three contemporary approaches to literary study: canonicity, historicism, and cultural—or ethical—theory. Each of these raises problems for, and challenges to, the notion of the literary.

Above all, Nietzsche's essay concludes, the problem with "culture" or "cultivation" is that it can too easily be seen as a mere "decoration of life," rather than—as in his own vision—"a unanimity of life, thought, appearance, and will."[30] This issue will come up again and again for us vis-à-vis the use of literature for life. Is it essential, intrinsic, internal, and formative (for thinking, for action, for character, for approaching the future as well as the past), or is it ancillary, decorative, an embellishment, a social accomplishment, an extra? Requirement or elective? Body or clothing? Sustenance or delicacy?

The Use and Abuse of Reading

There could hardly be a greater contrast between the bitter and eloquent passion of a young man like Alberti (who used the phrase *young man* constantly in *The Use and Abuse of Books*, especially in the passages where the books were speaking and offering advice to him) and the blithe and urbane tone of Sir Norman Birkett's lecture to the National Book League, "The Use and Abuse of Reading," in 1951, some five hundred years later. Birkett, who succeeded poet John Masefield as the league's president, was a celebrated jurist—a defense lawyer of note who had been a British judge at the Nuremberg war trials and later became a lord justice of appeal. Reading was a sign of class and culture, and the outreach activities of the league ("The Book Exhibitions, the Lectures, the discussions, the Book Information Bureau, the Reader's Guides and Book Lists") were all genially supported by the luminaries who offered these annual lectures, from historians R. H. Taney and G. M. Trevelyan to poet John Masefield and philosopher Bertrand Russell. Birkett addressed the group as an amateur, a "lover of books," and a member of the legal profession, and his lecture was ornamented with references to and quotations from works he clearly regarded as in the common possession of his hearers: from *Gulliver's Travels* and *Tristram Shandy* to the poetry of Shakespeare, Thomas Nashe, George Meredith, A. E. Housman, and Walter Scott. Toward the end of his talk, Birkett acknowledged that he had little appreciation for "what is sometimes termed modern poetry," and proved it by reading aloud the first verse of a poem by e. e. cummings.[31] Of "abuse," he had little to say: one abuse was to spend the limited time one has for reading "on the worthless and the inferior when the best is available—the reader should be selective"; another was "to read too much"—it was better to know a few authors well than many imperfectly; finally, "the wise reader will never make his reading a substitute for living. To do so is to abuse reading and to make it a drug or a narcotic." The "true use" of reading was "to enrich the actual life of the reader," "to refine in gladness and to console in sorrow," and to "stamp the life with high quality and with purpose."[32] To underscore his final points, he quoted, as many have done, a famous passage from Francis Bacon:

> Some books are to be tasted, others to be swallowed, and some few to be chewed and digested; that is, some books are to be read only in parts; others to be read, but not curiously; and some few to be read wholly, and with diligence and attention.[33]

Nowhere in this learned and amiable talk did Birkett mention literary criticism or scholarship, although many of the authors he cited also wrote essays and offered pertinent maxims. "Use and abuse" to him referred to the practice, and the life, of the reader.

The Use and Abuse of Criticism

A look at a twentieth-century public lecture on literary studies, one that would seem to be at the most genteel edge of discourse, far away from troublemaking, will provide us some evidence about the permeable borderline between use and abuse.

The author of this 1974 lecture, entitled "The Use and Abuse of Literary Criticism," was the eminent Shakespeare editor and literary critic Harold F. Brooks, and the occasion his appointment to a personal chair of English literature at Birkbeck College, London. The title of his talk suggests an urbane approach to pleasures and dangers, well suited to a celebratory event. Birkbeck, an institution committed to offering part-time undergraduate instruction for working people, was far away from the "theory revolutions" then under way at places like Yale, Berkeley, Johns Hopkins, and the University of Paris VIII. (Today's Birkbeck is another story, the theory revolution having come home to roost there, with the establishment of the Birkbeck Institute for the Humanities under the International Directorship of Slavoj Žižek.)

Brooks began with what he clearly regarded as some matter-of-fact statements about the role of criticism:

- "Literary criticism is meant to help us, either in writing literature; or in reading it with more enjoyment and discrimination; or in understanding, through the literature, the civilization it belongs to."[34]
- A good critic would help to provide a "known and sound text"[35] and "notes" to keep us from misunderstanding the words and context, especially if the work were of an earlier historical period.[36]
- The critic could also help the reader by "undermin[ing] your prejudices," developing a "fresh approach which we can then follow up ourselves"[37] and "reassur[ing] us" if we are repelled by novelties or obscurities.[38]
- Above all, "one of the greatest services a critic can perform" is "to enable us to recognize [a work's] coherence," since "a work of art needs to be seen in its unity."[39]

Having cataloged these useful "uses," Brooks moved on to enumerate some "pitfalls for the critic and his reader."[40] It becomes clear that there are more potential abuses than uses, and that the abuses are more appealing than the uses, for the same reason that Milton's Satan in *Paradise Lost* is a more interesting figure than his God, or Falstaff (to some people) a more engaging character than Hotspur or Prince Hal.

These included

- "the half-baked interpretation formed by attending to only part of the evidence in a text";[41]
- "hurrying on to say how good or bad a work is, before taking enough trouble to understand it";[42]

- "being too keen on ranking works of authors in order of merit";[43]
- running down one author in order to exalt another; expecting from one author or work what we admire in another;
- "the treatment of literature as no more than the raw material of sociology";[44]
- a skepticism that makes the critical "unable to believe that a great author . . . can have depicted a noble character or given a story a happy ending, without, as the fashionable phrase goes, 'undercutting it' ";[45]
- the Musical Fallacy, which claims that literature "works by direct appeals to the ear and to the mind's eye, rather than to logic and the reasoned progression of ideas," and that literature is an "impure art" because ideas get in the way of sensation and affect;[46]
- the Lyrical Fallacy, which holds, following Poe, "that a long poem is a contradiction in terms";
- the Anti-Historical Fallacy, whose adherents "take as their standard simply what the uninstructed modern reader can see in a work";[47]
- its twin, the Historical Fallacy, "where the critic's interpretation is governed by what he thinks an average audience of the author's day could have seen in the work";[48]

and finally,

- the abuse performed of the critic who takes the critical enterprise too seriously. "The final abuse of criticism . . . is to put its analysis in the place of the experience of art itself."[49]

For Harold Brooks, the "intellectual interpretation of imaginative literature is not an end in itself. It is a means to an end; and that end is the heightened and more finely tuned response to the work of art in its wholeness."[50] He was willing to acknowledge the possibility of both conscious and unconscious meanings—perhaps surprisingly, the first footnote (of only three) in this published lecture comes on the penultimate page and points the reader to Jung on phantasy and symbol—but he warned against "educating the intellect alone," rather than "the education of feeling, and of the sensibilities of the complete human being, which is the education offered by works of art."[51]

I find little to fault in this polished and gracious account, except to say again that it would be possible to reclassify the abuses as uses, and the uses as abuses, and to emerge with an equally viable and persuasive argument. In fact, the history of literary analysis from 1974 to the present may be seen to have followed all of these diverse "abusive" paths, from the sociology of literature and various avatars of historicism to a renewed interest in the passions, emotions, and positive and negative affect. The tendency to list and rank authors and works—as I will have occasion to discuss later—is a marketing device (for critics and for publishers) and a nostalgia for a literary canon. Skepticism, a resistance to closure (the happy ending), what Brooks called a "half-baked" interpretation "attending to only part of the text" but what might be as readily seen as a "strong reading," a reading "from the margins," or an argument for cognitive dissonance within the work—are among the most recognizable and fruitful critical activities of the past decades.

The interpretation of literature is itself always in dialogue with its own past. The elements of philology, close reading, myth, allegory, image and symbol, history, biography, context, and reception (or, to employ another familiar formulation, emphasis upon the *author,* the *text,* or the *reader*) follow upon one another cyclically. The sequence is not always the same: an interest in history can be provoked by an overemphasis on textual reading that seems to ignore context, but close textual reading can also lead to an interest in philology and the multiple, sometimes irreconcilable, roots and meanings of words. What is certain, if the past is any indication, is this: that no one way of reading or interpreting literature is the best. There are many good, or strong, ways of reading a literary text, and the more satisfying one mode of reading may be, the more likely it is to provoke a different kind of interpretation or approach from the next generation of readers. There is no way of solving a novel or poem or other piece of imaginative writing that will be definitive. We could say, borrowing a precept from physics, that every reading produces an equal and opposite rereading. (By *equal and opposite* I don't necessarily mean "just as good" or "completely the reverse" but, rather, a decided push in another direction. Perhaps it would be clearer to say that every *way* of reading produces an equal and opposite *way* of rereading, although individual readings are often flash points for such energized disavowals.)

Sometimes things in the world affect the nature and fortunes of literary analysis. The much ballyhooed disappearance of the printed book, supposed to be imminent with the arrival of the Internet and the e-book, has clearly helped generate an enormous interest in book history and the social—and technical—history of reading. Likewise, the current focus on human affect, the emotions and the passions, is in part a response to the discourse of cyborgs, cloning, genomics, and human/machine and human/animal boundaries. I think the interest in ethics by scholars in the immediate post-deconstruction days owed something to the insistence by opponents of deconstruction that it looked at nothing outside the text (despite Derrida's long-standing engagement with philosophy and politics). Certainly when, after his death and the discovery of his wartime writings, Paul de Man was accused of being a Nazi collaborator, ethical issues rose to the fore, as some critics suggested that the whole of deconstruction was a cover-up for collaboration during World War II. These are contributory causes, not explicit prompts or reasons, and few if any participants in such lively areas of thinking and research are likely to explain their interest as a result of any kind of cultural anxiety or psychological compensation rather than an intrinsic attraction to the field.

Nonetheless, looked at over time, social, political, and scientific events can be seen to nudge literary studies in various directions. Like every other intellectual activity or event, literary studies have an unconscious as well as a conscious. (Fredric Jameson's phrase "the political unconscious," like Richard Hofstadter's "paranoid style in American politics," has become a standard expression in cultural analysis, and the critical unconscious seems close to a pleonasm, since so much of what is most powerful in literary analysis begins with a hunch and goes on to seek evidence and proof. Without evidence and proof, there is no argument; but without intuition and risk, there is no challenge to verities and truisms, and thus no advance in thought.

Plainly, though, the use of literary criticism is not the same as the use of literature. As Harold Brooks's opening remarks suggest, he views literary criticism as a helping discipline, one that will assist the "complete human being" in encountering and understanding literary works. Whether the purpose of such an understanding is completed and fulfilled by this encounter ("the education of feeling, and of the sensibilities"), or whether it requires and expects a further application "in understanding, through the literature, the civilization it belongs to," has itself been the matter of considerable debate. As for the transgression Brooks calls "the final abuse of criticism," which he describes somewhat tendentiously as "to put its analysis in the place of the experience of art itself"[52]—this creates a dichotomy between *analysis* and *experience* that is worth unpacking. A truly unmediated experience of art would stand apart from all the helping mechanisms Brooks enumerates, from explanatory footnotes to kindly reassurance. "My toddler can paint (write, play, act) better than that" or "I don't know much about art (poetry, novels, movies), but I know what I like" is, arguably, the experience or, rather, an experience of "art itself." In fact, what is the "itself," the self-identity, of literature?

The literary critic, in this model, is an intermediary, a translator, a guide. Like other members of "helping professions" (medicine, social work, therapy, counseling, clinical psychology), the critic enables, intercedes, advises, nurtures, ministers, sometimes even corrects. But this is not the role, or the only role, that literary and cultural critics, scholars and theorists play either in today's academy or in today's journals, magazines, blogs, or electronic media. Since the time of Sidney, Ben Jonson, and Samuel Johnson, extending through Samuel Coleridge, William Hazlitt, Oscar Wilde, T. S. Eliot, to the present day, strong critics have been read and considered "primary" as well as "secondary" authors. Any serious inquiry into the use of literature must take into consideration the idea that criticism and interpretation are not inevitably helping or parasitic behaviors, but part of the life of the work of art.

———

The fortunes of literary studies have gone up and down during the twentieth and twenty-first centuries with the same volatility as the stock market. And like the stock market, the market in literary studies can be charted with confidence only with the benefit of hindsight.

English studies held the comfortable middle ground of the humanities in U.S. and Anglophile/Anglophone universities through the middle part of the twentieth century. The combined heritage of belletrism and the "little magazines" imparted a certain gloss of creativity and artiness to the practice of reading and writing about poems, novels, plays, and what was then often described as "intellectual prose"—works like Robert Burton's *The Anatomy of Melancholy,* for example, or Samuel Johnson's *Lives of the Poets.* Practices like textual explication, often cognate with or imported from the study of other European languages and literatures—were partnered with literary history, thematic criticism, and the study of images, tropes, and what was called literary influence (the indebtedness and echoes of one literary work to another) whether such influence was deemed serene or "anxious." *Intertextuality,* a term borrowed from the French, offered an adjustment to the question of influence by seeing it as a two-way street, and by emphasizing the agency of the text over that of the controlling author. Texts could converse with one another whether or not the author was consciously speaking or listening. The conscious/unconscious borderline was a natural topic for scholars steeped in the heritage of romanticism, whether or not they acknowledged the pervasive influence of Sigmund Freud's writings on the development of twentieth-century art and culture.

An infusion of exciting and provocative theoretical writing, again largely continental in origin, coming to the United States from France, Germany, and the UK, made "literary studies"—or, more properly then, "literary theory"—the star, and in some views the bad child, of humanistic work in the 1970s and 1980s. Intellectual practices like semiotics, phenomenology, and structuralism changed the way critics and scholars read literature, and literature itself changed with the onset of lively debates about the literary canon, cultural inclusiveness, and popular culture. Whether described under the heading of poststructuralism, deconstruction, or postmodernity, the work of European writers like

Roland Barthes, Pierre Bourdieu, Raymond Williams, Jacques Derrida, Jacques Lacan, and Michel Foucault shifted attention to issues of text and agency.

A phrase like *the linguistic turn* (later transformed into *the cultural turn*) signaled a high-water mark for the prestige of this particular mode of literariness in the late twentieth century. As Lynn Hunt and Victoria Bonnell note in their introduction to *Beyond the Cultural Turn* (1999), the publication of two key works in 1973—Hayden White's *Metahistory: The Historical Imagination in Nineteenth-Century Europe* and Clifford Geertz's *The Interpretation of Cultures: Selected Essays*—established the importance of techniques derived from literary studies for the disciplines of history and cultural anthropology. White's book used terms like *trope* and *emplotment* to argue for a deep structure of thought that organized historical research at the linguistic level, working with categories derived from the literary scholars Kenneth Burke and Northrop Frye. Geertz's idea of a "thick description" of cultures presented symbols, artifacts, social arrangements, and rituals as texts that could be read as a consistent story or interpretation—a word itself grounded in literary study. The powerful influence of Geertz has naturalized the phrase *interpretation of cultures* so that it no longer offers any hint of the jostling of disciplines.

White introduced his study with a strong claim about the relationship of history to language that established the first as dependent upon the second: "In this theory I treat the historical work as what it most manifestly is: a verbal structure in the form of a narrative prose discourse." Histories, he maintained, "contain a deep structural content which is generally poetic, and specifically linguistic, in nature, and which serves as the precritically accepted paradigm of what a distinctively 'historical' explanation should be."[53] His table of contents was explicitly indebted to Frye's structuralist account of genre, with chapters on topics like "Michelet: Historical Realism as Romance," "Ranke: Historical Realism as Comedy," "Toqueville: Historical Realism as Tragedy," and "Burckhardt: Historical Realism as Satire."

"The culture of a people is an ensemble of texts," wrote Geertz in his celebrated essay on the Balinese cockfight.

Such an extension of the notion of a text beyond written material, and even beyond verbal, is, though metaphorical, not of course, all that novel. The *interpretation naturae* tradition of the middle ages, which, culminating in Spinoza, attempted to read nature as Scripture, the Nietzschean effort to treat value systems as glosses on the will to power (or the Marxian one to treat them as glosses on property relations), and the Freudian replacement of the enigmatic text of the manifest dream with the plain one of the latent, all offer precedents, if not equally recommendable ones. But the idea remains theoretically undeveloped; and the more profound corollary, so far as anthropology is concerned, that cultural forms can be treated as texts, as imaginative works built out of social materials, has yet to be systematically exploited.[54]

"A deep structural content which is *generally poetic, and specifically linguistic*"; "An *extension of the notion of the text* beyond written material, and even beyond verbal." Both Hayden White and Clifford Geertz found the models of linguistic and literary analysis instrumental and clarifying as they grappled with fresh ways of understanding the methodologies of their own disciplines. Indeed, as such passages from their work make evident, these scholars would come to argue that history and anthropology were modes of reading and writing. "As in more familiar exercises in close reading," Geertz wrote in his concluding paragraph to the cockfight essay, "one can start anywhere in a culture's repertoire of forms and end up anywhere else." Later, he would sum this up in the phrase "the text analogy," which, when linked with "interpretive theory," allows for new reconfigurations of social thought.[55]

The idea of a master discourse has fallen into disuse and even into disrepute, but if there is any discourse that holds the mastery in these excerpts from two groundbreaking works of cultural theory, it is *literary studies*.

How quickly we forget.

In the years that followed these brilliant appropriations from literary studies, the appropriators were themselves reappropriated *by* literary critics and established in the rhetorical position of mastery. New historicists Steven Mullaney and Stephen Greenblatt invoke Geertz's methodology: "Employing a kind of 'thick description' in Clifford Geertz's sense of the phrase," Mullaney writes, "I examine diverse sources and events, cultural as well as literary, in an effort to situate the popular stage within the larger symbolic economy of Elizabethan and Jacobean England."[56] Greenblatt cites a passage from Geertz comparing Elizabethan and Majapahit royal progresses at a key turning point in his own essay on Shakespeare's Henry IV plays.[57] J. Hillis Miller, a specialist in the British nineteenth-century novel, lists Hayden White as an important figure in the development of modern theories of narrative. "The inclusion of Hayden White," he writes, "is testimony to the fact that in recent years history writing as well as fictional narratives have been addressed by narrative theorists."[58]

Authority in literary critical—and literary theoretical—writings increasingly began to derive from such voices. Not only White and Geertz but the anthropologist Mary Douglas *(Purity and Danger)*, the sociologist Pierre Bourdieu, the cultural historian Robert Darnton, and others were cited in argument and epigraph, and a new vocabulary became the common medium of exchange: "*Culture, practice, relativism, truth, discourse, narrative, microhistory,* and various other terms," note Hunt and Bonnell, were in general use across many of the social-science disciplines. But these same terms became words to conjure with in literary studies as well, together with others that originated in social-scientific or scientific disciplines: genealogy, archaeology, agency, paradigm.

Not long after their eager engagement with the linguistic turn, historians and others drew back, returning to an emphasis on empirical data, sometimes in conjunction with theoretical arguments and sometimes to trump them. In a book pointedly called *Telling the Truth About History,* Joyce Appleby, Lynn Hunt, and Margaret Jacob noted the difficulties of aligning postmodern theory with historical practice:

> If postmodern cultural anthropology is any guide, the concern with developing causal explanations and social theories would be replaced in a postmodernist history with a focus on self-reflexivity and on problems of literary construction: how does the historian as author construct his or her text, how is the illusion of authentic-

ity produced, what creates a sense of truthfulness to the facts and a warranty of closeness to past reality (or the "truth-effect" as it is sometimes called)? The implication is that the historian does not in fact capture the past in faithful fashion but rather, like the novelist, gives the appearance of doing so.[59]

The authors were at pains to say that they did not reject all the ideas of postmodernist thinkers, noting that the text analogy and various cultural and linguistic approaches had helped to disengage historians from some other models, like Marxism and other economic and social determinisms, while also "puncturing the shield of science behind which reductionism often hid." But linguistic determinism also presents a problem, they argued. And since postmodernism "throws into question the modern narrative form," key methodologies for history writing, including historiography, narrative, and storytelling, were all subject to critique. Yet historians have to tell stories, they claimed, in order to make sense of the past, as well as to reach toward practical political solutions for the future. So these authors, themselves historians, suggested that there was a point when members of the historical profession, however initially energized by the likes of Derrida and Foucault, had to part company with them, to rejoin the referent and leave the play of the signifier, or to leave the text and rejoin the world. In fact, they wrote in 1994, "a similar kind of crisis that foreshadows a turning away from the postmodern view can be seen in almost every field of knowledge or learning today."[60]

A few key observations might be made about the foregoing: first, that it ties "the linguistic turn" (quickly broadened, to accommodate anthropology, into "the cultural turn") to postmodern theory, thus eliding the linguistic, the literary, the cultural-anthropological, and the philosophical. Second, that it ultimately sets aside postmodernism as antifoundationalist and thus is likely to pose questions rather than seek solutions. ("In place of plot and character, history and individuality, perhaps even meaning itself, the most thoroughgoing postmodernists would offer an 'interminable pattern without meaning,' a form of writing closer to modern music and certain postmodern novels.")[61] Third, that it generalizes a crisis—supplementary to the fabled "crisis in the humanities"—which led, or would lead, or was then currently leading, participants "in almost every field of knowledge or learning" to turn away from the postmodern view, and thus from the temporary hegemony of humanistic and literary critical studies.

The return of the empirical after the heady attractions of the ungrounded "theoretical" had its effects upon literary scholars as well as upon historians, anthropologists, and sociologists.[62] Inevitably, perhaps, chroniclers began to contemplate "the historic turn." The editor of the volume *The Historic Turn in the Human Sciences* noted that there had been a proliferation of historical emphases across the disciplines: "the 'new historicism' in literary and legal theory, a revived interest in 'history in philosophy,' a historically oriented 'new institutionalism' and other historical approaches in political science and economics, 'ethnohistory' in anthropology."[63]

As the century drew to a close, the question of literary study's place in the intellectual and academic hierarchy was an unsettled matter. Suddenly, the word *material* was everywhere (to be contrasted, presumably, with its antonym *formal*, but also with the complicatedly intellectual and highly verbal playing fields of theory). *Material culture* and *the material book* were phrases to conjure with, as book series on "art and material culture," "design and material culture," "American material culture and folklore," "gender and material culture" proliferated *The Body as Material Culture, Children on Material Culture, Chimpanzee Material Culture,* and *Cognition and Material Culture* crowded the bookshops—and these titles are only the briefest of selections from the B's and C's. Literary critics, once to be styled by preference literary theorists, were now increasingly scholars of material culture.

Furthermore, the rise of cultural studies and other interdisciplinary approaches to social and cultural practice caught the eye, and the disapproving glance, of many former, retired, or disgruntled academics, some transformed into journalists or government officials, who unilaterally declared a culture war. Wielding the three most effective weapons for such a battle, intolerant anti-intellectualism, jingoistic super-patriotism, and nostalgia for a past that never was, these self-appointed guardians ridiculed what they did not demonize and demonized what they did not ridicule. Deconstruction, a reading practice developed directly out of the New Criticism, was parodied as a plot of the left. When deconstructive critic Paul de Man was discovered to have had a complicated past involving possible collaboration with the Germans during World War II, deconstruction also became a fascist plot. Race-class-and-gender, or race-class-gender-and-sexuality, were deemed unworthy "political" objects of humanistic attention, and attention to colonialism (even for a discipline like English studies, which emerged as a university subject at the height of the British empire) was likewise dismissed as irrelevant political meddling by scholars who would be better off restricting their activities to the library, the archive, the museum, and the (undergraduate) classroom. What was most disturbing about these attacks was their mean-spiritedness and the shoddiness of the "research" that produced them, often consisting of sitting in on a single class by a given professor, or listing and belittling the titles of courses or conference papers, many never read in their entirety by those who mocked them. But there is no doubt that this strategy was effective, and doubly so, since those targeted began to retaliate, providing precisely the kind of partisan evidence their critics had wished into being.

Few who lived through this period would welcome a resumption of such hostilities, which now seem both fevered and distant. But I mention these developments for a reason: to point out that the scholars singled out for particular opprobrium in these books of the late 1980s and early 1990s were, almost all of them, professors of literary studies. Roger Kimball's grumpy but highly successful diatribe, *Tenured Radicals,* begins in the spirit of a manifesto: "It is no secret that the academic study of the humanities in this country is in a state of crisis."[64] He then proceeds, in the second paragraph of his book, to name some of the principal culprits, all of them professors of literature: "Princeton University's Elaine Showalter" (gender), "University of Pennsylvania's Houston Baker" (race), and "Duke University's Fredric Jameson" (Marxist politics). Other humanistic disciplines also sustained periodic swipes, especially those that led to a concern with politics (as in the work of University of Virginia philosopher Richard Rorty) or popular culture (Harvard philosopher Stanley Cavell). But the academics these critics loved to hate were more often than not trained as literary critics.

As I've noted, this strategy was successful. Not only did the country take notice that the sky was falling, so, too, did the critics and scholars mentioned, and even those scholars watching the debates from the side-lines (not the margins, which were now at the center) began to feel the pressure. Once a suspicion is planted, it is very difficult to uproot it; *tenured radicals*, spiffy phrase that it was, had changed the way the academy regarded itself. Like the insinuations of Iago ("It speaks against her with the other proofs" [*Othello,* 3.3.44]), these proofs of nothing multiplied to produce a firm conviction that something had gone wrong. Partially as a result, the place of literary studies in the pantheon of the humanities came under tacit and explicit critique. Younger—and older—scholars of literature shifted their interests, whether consciously or (more likely) unconsciously, away from the play of language, the ambivalent ambiguities of the signifier, and the modes of counterintuitive argument that had marked the most brilliant literary work of the 1970s and 1980s (and, indeed, the 1940s and the 1950s), toward less controversial terrain and more supposedly objective (and even scientific) methodologies like history, the sociology of knowledge, and cognitive theory. Literary study was in the process of disowning itself.

Genteelly, professionally, persuasively, and without an apparent consciousness of what might be lost in the process, departments of literature and literary study have shifted their emphasis. This return to history is in fact a return, not a leap or an evasion. Trends in intellectual work tend to be cyclical, with attention shifting from text to context, from author or artist to historical-cultural surround, from theory to practice and from micro- to macro-analysis (in literary study, close reading versus meta-narratives). A great deal of the most recent work in literary studies is deeply informative, much of it represents what used to be called "a contribution to knowledge," and almost all of it is professionally honed if not glossy. If little is provocative, perhaps that is to be expected after a couple of decades of high-profile contestation. There are many ways of doing inventive scholarship. Painstaking literary-historical work (like the kind of literary work that admires and imitates the scientism of cognitive theory) can at its best also be imaginatively interesting.

Nevertheless some literary historians and historicist critics within departments of literary study are in danger of forgetting or devaluing the history of their own craft and practice, which is based not only on the contextual understanding of literary works but also on the words on the page. Counterintuitive interpretation, reading that understands the adjacency of literature, fantasy, and dream, the subliminal association of words through patterns of sound or tics of meaning, the serendipity of images and ideas, the sometimes unintended echoes of other writers, the powerful formal scaffolding of rhetoric or of genre—all these are as richly transgressive as any political interpreter might desire, and as elusively evocative as any archive-trained researcher could wish to unearth or detect.

A passage from T. S. Eliot's "Burnt Norton" has always seemed to me to describe with particular eloquence what we do as critics when we study how writing works:

> Words move, music moves
> Only in time; but that which is only living
> Can only die. Words, after speech, reach
> Into the silence. Only by the form, the pattern,
> Can words or music reach
> The stillness, as a Chinese jar still
> Moves perpetually in its stillness.
> Not the stillness of the violin, while the note lasts,
> Not that only, but the co-existence,
> Or say that the end precedes the beginning,
> And the end and the beginning were always there
> Before the beginning and after the end.
> And all is always now. Words strain,
> Crack and sometimes break, under the burden,
> Under the tension, slip, slide, perish,
> Decay with imprecision, will not stay in place,
> Will not stay still. (137–153)

The specific contribution of literary studies to intellectual life inheres in the way it *differs from* other disciplines—in its methodology and in its aim—rather than from the way it *resembles* them. What literary scholars can offer to the readers of all texts (not just those explicitly certified as literature) is a way of *asking literary questions:* questions about the *way* something means, rather than *what* it means, or even *why*. It is not that literary studies is uninterested in the what and the why—in recent years, such questions have preoccupied scholars whose models are drawn from adjacent disciplines like history and social science. But literariness, which lies at the heart of literary studies, is a matter of style, form, genre, and verbal interplay, as well as of social and political context—not only the realm of reference and context but also intrinsic structural elements like grammar, rhetoric, and syntax; tropes and figures; assonance and echo. A manifesto for literary studies will claim for it an unapologetic freestanding power to change the world by reading what is manifest, and what is latent, within and through the language of the text.

The best way for literary scholars to reinstate the study of literature, language, and culture as a key player among the academic humanities is to do what we do best, to engage in big public questions of intellectual importance and to address them by using the tools of our trade, which include not only material culture but also theory, interpretation, linguistic analysis, and a close and passionate attention to the rich allusiveness, deep ambivalence, and powerful slipperiness that is language in action. The future importance of literary studies—and, if we care about such things, its intellectual and cultural prestige both among the other disciplines and in the world—will come from taking risks, not from playing it safe.

TWO

The Pleasures of the Canon

The notion of a literary canon, a body of works considered centrally important and worthy of study, is—linguistically, at least—a fairly recent idea. Canon law, canons of saints, and canonical books of the Bible were all familiar concepts from the medieval period on. The word *canon* itself means *rule,* and it came to indicate a standard of judgment or authority, a test or criterion. But it's really only in the twentieth century that the term regularly began to be applied to a list of modern books. (In effect, the literary canon was a secular version of the biblical canon: a system for designating books that were authentic and merited inclusion.) The development of Great Books curricula at places like Columbia University, the University of Chicago, and St. John's College, and the publication of projects like the fifty-four-volume *Great Books of the Western World* in 1952, made such lists of major writers and thinkers widely available.

In this connection, it's of some interest to note that the Chicago Great Books course, devised by university president Robert Hutchins and philosopher Mortimer Adler, was initially aimed at businessmen, and was intended to fill in gaps left in their education. This was not, that is to say, initially a freshman "core" course but a program intended to allow "successful business and professional men" to remedy the omission of literary reading in their earlier years of study by meeting "in a relatively painless fashion in congenial surroundings." The year was 1943.

The concept met with immediate approval, and within a month the Great Books seminar, nicknamed by participants the "Fat Man's Great Books Course," began to meet once a month at the University Club.[1] It was one of these businessmen, William Benton, the CEO of the Ency-clopaedia Britannica (and later a U.S. senator from Connecticut), who had the idea of marketing a set of Great Books in conjunction with the encyclopedia. It was only when the *Great Books of the Western World* were sold *like* encyclopedias—by door-to-door salesmen explicitly rec-ommending them as an instant educational upgrade for middle-class American households—that the set turned the corner from steep defi-cit to (modest) profit. To save money, the editors had chosen inferior translations in the public domain. Some nineteenth-century translations of the Greek classics were imbued with ejaculations and false archa-ism—"Ay me!" "Why weepest thou!"—at the same time these plays by Sophocles and Euripides were being translated by a brilliant new genera-tion of scholars and published as *The Complete Greek Tragedies* by the University of Chicago Press.[2]

For decades the Great Books movement—which Dwight Macdonald, in a scathing review of the Adler-Hutchins venture, called "the fetish for Great Writers"[3]—had been tied to a notion of general education that promoted these texts as essential building blocks for college freshmen and sophomores. Today, however, many freshmen and sophomores rush straight ahead to professional training, skipping literature altogether, or taking only one or two literature courses over the four years of their undergraduate education. Some later come to regret the lost opportu-nity to learn about the humanities and the arts. As a result, the interest in brushing up the classics that animated executives in the 1940s and 1950s is again alive and well: an idea that began as a pick-me-up for businessmen has found a new audience among modern-day profession-als. Very often readers who read these authors with pleasure in high school will return to an interest in literary culture only after establish-ing themselves in positions of professional—and financial—security through college and post-college training. Book clubs, leadership insti-tutes, post-performance audience talk-backs in regional theaters, cruise-ship lectures, and alumni colleges are among the ways adult readers now encounter the literary classics. Business schools teach the plays of Shakespeare to exemplify good (and bad) business practices, management skills, and group motivation, and programs in medical humanities likewise use Shakespeare to illustrate key themes about life, death, and humanity. It is in extension courses and lifelong learning, though, that the appetite for reading great works of literature seems most directly expressed.

But what does it mean to read the classics or to study them? Dwight Macdonald's review of the Hutchins-Adler Great Books series—a review that must have been real fun for him to write—takes note of the deliberate absence of a "scholarly apparatus" accompanying a set of books that span the disciplines of literature, philosophy, history, and science, and range from ancient Greece and medieval England to Freud and (inadequately selected works of) Marx. "The Advisory Board," Robert Maynard Hutchins wrote, "recommended that no scholarly apparatus be included in the set. No 'introductions' giving the editors' views of the authors should appear. The books should speak for themselves, and the reader should decide for himself. Great books contain their own aids to reading; that is one reason why they are great. Since we hold that these works are intelligible to the ordinary man, we see no reason to interpose ourselves or anybody else between the author and the reader."[4]

Macdonald found this particularly vexing in the case of the six volumes of scientific writing, which posed a problem "so urgent that almost no expository apparatus would suffice. A scientific work differs from a literary, historical, or philosophical work," in his view, "partly because it is written in a language comprehensible only to the specialist (equations, diagrams, and so on) and partly because its importance is not in itself but in its place in the development of science." Thus, while Milton "does not supersede Homer," and the historian Edward Gibbon "represents no advance over Thucydides," scientific writing is "often revised, edited, or even superseded by the work of later scientists."[5] To underscore this point, Macdonald offered some quotations from Hippocrates that were meant to show how out of date he was as a scientist—for instance, "In women, blood collected in the breasts indicates madness." But as this example makes clear, such observations are very much of interest today in the history of science and medicine, and as well in the fields of women's and gender studies. It has become a critical truism that the works of Freud, Marx, and Nietzsche are taught more often in literature courses than in the original disciplines (science, economics, philosophy, or philology) in which those writers began their work. This does not make them failures but, rather, successes—"crossover" successes. Hippocrates, likewise, has found new readers, new contexts, and new relevancies, even if physicians do not consult him on the treatment of ulcers and broken bones. These writers have become literary and historical. That does not mean they are useless but that they have found, or made, new uses. The literary is not the category of last resort (or of lost causes) but the category of textual richness and multiplicity of meanings.

Let's return, though, to the purist claim made by Hutchins and Adler—that the omission of a scholarly or expository apparatus was a plus, morally, ethically, and literarily, for their Great Books series, removing a barrier between reader and writer. Dwight Macdonald quite sensibly suggests that "surely, without distracting the reader from the text," a scholarly apparatus could have given the essential information about the historical and cultural context in which each work appeared and have translated terms and concepts whose meaning has changed with time.[6] The word *apparatus* is an unlovely word, conjuring up as it does a kind of mechanical contraption or scaffolding. In fact, *apparatus* comes from the same root as *prepare*, and means a way of getting ready A scholarly apparatus, however, sounds particularly menacing and constraining, like a harness (or a HAZMAT suit).

This idea, that scholarship and criticism somehow got in the way of and impeded the direct interaction between reader and work, is an artifact of the times—the late forties and early to mid-fifties. It is related to the romance of the Great Books as part of a theory of general education, a theory that was, in turn, indebted to concepts of American individualism, self-realization, and the spread of democracy in the post–World War II period. It is, in fact, the forerunner of the "culture wars" of the 1980s and the resistance to literary theory, which was widely regarded as a dangerous foreign import.

Specialists and Generalists

One of the recurrent flashpoints in the public discussion of the humanities is whether specialization is ruining literary studies, replacing generalists who know and love the canon and the great (and small) works across periods and genres with specialists, intensely localized and professionalized, who know every inch of a particular piece of literary terrain (the American nineteenth-century novel, or seventeenth-century religious poetry, or medieval drama, or Dickens) but who no longer command—or, it is implied, much care about—the larger picture.

Not long ago, that larger picture would have included the classics of ancient Greece and Rome (preferably read and studied in the original languages), Dante and Petrarch, French literature from (at least) Corneille and Racine through the nineteenth-century novel and the twentieth century, and many other works from what came to be known, too broadly, as the Western tradition. Time moves on, and—happily—writers keep writing, and so we now have not only a more global sense of world literature but also a constant consciousness of new work, poems and plays and novels and essays, that is published, reviewed, and read every day. No one can read all of this; no one can command it. And certainly no scholar can read the preponderance of scholarly work being produced today. A century ago the world of literary scholarship was smaller, more intimate, clubbier—riven by factions and sometimes astonishingly personal and intemperate in its expression, but at the same time rather self-protective, insulated as well as isolated.

We can't go back to that time, nor—in the main—should we want to do so. The world of literary studies has become, to a great extent (though not completely), democratized and pluralized, with beneficial effects for scholarship and teaching. But the question remains about that elusive, and to some extent delusory, "larger picture." The old divisions and categories—period, genre, author, nation—have all been questioned, their borderlines exposed as permeable (when does medieval begin or end? Do terms like *epic* and *pastoral* have modern and postmodern equivalents? How do we assess collaborative or collective authorship? Does it matter whether Beckett is an Irish author or a French author?). After decades in which master narratives were set aside in favor of the local, the particular, the outsider, and the idea of bricolage, there is an understandable longing on the part of students, and of some teachers and scholars, for a broader arc, a story if not a picture.

The language of specialist and generalist is sometimes deployed as a kind of code, implying that members of the former are technocrats (or even bureaucrats) and careerists, while the latter are genuinely committed to literary study and, as a strong and insistent subtext, to teaching, by which is meant the teaching of undergraduates (and non-majors) rather than graduate students. This divide, too, I think is false, and not only inaccurate but meretricious. It sets up the terms of apparent difference in a way that fails to understand or to value the continuum between teaching and scholarship, intellectual excitement and painstaking research, pleasure and profit, learnedness and learning.

My own education was as a generalist, and I am to a certain extent a generalist still, "dabbling," as the dismissive term has it, in periods and others not "my own." From time to time I have taught courses on Jane Austen as well as Shakespeare and Renaissance drama, on modern and postmodern drama as well as sixteenth- and seventeenth-century poetry, on detective fiction (from *Oedipus* to Agatha Christie to Crick and Watson's double helix), on literary and cultural theory, and on ghosts in literature, as well as what used to be called survey courses in English literature, the epic and the novel, and drama from the Greeks to the present day. If we were to try to adapt the terms of Isaiah Berlin's essay "The Hedgehog and the Fox" to the realm of literary study, rather than of literary production, I would be pretty clearly on the side of the fox rather than the hedgehog.[7] Or, to put it another way, my interests are transhistorical, eclectic, thematic, and theoretical. I am less interested in thick description and period-based work, more intrigued by following out an idea, an intuition, a hunch, or a series of associations wherever they lead me. But I am deeply committed to research, to evidence, to documentation, to the acknowledgment of prior scholars' work, and to other things that belong to the apparatus of scholarship.

So for me, the dichotomy between so-called specialists and so-called generalists is a false divide. Since I believe, along with many of the critics I have cited in these pages, that the colloquy is always being held across the centuries between and among writers, whether of fiction, poetry, drama, or any other genre, to specialize will mean to know the intellectual surround (as well as the historical background) of any given author's work, its precursors and successors, its effects and affects. What I want to emphasize here, though, is the distinct kind of pleasure that comes from connecting one literary work or phrase or character or passage with another—the experience that is sometimes called getting, or catching, or recognizing a literary allusion.

The Fate of an Allusion

The title of Edward Albee's play *Who's Afraid of Virginia Woolf?* (1962) is a reference to the theme song of Disney's *Three Little Pigs* (1933), but it would have no resonance if the name Virginia Woolf didn't already carry some important connotative power (feminist writer; major twentieth-century novelist; innovative stylist; Bloomsbury icon). Albee apparently said that when he saw the phrase scrawled on a mirror, he thought of it as "a rather typical, university intellectual joke."[8] It's hard to know whether such a joke would today be the typical product of college wit. Or take a slightly different kind of example, T. S. Eliot's play *Sweeney Agonistes*, which offers a wry reference to John Milton's verse tragedy *Samson Agonistes* (1671). The titles of both *Sweeney Agonistes* and Gary Wills's biography *Nixon Agonistes* (1969) assume at least a fleeting familiarity with Milton's poem, or at least with its title. As with Albee's *Virginia Woolf,* the wit lies in the apparent disjunction between the original and the subsequent allusion.

But the practice of allusion seems to have moved from the realm of classic literature to popular culture and politics. The old-style literary allusion required that the reader or hearer identify the reference. Thus, the American poet Amy Lowell could, in 1912, title a poem "Fresh Woods and Pastures New" and assume that her readers would understand the allusion to the last line of Milton's "Lycidas." An exhibition of Dutch seventeenth-century landscape drawings with that title toured in 2000, having originated in a university art gallery. *Slate* used the same phrase appositely as the title of a posted item on the move of a professor from one law school to another; the professor, it turned out, was writing a book on law and Shakespeare, so he was twice embarking on a new venture, field, and vocation.[9] But these audiences of readers are comparatively cognoscenti. How many readers would catch a witty reference to "fresh woods and pastures new" today?

Let's take another example, perhaps a more familiar one to modern readers, the phrase "miles to go before I sleep" from Robert Frost's "Stopping by Woods on a Snowy Evening." (The alert reader of this book will see that I got from Milton's woods to Frost's woods by a process of association, though it is more conventional to associate Frost's entry into the woods with that of Dante in his *Inferno*.) In any case, "miles to go before I sleep" has had a lively itinerary, having been used in 1974 as the title of a movie about a lonely senior citizen (played by Martin Balsam) and, with signifying parentheses, as the title of a love song, "Miles to Go (Before I Sleep)," which appears on a 1997 CD by Celine Dion. Arguably, audiences for both works would recognize the allusion to Frost, one of the most frequently taught lyric poets in the high school curriculum.

Some authors—like Laurence Sterne, for example, or T. S. Eliot, or James Joyce—demonstrably use allusion as a major constituent part of their own creative work.[10] Sterne's *Tristram Shandy* is, in formal and intellectual terms, both a tapestry of allusions and a send-up of, or a challenge to, the very idea of allusion. But if an allusion falls (or is dropped) and no one catches it, does it really allude?

T. S. Eliot famously added learned footnotes to his poem *The Waste Land* when it was published in 1922. References to Virgil, Dryden, Pope, Spenser, Shakespeare, Chaucer, Ezekiel, Dickens, etc., are essential to the structure, tone, and content of the poem, but the footnotes are selective, didactic, and (deliberately?) pompous and condescending. In a preliminary note, for example, Eliot cites "Miss Jessie L. Weston's book on the Grail legend: *From Ritual to Romance* (Cambridge)" and "another

work of anthropology . . . one which has influenced our generation profoundly: I mean *The Golden Bough*."[11] (No author is cited here; those
who don't know, don't know.) Eliot proceeds to comment that "Anyone
who is acquainted with these works will immediately recognize in the
poem certain references to vegetation ceremonies." The tone is droll,
deadpan: there are sheep and goats, insiders and outsiders. And the language is scholarly piling-on: "anyone," "immediately," and the tantaliz-
ingly vague "certain references." Again, if you know, you know. These
are parody footnotes, allusions to footnotes, allusions to allusions. Yet,
like many others of my generation, I wanted to know what the poets
knew. Eliot's poem and its footnotes were my homeschooling. I went in
quest of the works of Mr. Frazer, *The White Devil*, and the philosophical
writings of F. H. Bradley. I read Dante and Spenser and whatever translations of the Upanishads I could find. I also bought and read Weston's
From Ritual to Romance, a slim book that became a must-have on the
bookshelves of the time, right next to all those New Directions poetry
paperbacks.

Much critical sport has been made of Eliot's learnedly mocking footnote on the song of the hermit-thrush, which cites the bird's Latin name
(*Turdus aonalaschkae pallasii*), Chapman's commentary on it in the
Handbook of Birds of Eastern North America, and a further ornithologi-
cal observation from the annotator-poet: "Its 'water-dripping song' is
justly celebrated." What Eliot doesn't mention is that the hermit-thrush
is Whitman's bird and plays an important role in two of the best-known
poems in the American canon, "Out of the Cradle Endlessly Rocking"
and "When Lilacs Last in the Door-yard Bloom'd," Whitman's poem on
the death of Abraham Lincoln, in which the solitary thrush becomes an
American elegist and muse. This is a kind of allusion by omission, even
a misdirection ploy, as the diligent student is invited to hunt down Frank
Chapman's field handbook to regional birds (not even the author's full
name is given) rather than to speculate upon the canonical place of the
hermit-thrush in poetry.

But these notes, however belatedly added to the poem, are themselves
works of art rather than of scholarship, as the next footnote makes clear.
"The following lines," writes Eliot, "were stimulated by the account

of one of the Antarctic expeditions (I forget which, but I think one of Shackleton's) . . ." No academic could get away with this insouciance or this inexactitude. Despite my early eagerness to follow the track of the poet's reading—rather like J. L. Lowes's exhaustive study of Coleridge's reading in *The Road to Xanadu*—such notes are tantalizing digressions rather than allusions, since their associations (assuming them to be truthful rather than completely fictive) are personal rather than public.

Ernest Shackleton's Antarctic expeditions were much of the moment when Eliot was writing. The unsuccessful but heroic *Endurance* expedition took place in 1914–16, and Shackleton died on yet another voyage to Antarctica in 1922, the year *The Waste Land* was published. But it's also the case that the "delusion" to which Eliot here refers, on the part of the explorers in extremis, "that there was *one more member* than could actually be counted," has its familiar literary-historical counterpart in the famous stories told about the early performances of Marlowe's *Doctor Faustus*, when "the visible apparition of the Devill" was said to have joined the actors onstage.[12] (The fact that Shackleton was educated at Dulwich College, founded by Edward Alleyn, the Elizabethan actor who played Faustus on this occasion, may be put down to one of those coincidences it is perhaps not worth considering too curiously.)

What I want to emphasize is not the creative process, the ways— direct and oblique—that poets and writers get their ideas and find their words, but, rather, the difference between a reference and an allusion, indeed between a *literary* allusion (pointing toward another literary work or phrase) and a historical allusion. The borderline is tricky and fluid: if the phrase "who is the third who walks always beside you?" were taken by Eliot from the language of one of the Antarctic accounts, it would be—by my admittedly ad hoc standards—a literary, or perhaps better, a textual allusion. But if Eliot is imagining the phrase, taking an idea and bringing it to verbal life, then (for me) he is using Shackleton as a source, the way Shakespeare uses Holinshed's *Chronicles* as a source, not as an allusion.

Why should this distinction matter? you may well ask. Because, I might reply—assuming we were to remain in this subjunctive mood— it speaks again to the heart of the literary enterprise. A conversation among texts is different from a conversation among persons, and a literary allusion is different from a historical reference. To take up the third, and manifestly overdetermined, case I mentioned above, that of James Joyce, whose range of literary and cultural allusion is simply staggering: to identify the Irish physician, poet, footballer, and wit Oliver St. John Gogarty as Joyce's inspiration for the figure of Buck Mulligan in *Ulysses* is perhaps an interesting piece of historical fact. But when Stephen Daedalus in the same novel is obsessed with the phrase "Agenbite of inwit," that is a literary allusion—as, indeed, is Stephen's surname (and, if we want to pursue the question, his given name). The *Ayenbite of Inwyt,* as the title is usually spelled, is a Middle English work, the title of which means *Prick of Conscience* or *Remorse of Conscience. Againbite* and *in-wit* are nicely Joycean terms that originate, here, in a mid-fourteenth-century Kentish dialect.

Allusion as a literary practice differs from the concept of intertextuality in that it ordinarily presumes an intention on the part of the author, whereas intertextuality—a term coined by the theorist Julia Kristeva—posits a relationship between or among literary works, a kind of textual conversation that is observed, participated in, and augmented by the reader. Now, obviously, the reader also participates, as we have seen, in getting or catching an allusion, and it is conceivable that some allusions are unconscious rather than conscious on the part of the author. Some of the most basic questions about authorial intention and authorial control of meaning touch upon this kind of issue: did the writer intend an allusion to poem X or author Y? If he or she cannot be said to have done so, then the claim is sometimes made that the critic is "reading too much into" the work, as if that intensive reading process were not legitimate, were not, in fact, at the very heart of the literary enterprise (and the "use" of literature).

Literary allusions may be overt or covert, manifest or hidden, direct or indirect, faithful or parodic. But there is a dog-whistle aspect to the process: some readers will hear the signal, and some will not. A reader who has never encountered the classical epic (or read any of the critical scholarship) may miss the fact that Joyce's *Ulysses* is based on Homer's *Odyssey.* More basically yet, that reader may not register the importance of an English-language poem designed or written in twelve books (Spenser's plan for the unfinished *Faerie Queene*, Milton's *Paradise Lost,* both reflecting on Virgil's *Aeneid*), or hear the echoes and revisions of Milton's poem in Wordsworth's *Prelude.* All of these were standard literary-historical expectations for students of the canon in the middle of the twentieth century—as indeed was the Virgilian sequence of pastoral elegy, eclogue, and epic in the evolution of a poet. Or the notion of the "elegy on the death of the poet," written by a mourning, and surviving, successor.

Such allusions are formal, not verbal, although some tropes can be both, like the opening lines of *The Canterbury Tales,* or of *Paradise Lost,* passages the English student was in the past often expected to memorize and know by heart (in an idiom that goes back to Chaucer). Even the number of lines—the first eighteen lines of *The Canterbury Tales,* the first twenty-six lines of *Paradise Lost*—were engraved upon memory. Here they are:

Whan that Aprill with his shouers soote
The droghte of March hath perced to the roote,
And bathed every veyne in swich licour
Of which vertu engendred is the flour:
Whan Zephirus eek with his sweete breeth   5
Inspired hath in every holt and heath
The tender croppes, and the younge sonne
Hath in the Ram his halve cours yronne,
And smale fowles maken melodye,   ·
That slepen al the nyght with open ye   10
(So priketh hem nature in hir corages);
Thanne longen folk to goon on pilgrimages,
And palmeres for to seken straunge strondes,
To ferne halwes, kowthe in sundry londes;
And specially from every shires ende   15
Of Engelond to Caunterbury they wende,
The hooly blissful martir for to seke,
That hem hath holpen whan that they were seeke.

                                        —Geoffrey Chaucer,
                  "General Prologue," *The Canterbury Tales*

Of man's first disobedience, and the fruit
Of that forbidden tree, whose mortal taste
Brought death into the world, and all our woe
With loss of Eden, till one greater Man
Restore us, and regain the blissful seat,   5
Sing, Heavenly Muse, that on the secret top
Of Oreb, or of Sinai, didst inspire
That shepherd who first taught the chosen seed
In the beginning how the heavens and earth
Rose out of Chaos: or, if Sion hill   10
Delight thee more, and Siloa's brook that flowed
Fast by the oracle of God, I thence
Invoke thy aid to my adventurous song,
That with no middle flight intends to soar
Above th' Aeonian mount, while it pursues   15
Things unattempted yet in prose or rhyme.
And chiefly thou O spirit, that dost prefer
Before all temples the upright heart and pure,
Instruct me, for thou know'st; thou from the first
Wast present, and, with mighty wings outspread,   20
Dovelike sat'st brooding on the vast abyss
And mad'st it pregnant, what in me is dark
Illumine; what is low raise and support;
That, to the height of this great argument
I may assert Eternal Providence,   25
And justify the ways of God to men.
                            —John Milton, *Paradise Lost,* Book 1

I print these two blockbuster passages together not because one refers
to or alludes to the other but because between them, they could be said
to author the English literary canon. How many students, even graduate students, can recite them now? Memorization, learning by heart, is
out of fashion as a pedagogical skill, though students of all ages regularly memorize the lyrics of popular songs, the Pledge of Allegiance, and
"The Star-Spangled Banner"—although the latter is often committed
to memory phonetically rather than in terms of units of sense, like the

famous and comical rendition of a religious hymn as "Gladly the Cross-eyed Bear."

But there is much to learn from these passages committed to memory and recited out loud. The sequencing of ideas and rhythms in the Chaucer ("when," "when," "then," as if there were an inescapable seasonal logic to these human migrations) and the Google Earth–like literary zoom lens, zeroing in on a tighter and tighter focus (from the calendar and the heavenly constellations to the desire for pilgrimage and the Canterbury pilgrims), are superbly indicative not only of the economy of art but of the wit of the poet. His ability to paint genre images comparable to that of Breugel (the birds are sleepless with spring fever and desires of their own) is matched by a poetic daring—and humor—that allows the last line to flirt with bathos, nine simple single-syllable words and a past participle expressing the homeliest of sentiments ("That hem hath holpen whan that they were seeke"). "Seeke" and "seke" may rhyme, but aren't they also homophones, words that share the same pronunciation? If so, what does that doubled relation (rhyme and homophony) do to the poetic logic? Does it make the sentiment seem redundant? Does it make the fictional poet-speaker sound unartful? And did I mention that this long unfolding pageant occurs over the course of a single sentence? Many critics have noticed that the weather report seems off: March in the environs of Canterbury is distinctly not a month of drought. This is a classical trope, the meteorology of Virgilian Rome, maybe, but not an accurate forecast for England. And yet those small birds are so distinctly native. Eighteen lines. And we have just begun to talk about them.

It would be possible to pose a similar set of initial questions and observations about the opening lines of *Paradise Lost*. A reader needs to start somewhere: since few English majors these days come to Milton with a prior knowledge of Homer and Virgil, of the traditional epic *invocatio* (address to the Muse) or *principium* (statement of the poem's scope of action), or, indeed, of Latin syntax, will a close-reading strategy work for unpacking this powerful and moving passage? To begin a sentence or a work with *of* would be familiar structure in Latin, or in early-modern English (think of Bacon's essays titled "Of Studies" or "Of Fame," "Of

Youth and Age," "Of Truth," and so on, themselves based on classical models). But—or and—for a modern reader, the experience of waiting six lines to get from the prepositional clause ("Of man's first disobedience") to the verb ("sing") is a powerful tactic of suspension and delay. Milton's enjambments (the carrying over of the sentence from one line to the next) are celebrated, and they teach a great deal about how literature works. What is the effect of ending the first line of verse with "the fruit" and then carrying the sense over to the next ("Of that forbidden tree")? The effect of double take here is similar to the enjambment of Richard III's opening lines: "Now is the winter of our discontent / Made glorious summer by this son of York" (1.1.1–2). In both cases, the listener needs to rethink the syntax, and therefore the meaning, of what has gone before. "Fruit" refers both directly to the fruit of the tree of knowledge, and also to the results, or consequences, of this transgression. And so on. The personal "I" appears in the middle of line 12, after the caesura, or the pause in the verse. The commas, line breaks, caesurae, personal pronouns, and verb forms (invocations, assertions, declarations) are all underscored in the process of reciting aloud. So "having" these twenty-six lines may give the reader—even, or especially, the reader largely unfamiliar with Milton—a template for interpreting, understanding, analyzing, and responding to the rest of this long poem.

Memorization and Its Discontents

The arts of memory go back thousands of years, to cultures and literatures that flourished before printing, and before sophisticated systems of number and placement were developed to assist in retaining and collecting ideas, words, lists, and places so they could be readily and systematically recalled. What people memorize is culturally indicative, whether it's words to a pop song or lines from a political treatise. But to a large extent, memorization has faded from the practices of higher education in literature, even as research on historical memory, medieval "memory theaters," and other mnemonic devices, architectural memorials, and false memory syndrome have increasingly interested scholars in other disciplines. Being asked, or required, to memorize passages of poetry became associated with lack of imagination on the part of the teacher and lack of freedom on the part of the students.

When I began teaching a lecture course on Shakespeare many years ago, I initially thought of the memorization requirement as an old-fashioned practice that was basically a waste of time. How wrong I was. After a year or two, wanting my students to get closer to the text and to feel ownership of it, I restored the requirement that each student memorize twenty consecutive lines of text—any twenty but preferably a single speech—and perform it in the section, or small-group, part of the course. If a student were really reluctant, he or she could recite the lines in office hours, but once it became normalized, students were usually agreeable to, and often eager for, the chance to perform in front of their classmates. Some of the performances were simply stunning and taught me things I had not known about the plays. I remember with particular pleasure a young man who performed Cassius's speech about Brutus ("Why man, he doth bestride the earth / Like a Colossus") with an unbelievably strong outburst of bitter feeling toward the end, when Cassius reports having once rescued "the tired Caesar" from drowning. "And this *man* / Is now become a *god*." I never read these lines now without hearing that student's voice behind them, and he was only one of hundreds who did this exercise every year. I tell my students that they will always remember the lines they have memorized—that at their twenty-fifth class reunions, long after they have forgotten what I said about the plays in lecture, they would still be able to call up "their" Shakespeare speech from deep memory and recite it. I've asked some reunion classes about this, and they've said it is true. The lines had become their lines. They owned a piece of Shakespeare.

Memorization is often conflated with rote learning, in which nothing is really learned but only repeated. Lately, in the press, this kind of memorization has been associated with indoctrination or even with terrorist ideology, as in the account of madrassas (Islamic religious schools) that teach their students to memorize passages from the Koran. Of course, the United States has some texts that are routinely memorized as well, like the Pledge of Allegiance, the Gettysburg Address, and "America the Beautiful." Rarely do we subject any of these to textual analysis—as we would certainly do with poetry or other memorized passages in a literature class—and it might make for some very lively discussions to compare the merits, for example, of "purple mountain majesties" (which is what Katharine Lee Bates wrote in 1895) to "purple mountain's majesty," which is what many people sing.

The tenor of the Pledge of Allegiance as a recitation piece, and a political document and a loyalty oath, was changed when the phrase "under God" was inserted in 1954. From a poetic point of view, the rhythm was altered, as the line comes to a thudding halt: "One nation [heavy pause], under God [heavy pause], indivisible [heavy pause], with liberty and justice for all." Equally significant and equally forgotten are (1) the fact that the pledge was originally written by a Baptist minister and Christian socialist and was distributed as part of a marketing ploy for a popular children's magazine, *The Youth's Companion*, in connection with the sale of flags in the public schools; and (2) the fact that from 1892 to 1942 the recitation of the pledge was accompanied by a stiff salute, the arm outstretched and the palm upward, that looked disconcertingly like the Nazi salute and was therefore changed, by President Franklin D. Roosevelt, to the now familiar hand over the heart.

Or consider the case of "God Bless America." We seldom if ever acknowledge that this song, which has become an informal but universal favorite, sung now at ballparks (especially after the September 11, 2001, terrorist attacks) as well as in classrooms, was originally written in 1918 for an army revue called *Yip Yip Yaphank* and was popularized in 1938 by Irving Berlin and the singer Kate Smith as part of the home front resistance to Hitler. There is a tendency to think that it has always been part of the national spirit. We worry so much about performers hitting the high notes in the national anthem, and about their remembering the words, that we don't ordinarily discuss questions like voice and address (who is speaking when we sing "O say can you see?," and to whom?) or the fact that "The Star-Spangled Banner" is based on a particular historical event (the defense of Fort McHenry during the War of 1812).

In other words, memorization can either replace analysis and context or be combined with them. Without some sense of what the words mean, have meant, and might come to mean (Irving Berlin changed a key phrase in "God Bless America" from "to the right" to "through the night," to avoid the sense that "right" meant the political right wing, not "impartial justice"), these are formulas, not texts. The same is true of works we consider part of a *literary* canon rather than a *national* (or *religious*) canon.

Here I want to stress a point I've made before about literary analysis— that it does not damage but tends to strengthen the status of the texts being analyzed. Their greatness, however we want to define that term, is enhanced rather than undercut by the discussion, interpretation, and examination of historical context. The works of Chaucer do not need to be protected from feminist analysis—just to give one example—any more than the Pledge of Allegiance needs to be protected from its origins in advertising tie-ins and marketing. The more we know, the more we discuss, the more we interpret, the more familiar we become with the language, nuance, history, and meanings (in the plural) of these texts, the better. And this is especially the case, I'd contend, with works that have achieved canonical status. They should be alive to us, which means that they grow and change as the times change and readers change. If they are immobile, marmoreal, and untouchable, venerated rather than read and interpreted, then they are no longer literary and no longer living.

Recognizing Literature

Re-cognition is cognition. You never go anywhere for the first time—you have always somehow imagined or "experienced" it before, in dreams, in images, in novels, in travel documentaries, in fantasy. *Hamlet* is often described in just this way—as a web of quotations, a play that cannot be read for the first time because it has so permeated cultures around the world. The indubitable and indisputable pleasures of the canon are pleasures of rereading, and pleasures of recognition, and pleasures of shape-shifting, as "literary allusions" and "literary influence" and "swerving

from strong predecessors" and "the burden of the past" have all made—
as, again, is often said—the Western tradition into a single gigantic work
of literature.[13]

The invocation of the phrase "Western tradition" raises a few central questions. First, is there a literary canon anymore? Was there ever?
With fewer and fewer readers commanding the classical languages, and
fewer studying French and German (instead of, for example, Spanish,
the language of much of the Western Hemisphere, or various languages
deemed politically or commercially important, like Mandarin, Japanese,
or Arabic), has the idea of a literary canon lost its meaning or its cachet?
The moves toward what was called "opening up the canon" (to women,
to ethnic writers, to the token text from India or China) now look like
a medial step—as doomsayers warned—toward discarding the notion
altogether, since an inclusive canon cannot also be exclusive.[14]

It's been remarked that any Web search under *canon* produces dozens of sites about photographical and digital products before you reach
the first timid citation for literature. But perhaps this hieroglyphic is
itself a lesson. The canon has changed. It has intersected, precisely, with
the photographic, the reduplicative, the digital, the electronic. If you are
looking for a copy of a poem—say, one of those I have discussed above—
you can find it, often in many iterations, on the Web.

Yet ultimately this may be one reason to cherish the canon, or *a*
canon, especially if we think of it as something like an interconnected
reading list, rather than only as a list of Great Books. Mortimer Adler's
rather grandiose phrase "The Great Conversation," used to advertise
and publish his Encyclopaedia Britannica Great Ideas series, may seem
to belong to a different era, but perhaps for that very reason the concept
of a literary canon conversation across the continents and centuries *is*
more important than ever.

THREE

What Isn't Literature

There's no accounting for taste. We might say that whatever we find tedious, banal, sloppy, ill formed, or opaque isn't literature. Or we could say that literature has to pass some kind of test, like the test of age, or having once been in someone's canon, or winning a literary prize. Or we could say that it has to be fictive (or creative or imaginative) in order to be called literature. I don't share any of these views, although I acknowledge their appropriateness in various situations. Instead I think it's productive to look at the boundaries and limits of literature. If we do this, we see a fairly constant centripetal movement from the edges to the center, from the outside to the inside, incorporating once disparaged genres and authors into respectable, canonical, and even classic status.

What once wasn't literature (Renaissance stage plays; novels; high-quality pornographic writing) is now at the heart of the canon, as are works previously defined as "women's literature" or "Afro-American literature." Does the term *literature* in the sense of "worthy of rereading, worthy of study" have any agreed-upon meaning today? Who judges this? Who should?

The word *literature* now seems to have two distinct regions of meaning: one belonging to so-called high culture and print culture, and the other to handouts, throwaways, documents on flimsy paper and in tiny print, among them those providing medical and statistical legalese aiming to shield drug companies from potential lawsuits. ("I'll see what's in the literature on that subject . . .").

Whenever there is a split like this, it is worth pausing to wonder why. High/low, privileged/popular, aesthetic/professional, keep/throw away. It seems as if the category of literature in what we might inelegantly call the literary sense of the word is being both protected and preserved in amber by the encroachment, on all sides, of the nonliterary literature that proliferates in professional-managerial culture. But literature has always been situated on the boundary between itself and its other.

We might want to make the (slightly overreaching but nonetheless interesting) claim that this boundary status is part of what enhances the status of the work/text as literature. Here, our authority, if we need one, is again Immanuel Kant, this time on the topic of genius: specifically, his dictum that genius gives the rule to art. The genius—according to Kant—doesn't follow rules. Indeed, he (for Kant, the masculine pronoun would have been taken for granted) doesn't often make or ordain rules unless he is, for example, Aristotle. To the contrary: rules are made in imitation of, or in consequence of, the rule-breaking performances of artists (including writers). Innovation—breaking the rules—produces rules for the next generation: Sophocles' third actor, Petrarch's love sonnet, Dante's poetry in the vernacular, and Wordsworth's decision to write an epic poem about the growth of a poet's mind—all these innovations changed the course of literature. Brilliant success is often adjacent to failure, as pathos is to bathos. What this means when we come to ask the question "What isn't literature?" is that, all too likely, today's answer will not suit the circumstances of tomorrow—or perhaps of yesterday.

Let me offer two contrasting examples: the graphic novel and the well-made play.

Low and High

The graphic novel is a descendant of the much maligned comic book, a genre so ubiquitous and so reviled in the 1940s and '50s that the Senate Subcommittee on Juvenile Delinquency held hearings on the subject, and an alarmed industry moved toward self-censorship by adopting a Comics Code banning words like *terror* and *zombie* and decreeing that all criminals must be punished. (Unlike, we might note, all criminals in literature . . .) The catalyst, or we might say the reagent, for these hearings was a book called *Seduction of the Innocent* (1954) by the German-American psychiatrist Fredric Wertham. Wertham, who had previously published the essay "The Psychopathology of Comic Books" in the *American Journal of Psychotherapy,* complained of hidden sexual themes, perversion, violence, and morbidity in the comic books of the era, and urged that comics be prohibited to children under the age of fifteen.

"What is the social meaning of these supermen, superwomen, super-lovers, superboys, supergirls, super-ducks, super-mice, super-magicians, super-safecrackers? How did Nietzsche get into the nursery?"[1] Some of Wertham's most derided observations, like the gay themes he detected in *Batman & Robin,* and the dominatrix image of Wonder Woman, are now, minus the moral disapproval, commonplaces of critical interpreta-tion. I was interested by his strong reaction to the publication of *Mac-beth* in comic book form—a mode that is now familiar but at the time provoked Wertham's disapproval and also, as he notes, that of a distin-guished American drama critic:

Another important feature of a crime comic book [Wertham wrote] is the first page of the first story, which often gives the child the clue to the thrill of violence that is to be its chief attraction. This is a psychological fact that all sorts of children have pointed out to me. *Macbeth* in comic book form is an example. On the first page the statement is made: "Amazing as the tale may seem, the author gath-ered it from true accounts"—the typical crime comic book formula, of course. The first balloon has the words spoken by a young woman (Lady Macbeth): "Smear the sleeping servants with BLOOD!"

To the child who looks at the first page "to see what's in it," this gives the strongest suggestion. And it gives the whole comic book the appeal of a crime comic book. As for the content of this *Macbeth,* John Mason Brown, the well-known critic, expressed it in the *Sat-urday Review of Literature:* "To rob a supreme dramatist of the form at which he excelled is mayhem plus murder in the first degree . . . although the tale is murderous and gory, it never rises beyond cheap horror . . . What is left is not a tragedy. It is trashcan stuff."[2]

"Trashcan stuff" is very like what the detractors of Renaissance drama had to say about the literary merit of the entire genre in Shakespeare's time, and of course *Macbeth* as a play *is* violent, bloody, and based on true accounts. That has long been part of its appeal to audiences—in addition to, or sometimes despite, Shakespeare's language. But it's the novelization aspect, the transformation of the play into another form and other words, that the drama critic finds most offensive.

Such translations of the plays into a form that might appeal to children have been popular at least since Charles and Mary Lamb's 1807 *Tales from Shakespeare,* although the Lambs stay much closer to Shakespeare's language: in their tale of *Macbeth,* we read that "she took his dagger, with purpose to stain the cheeks of the grooms with blood, to make it seem their guilt," and that "the proofs against the grooms (the dagger being produced against them and their faces smeared with blood) were sufficiently strong."[3]) For Wertham, a psychiatrist who served as an expert witness in numerous medico-legal cases, the chief issue is the danger he thought sex and sensationalism posed for children—or, as the title of his book declared, the seduction of the innocent. In the classic comic version of *Macbeth,* described by its publisher as "a dark tragedy of jealousy, intrigue and violence adapted for easy and enjoyable reading," he found that "Shakespeare and the child are corrupted at the same time."[4]

Graphic novels, which trace their forebears not only to comic books and comic strips but also to the medieval woodcut, have been published in the U.S. and in Europe since the 1930s. The term *graphic novel* has been in use at least since the 1960s and became popular with Will Eisner's *A Contract with God, and Other Tenement Stories* (1978), in which the word *graphic* was intended to distinguish it not only from what we might call, in a back-formation, the *verbal novel,* but also from other kinds of graphic illustration, like—of course—comic books. These works were thus both *graphic* novels and graphic *novels,* depending upon what the selected comparison (or contrast) group might be. "The American graphic novel considers itself a literary genre," wrote one scholar of the field, "a novel, not made by words, but by images, balloons, and captions," so that "in 'graphic novel,' the important word is 'novel,' not graphic."[5] By contrast, he suggested, in the French-speaking parts of Europe, the emphasis is put much more on the word *graphic,* and the genre as a whole is regarded as a new kind of storytelling where a visual logic motivates both the plot and the narration. But as the form itself has internationalized, these distinctions may be seen to be breaking down.

Some authors of highly regarded graphic novels, like Art Spiegelman, the creator of *Maus,* a graphic novel about the Holocaust, also teach and write about the history of comics—or, as Spiegelman prefers to call them, comix. *Maus,* published in two volumes (*Maus I: A Survivor's Tale* and *Maus II: My Father Bleeds History*) won Spiegelman a Pulitzer Prize in 1992 and was the topic of an exhibition. Spiegelman's graphic novel about the World Trade Center bombing on 9/11, *In the Shadow of No Towers,* was published in 2004.

That *Maus* is a work of literature, whatever literature is thought to be today, is inarguable (though this will doubtless lead someone to argue it). Charles McGrath, in his account of the graphic-novel phenomenon, notes that the genre really took off in the 1990s. Books like Chris Ware's *Jimmy Corrigan: The Smartest Kid on Earth* and Daniel Clowes's *David Boring* have, says McGrath, achieved cult status on many campuses. "These are the graphic novels—the equivalent of 'literary novels' in the mainstream publishing world—and they are beginning to be taken seriously by the critical establishment. *Jimmy Corrigan* even won the 2001 Guardian Prize for best first book, a prize that in other years has gone to authors like Zadie Smith, Jonathan Safran Foer and Philip Gourevitch."[6] Such novels are, he thinks, especially suited for portraying "blankness and anomie," "spookiness and paranoia," and "cartoonish" exaggeration and caricature. "How good are graphic novels, really?" McGrath asks. "Are these truly what our great-grandchildren will be reading, instead of books without pictures? Hard to say." But the genre has gained enormous respect and corresponding review attention.

In a pun that comics and graphic novel writers were quick to exploit, the word *gutter,* a technical term for the space between the panels of a comic strip (as well as for the blank space between two facing pages in a printed book), came to emblematize both the supposed low origins of the genre and its defining formal characteristic. The graphic novel is a growth stock in both the publishing and the academic worlds, the topic of much discussion and of several critical anthologies. The trade paperback version of the collected *Watchmen* comics written by Alan Moore and drawn by Dave Gibbons was marketed as a graphic novel and appeared on *Time* magazine's "All-TIME 100 Novels list" of the "best English-language novels from 1923 to the present," together with works like *All the King's Men, To the Lighthouse, Midnight's Children, The Catcher in the Rye,* and *Gravity's Rainbow.*[7] Increasingly, book awards are being added or expanded to recognize the growth in number and in quality of collaborative graphic fiction. Neil Gaiman's comic book series *The Sandman* included a stand-alone issue, "A Midsummer Night's Dream," which won the World Fantasy Award for Best Short Fiction in 1991. *The Watchmen* was awarded a special Hugo Award in 1988 by the World Science Fiction Society, and a new Hugo category, called Best Graphic Story, was added in 2009 to accommodate and honor the increasing number of graphic works in science fiction or fantasy form.

An enthusiastic front-page review in the weekend arts section of *The New York Times* (A SUPERHERO IN A PRISM, ANTIHEROES IN DEEP FOCUS) spoke glowingly of three new graphic novels that "display the ambition behind an evolving format," and was accompanied by extensive illustrations.[8] Wertham had considered the popularity of the comic book a sign of the loss of interest in reading. He quoted a publisher who, asked about the spread of the comic style to regular publications, answered, "We are retooling for illiteracy," then said flatly, "Comic books are death on reading."[9] He was speaking of children's reading habits. But in a more visual age, and with extraordinary graphics, the comic book has come of age.

As for the term *well-made play,* who uses it today as a term of praise? Yet in the nineteenth century, the well-made play was an extraordinarily successful mode of tight construction, developed by the French dramatists Eugène Scribe and Victorien Sardou, influencing even those who professed to scorn it. In Scribe's typical formula, a plot complication—like letters or documents coming suddenly to light or to hand—brings about a reversal of fortune, sometimes revealing a major character to be a fraud or impostor, which in turn leads to a denouement in which there is at least a semblance of return to order. Dismissed by George Bernard Shaw as "sardoodleism" or "sardoodledom," a contrived plot structure with stereotyped characters, the well-made play *(pièce bien faite)* nonetheless had its effect upon Shaw's plays, as well as those of Ibsen, Strindberg, Chekhov, and other dramatists. (Oscar Wilde's *The Importance of Being Earnest* is a deliberate send-up of the genre that profits both from following and from exploding its by then familiar conventions.) Many of these responses to the well-made play are enrolled in the canons of literature, but the genre, though dutifully taught in courses on the history of the drama, has pretty much disappeared from view. By contrast, this genre's near historical neighbor, melodrama, has enjoyed a recent revival, spurred by film studies but extending back into studies of the Victorian stage and emerging side by side with the sensation novel as an area of intense interest for scholars, audiences, and readers. *Sweeney Todd, The Woman in White, Lady Audley's Secret*—none of these was literature when first written, published, or performed. All are now regularly taught in college and university courses, and feature centrally in well-regarded scholarly books.

While *melodramatic* retains its negative force as an adjective, courses in Hollywood melodrama, American melodrama, melodrama and modernity, melodrama and race, etc., attract both students and teachers. (One indicative text would be *Uncle Tom's Cabin*, an instant best seller when it was published in 1852, having first appeared in serial form in an abolitionist magazine.)

Recent years have witnessed the migration of things that once weren't considered literature into the privileged fold, ranging from essays (Montaigne, Bacon, Addison and Steele, Barthes, Sontag) to what was once called intellectual prose (philosophy, politics, economics, via—for example—Francis Bacon again, or John Milton, or Edmund Burke) to the graphic novel (scion of the humble comic book). This period has seen the emigration of things that once were literature into the discard pile, which has been the fate of not only the well-made play, but also of the long didactic poem. These entities are still arguably literature, or at least literary, if we use those terms in the broadest sense. But they are out of favor at present: a circumstance almost guaranteeing that at some time or another, each will make a triumphant return.

Some genres that have become central to a contemporary understanding of literature, like the novel, were down-market upstarts until fairly recently in modern Western history. The word *novel* began to appear consistently in the 1680s, replacing or competing with *romance;* both terms are used throughout the eighteenth and nineteenth centuries, as what had once been trivial became literature, an instrument of national pride, identification, and cultural advocacy. The study of literature, together with that of the sciences, gained an important place in public culture, and fictions of the self, the individual, and the bildungsroman or novel of personal development, became an influential, as well as a well-regarded, mode of literary writing. This kind of prose fiction differed from the old ideal of the national epic in verse, though—as many critics have noted—it shared some of its goals and techniques. Much more could be said on this topic, about which there exists an extensive and informative body of critical history.[10]

But the point here is straightforward: with the novel, as with the drama, the lyric poem, the satire—indeed, just about every genre we think of as foundational to the notion of literature—we are dealing with a form that has evolved over time, that had some antecedents that were distinctly low, popular, and unrespectable, and in short, *became* literature, for reasons variously aesthetic, political, situational, and cultural. The establishment of a literary canon requires both the forgetting and the selective remembering of these sometimes low origins.

"Baggage Books," Ephemera, and the Ballad

It's not a surprise that texts first regarded as extra-literary should be brought, after the fact, into the canonical fold. Ben Jonson scandalized some of his contemporaries by publishing his plays in folio form in 1612. The publication of Shakespeare's plays in folio eleven years later was a similar act of confidence, or bravery, on the part of his friends. Playbooks were not works, a term of honor reserved for sermons, didactic writings, and other serious endeavors. And the large folio format was reserved for writings of enduring importance, the opposite of stage plays. Sir Thomas Bodley, the founder of Oxford's Bodleian library, instructed his librarian not to include any plays, which he called "riffe raffes" and "baggage bookes."[11] Such things could create a scandal. In any case, plays were comparable, he thought, to items like almanacs and proclamations, useful written objects that, once used, could be thrown away.

The technical term for throwaways of this kind is *ephemera,* from a word meaning "lasting only a day." In general, the word refers to items like posters, greeting cards, seed packets, advertising mailers, air transport labels, printed handouts, and probably everything we now call second-class mail. Perhaps inevitably, ephemera have now become collectibles, highly valued by museums, galleries, auction houses, and libraries. What was once discarded is now purchased, donated, preserved, cataloged, and exhibited. The Ephemera Society of America, formed in 1980, encourages "interest in ephemera and the history identified with it" and publishes *The Ephemera Journal;* a recent issue contained articles on "an important collection of paper ephemera with Shakespearean themes" at the Folger Shakespeare Library; a collection of antiquarian playing cards from the Netherlands that had second lives as "promissory notes, clothing reinforcement, and even heart-wrenching notes from destitute mothers forced to abandon their infants"; and nineteenth-century scrapbooks.[12] There are ephemera collections at the British Library and the National Library of Australia, and an Ephemera Society in New Zealand, as well as archives of video and audio ephemera. Bearing in mind Thomas Bodley's strictures on the ephemerality of playbooks, it is intriguing to note that one especially significant archive today is the John Johnson Collection of Printed Ephemera—located at the Bodleian library, Oxford.

Ephemera also includes specimens of oral art, like ballads, which need to be collected lest they disappear. As the critic Susan Stewart suggests, the justification for the act of collection is the anxiety about disappearance, loss, or contamination, the waning of a supposed authenticity which, paradoxically, will itself be lost when the artifact, having become a work of literature, is removed from the context of performance and placed in the context of art.[13] What this changed status for ephemera means is that items gathered under this rubric are not—if they ever were—ephemeral.

"Folkupmanship" and the Ballad

A ballad is a simple song or narrative that tells a story in verse. The category encompasses everything from medieval minstrelsy to printed broadside ballads celebrating or attacking individuals, events, and institutions.

Two familiar examples from Shakespeare will show something of the low or popular status of the ballad in the English Renaissance, and its complicated relationship with true reporting. In *The Winter's Tale*, the rogue Autolycus presents himself as a peddler selling ballads, several of which, from their description (here offered by a clueless country servant who comically misstates the case), are of the sort that a modern newspaper might call unsuitable for family fare.

> He hath songs for man or woman, of all sizes: no milliner can so fit his customers with gloves: he has the prettiest love-songs for maids, so without bawdry (which is strange); with such delicate burdens of dildoes and fadings, jump her and thump her.
>
> *The Winter's Tale*, 4.4.193–197

The ballads include one about a usurer's wife who gave birth to twenty moneybags, and another about a woman who was turned into a cold fish because she would not sleep with her lover. The latter one sung by the fish, its veracity attested to by "historical" detail: it "appeared upon the coast on Wednesday the fourscore of April, forty thousand fathom above water, and sung this ballad against the hard hearts of maids" (276–279). One eager consumer is a shepherdess, who declares that she "love[s] a ballad in print, a life, for then we are sure they are true" (261–262). Her confident assertion might well serve as a warning to readers of all eras with respect to the automatic credibility of the media, whether printed or electronic. If art is in print, does it mean it is true?

Shakespeare's other unquestioning believer in the truth-telling capacity of ballads is Bottom the weaver, in *A Midsummer Night's Dream*. Having experienced with remarkable aplomb and lack of anxiety a physical transformation into an ass, an erotic relationship with the fairy queen, and a subsequent return to fully human form, Bottom decides that the best way to report the events he thinks he has dreamed is to transform them into a ballad. "I will get Peter Quince to write a ballad of this dream; it shall be called 'Bottom's Dream,' because it hath no bottom; and I will sing it in the latter end of a play, before the Duke" (*MND*, 4.1.212–16). The ballad both contains the marvelous events and defuses them: art here makes the unbelievable believable, converting danger into pleasure.

Ballads began to be collected and published in the late eighteenth and early nineteenth centuries. Among these early collectors were Samuel Pepys and Robert Harley, the First Earl of Oxford, and Mortimer, whose "Harleian Collection" is a main part of the British Library. Bishop Thomas Percy's collected *Reliques of Ancient English Poetry* (1765) inspired Wordsworth and Coleridge to publish their *Lyrical Ballads* (1798), which entered the world as what we would now call literature. Sir Walter Scott, similarly intrigued by Percy's *Reliques*, set about collecting the ballads he would publish in 1802 in *The Minstrelsy of the Scottish Border*. But the popular appeal of Percy's collection also motivated studies of folklore and folk tales by the brothers Jacob and Wilhelm Grimm, and in Germany as well as in Scotland, the ballad craze contributed to the growth of what is sometimes called romantic nationalism. It was not until the Harvard professor Francis James Child produced his collection *English and Scottish Popular Ballads*, however, that the study of these ballads became scholarly, in the sense of collecting variants, classifying and numbering them, and (no small factor) establishing them within the vernacular literature tradition taught at a major university. During the folk music revival of the 1950s and 1960s, it became de rigueur to point toward the authenticity of song lyrics by citing Child's filing system for ballads. Thus, *Time* magazine, in an article about folksinger Joan Baez, noted that "Folkupmanship absolutely requires that a ballad be referred to as Child 12, Child 200, or Child 209 rather than Lord Randal, Gypsie Laddie, or Geordie."[14]

So "what isn't literature?" may depend upon who is asking, and who is answering, and for what ends: institutional, social, aesthetic, and so on. As Susan Stewart observed, "the literary tradition, in rescuing a 'folk' tradition, can just as surely kill it off." For example, "in order to imagine folklore, the literary community of the eighteenth century had to invent a folk, singing and dancing 'below the level' of 'conscious literary art.'" Stewart adds, equally perceptively, that this development has hardly ceased. "The advent of modern literary scholarship, with its task of genealogy—the establishment of paternity and lines of influence—and its role in the legislation of originality and authenticity, depended upon the articulation of a 'folk' literature that 'literature' was not."[15] Meantime, the saga of the ballad continues. While one branch of this field has reconverged with the public and with performance, through folk singers, blues ballads, and the ballad traditions of America, Australia, and other geographical areas, another branch has taken on a new energy within academic work, with the founding of the English Broadside Ballad Archive at the University of California, Santa Barbara. The archive aims to make these fragile objects, often printed on cheap, degradable paper, accessible to scholars worldwide, by transcribing the black-letter font into more easily readable Roman type, and providing online audio recordings, visual facsimiles, and essays that place the ballads in a historical context. Whether any of these uses are "literary" will depend, still, on whether the ballads are being interpreted as signs of the times or as works of art.

Redeeming Social Value

Books banned as indecent, obscene, or pornographic are often remanded, at least by those who ban them, to the category of something other than literature. This has been the case with some of the most critically admired works of the twentieth century, including Joyce's *Ulysses,* D. H. Lawrence's *Lady Chatterley's Lover,* and Vladimir Nabokov's *Lolita.* From the point of view of critics, these were never, arguably, "not literature," but the customs and postal authorities of the United States, Britain, France, Australia, and other nations that have at one time or another outlawed them saw the matter differently. Here again, the question of use (and of abuse) enters the equation, since one of the criteria for a ruling of obscenity has been that a work has "no redeeming social value." In this case, it is probably unnecessary to add that *abuse* (whether self-abuse, child abuse, or some other kind) is sometimes suggested as the intended *use,* or outcome, of the reading or even the simple possession of the banned book.

Ruling in the case of *United States* v. *One Book Called* Ulysses in the U.S. District Court for the Southern District of New York in 1933, Judge John M. Woolsey memorably declared that the book nowhere exhibited "the leer of the sensualist."[16] Defending the frequency with which sex seemed to be on the minds of Joyce's characters, he observed drily, "it must be remembered that his locale was Celtic and his season Spring."[17] And on the question of whether reading the book led to "sexually impure and lustful thoughts," or provoked "sex impulses," Woolsey gave it as his opinion that although the effect of *Ulysses* was "undoubtedly somewhat emetic, nowhere does it tend to be an aphrodisiac," and that its "net effect" on some readers to whom he himself had given the book was "that of a somewhat tragic and very powerful commentary on the inner lives of men and women."[18]

Even to quote these phrases indicates how far we have come in accepting the aphrodisiac (and the emetic) as a commonplace effect of reading modern literature—and also how far we have come since the time when such felicitous phrases, generated on behalf of a book the judge had read and admired, would give evidence of an admirable literary style. By contrast, when the U.S. Court of Appeals reviewed Judge Woolsey's decision, they decided in advance, since they wanted to avoid publicity, that the opinion should, if possible, contain "not a single quotable line."[19] In a foreword to the Random House edition of *Ulysses,* Morris Ernst, the cofounder of the American Civil Liberties Union, noted that Judge Woolsey had "written an opinion which raises him to the level of former Supreme Justice Oliver Wendell Holmes as a master of juridical prose." But we might also want to add that he had mastered the art of the literary review and of literary criticism.

> In writing "Ulysses" [Judge Woolsey's opinion declared], Joyce sought to make a serious experiment in a new, if not wholly novel, literary genre . . . Joyce has attempted, it seems to me, with astonishing success—to show how the screen of consciousness with its ever-shifting kaleidoscopic impressions carries, as it were on a plastic palimpscst, not only what is in the focus of each man's observation of the actual things about him, but also in a penumbral zone residua of past impressions, some recent and some drawn up by association from the domain of the unconscious . . . What he seeks to get is not unlike the result of a double or, if that is possible, a multiple exposure on a cinema screen . . . Whether or not one enjoys such a technique as Joyce uses is a matter of taste on which disagreement or argument is futile, but to subject that technique to the standards of some other technique is absurd.[20]

Woolsey found Ulysses "an amazing *tour de force*," describing it as "brilliant and dull, intelligible and obscure by turns." Joyce, he thought, was "a real artist."[21] The question of law on which the judge was asked to rule was whether the book was written with pornographic "intent"—"that is, written for the purpose of exploiting obscenity." This he emphatically denied. *Ulysses* was "a sincere and serious attempt to devise a new literary method for the observation and description of mankind."[22] It was not obscene under the law.

By comparison, we might note that one of the judges in an earlier 1920 New York court case about the publication of the "Nausicaa" episode of *Ulysses* refused to allow passages to be read aloud in the courtroom because there were women present—including, as it happened, some of the editors of the book.[23]

The standard in the *Ulysses* case in the U.S. in 1933 was whether or not the work was written for the purpose of exploiting obscenity. In the U.K.

in 1960, the decision about *Lady Chatterley's Lover* rested, according to the Obscene Publications Act of 1959, on whether the work in question had literary merit. A group of recognized literary experts—Helen Gardner, E. M. Forster, Richard Hoggart, and Raymond Williams—were called to testify. The chief prosecutor, Mervyn Griffith-Jones, asked the members of the jury whether it was the kind of book "you would even wish your wife or servants to read."

> Would you approve of your young sons, young daughters—because girls can read as well as boys—reading this book? Is it a book that you would have lying around in your own house? Is it a book that you would even wish your wife or servants to read?[24]

This class breakdown doubtless contributed to the ridicule of the prosecution as out of touch with the times, although the mention of "your wife or servants" seems particularly and ironically germane to the plot of the novel. In any case, what was chiefly deplored was the danger such a novel posed to the moral character of readers. The defense, in general, preferred to move the debate away from the dangers of reading and toward either a standard of literary merit that presumably stood apart from and above the social, or a broad and impassioned articulation of the importance of freedom of expression. The jurors in the case returned a verdict of not guilty—and the 1961 Penguin edition of the novel was dedicated to them.

In both *Ulysses* and *Lady Chatterley* the index of the literary was determinative. Judge and jurors attempted to decide whether the works had literary quality and were written with literary intent. Probably the most cited piece of literature to come out of the trials was Philip Larkin's poem "Annus Mirabilis," with its well-known opening stanza:

> Sexual intercourse began
> In nineteen sixty-three
> (which was rather late for me)—
> Between the end of the Chatterley ban
> And the Beatles' first LP.

Similar issues had been raised in connection with Vladimir Nabokov's *Lolita,* which was banned in the United Kingdom and in France before its eventual publication. In an interview with the London *Times,* the novelist Graham Greene had called *Lolita* one of the best novels of 1955. The editor of the *Sunday Express* immediately denounced it as "sheer unrestrained pornography" and "the filthiest book I have ever read." Were these books literature, or were they "filth"? This was the question bandied in the court of public opinion and argued in the courts of law. From a present-day perspective, it would be possible to regard the contretemps as quaint, signs of a very different time. (Morris Ernst indeed compared the lifting of the ban on *Ulysses* to the end of Prohibition.)[25]

For these novels, *literary* was a qualitative honorific, borne out by subsequent critical judgment, and the binary alternative set up by the law as the opposite of obscene. Judge Woolsey's decision, as we saw, was itself an extended and effective piece of literary criticism. All three books are now regularly taught, and highly praised, in college courses. But what about works with a less certain or less acclaimed literary status?

Radclyffe Hall's lesbian novel *The Well of Loneliness* (1928) inspired support from writers and scholars despite doubts about its lasting merit as a work of literature. When *The Well* was condemned by the editor of the *Sunday Express* as "A Book That Should Be Suppressed" ("I would rather give a healthy boy or a healthy girl a phial of prussic acid than this novel"[26]), Leonard Woolf and E. M. Forster drafted a letter of protest and lined up other signatories, including T. S. Eliot, G. B. Shaw, Arnold Bennett, Vera Brittain, and Ethel Smyth. But as Virginia Woolf reported, Radclyffe Hall insisted that the letter should praise the book's "artistic merit—even genius,"[27] and the letter was never sent. Woolf herself, who privately regarded *The Well* as a "meritorious dull book,"[28] signed a briefer letter with Forster and appeared as a witness in court, where she was relieved, she wrote, that "we could not be called as experts in obscenity, only in art." The chief magistrate, Sir Charles Biron, ruled that the question of obscenity was one that he alone would determine, and he refused to permit testimony about literary merit. His decision—that the book was obscene and prejudicial to the morals of the community—was upheld on appeal, and the book was not legally available in the U.K. until twenty years later.[29]

In the United States, Morris Ernst headed the defense when *The Well* was accused of obscenity. A number of prominent authors, including Ernest Hemingway, Theodore Dreiser, F. Scott Fitzgerald, Sinclair Lewis, Ellen Glasgow, John Dos Passos, and Edna St. Vincent Millay, submitted statements in support of the book, and although a magistrate refused to consider the question of literary merit, the New York Court of Special Sessions decided that the book addressed a "delicate social problem" and was not written in a way that could be described as obscene.[30]

But if *The Well of Loneliness* was not obscene, did that make it literature? It has been much reprinted and has sold well; it is often taught in courses on sexuality, lesbian and gay theory, and feminism. Few critics have spoken up in admiration of its style, which is often regarded as overwrought and sentimental. The use of obscene works had been roundly decried: such works, it was said, provoked lustful thoughts, and lustful actions, and were "intended" by the authors to produce such thoughts and actions. What should we say about the use a work like *The Well*, which inspired identification, solidarity, strong and varied emotional responses, and political and social debate? The publicity that the trials brought to the book increased its visibility and its sales, to the pleasure of some and the dismay of others. Its celebrity, and its subsequent place in a historical canon of lesbian and gay writing, came about as a result of a kind of publicity we might want to call extra-literary, or nonliterary. But the publicity was inextricably tied to a debate about whether it was a literary treatment or some other kind of writing.

Moreover, the view that *The Well* addressed a "delicate social problem" comes close to the notion of "redeeming social value," which was laid down in the 1957 case of *Roth* v. *United States* (354 U.S., 476) as the limit standard for obscenity: "[a] book cannot be proscribed unless it is found to be utterly without redeeming social value." The conditions attached were two: the book had to be considered in its entirety rather than by particular parts; and it had to be judged according to contemporary community standards, the anticipated response of the average person. In a later case, *Jacobellis* v. *Ohio* (378 U.S. 184, 191, 194), Justice Brennan altered the phrase to "utterly without redeeming social importance." Whether there is a significant difference between "value" and "importance," legally speaking, is not unambiguously clear.[31] But what is clear is that when jurists and literary scholars go head to head in a courtroom—even, or especially, a Supreme Court room—a great deal depends upon the literary standards of the judge.

Supreme Court Justice Tom Clark, dissenting in the decision on John Cleland's eighteenth-century *Memoirs of a Woman of Pleasure* (usually known as *Fanny Hill*), found literary scholars' testimony about "the book's alleged social value" unconvincing, to say the least. He offered, with "regret," a summary of the book's plot, beginning, "*Memoirs* is nothing more than a series of minutely and vividly described sexual episodes." To the first expert witness's testimony that the book "is a work of art" and "asks for and receives a literary response," he countered with a flat statement of denial: "If a book of art is one that asks for and receives a literary response, *Memoirs* is no work of art. The sole response evoked by the book is sensual." Whether reviews spoke in favor of the novelist's writing style ("literary grace"), the history of the novel as a form, or the heroine's "enthusiasm for an activity that is, after all, only human," Clark dismissed their arguments as worthless: "The short answer to such 'expertise' is that none of these so-called attributes have any value to society. On the contrary, they accentuate the prurient appeal."[32] Despite the facts that Clark's opinion was a dissent and that *Fanny Hill* went on to have a successful commercial career (including films and a spinoff novel by Erica Jong), his views underscore the problem of calibrating "value to society" in terms of "literary merit"—especially when "literary experts" are rejected as lacking any substantive grounds for their expertise.

This was precisely the issue addressed by Justices Harlan and Douglas in their opinions in Memoirs v. *Massachusetts*, the case that addressed the status of Cleland's novel. Justice Harlan wrote, "To establish social value in the present case, a number of acknowledged experts in the field of literature testified that *Fanny Hill* held a respectable place in serious writing, and unless such largely uncontradicted testimony is accepted as decisive it is very hard to see that the 'utterly without redeeming social value' test has any meaning at all." Justice Douglas wrote, "If there is to be censorship, the wisdom of experts on such matters as literary merit and historical significance must be evaluated."[33]

The idea that a work of literature should have an identifiable "social value" to "redeem" it from the charge of obscenity ran counter to much thought about what art was and was not. Such an idea spoke, and speaks, to the continually problematic question of use. If use in this case was synonymous with "having social value," what kept the claim from being merely tautologous, or a matter of taste, whether lay or expert? The defense against the charge of obscenity was, to a certain extent, a defense against the idea that the author's intent had been to create a bad object, something that could be used (or misused, or abused) to generate lustful thoughts and even lustful actions. What was the proper, nonabusive, nonmisusing use of a novel? Was reading a sufficient use? Was it a social value? None of these novels has been at the forefront of social change or social improvement, except if we include—as maybe we should—a change in cultural taste or cultural norms. But this idea, that risky (and risqué) writing should push the envelope of community standards, was not the social value that the Justices had in mind. The notion of redemption, with its religious ring, further complicates the matter: is the sinner in this picture the work, or the author, or the reader?

As is often the case with sin, these putative acts of bad behavior on the part of works of literature seem to have required, or inspired, their foes to wallow in them in order to make their sinful nature clear. Thus, for example, in 1930 U.S. Senator Reed Smoot of Utah undertook a public reading of blue passages from "foreign literature" that brought crowds of spectators to the Senate galleries. Smoot had piled up a stack of works by non-American authors, works he thought should not be permitted to pass through customs. They included Frank Harris's *My Life and Loves,* Balzac's *Droll Tales,* the poems of Robert Burns, the memoirs of Casanova—and perhaps inevitably, *Lady Chatterley's Lover.* Smoot decried the books as "lower than the beasts" and averred that he would rather have a child of his "use opium than read these books." He was succeeded at the podium by Senator Bronson Murray Cutting, who represented New Mexico but had been born in New York and educated at Harvard. Cutting suggested that such liberties were often taken by works of literature: "the first page of *King Lear* is grossly indecent; the love-making of Hamlet and Ophelia is coarse and obscene; in *Romeo and Juliet* the remarks of Mercutio and the Nurse are extremely improper," and so on. "There may," he said, "be people whose downfall and degeneration in life have been due to reading Boccaccio, but I do not know who they are." Moreover, Cutting accused Smoot of having drawn attention to *Lady Chatterley's Lover* by his attacks, suggesting that Smoot had thereby made the book a "classic." This thrust brought Smoot back to his feet. "I resent the statement the Senator has just made that *Lady Chatterley's Lover* is my favorite book!" he said. "I have not read it. It was so disgusting, so dirty and vile, that the reading of one page was enough for me . . . I've not taken ten minutes on *Lady Chatterley's Lover,* outside of looking at its opening pages. It is most damnable! It is written by a man with a diseased mind and a soul so black that he would obscure even the darkness of hell!" In support of Smoot's position on censorship, Senator Coleman Livingston Blease of South Carolina rose to say that his priority was "the womanhood of America" and that "the virtue of one little 16-year-old girl is worth more to America than every book that ever came into it from any other country."[34]

This culture clash would seem completely trivial and forgettable, except that its upshot was to take the question of literary censorship away from the customs agents and leave the decisions, instead, to the U.S. District Courts. Senator Smoot was the co-sponsor of the Smoot-Hawley Tariff Act of 1930, to which the decision about the importation of foreign books was an amendment, so the obscenity trial of Joyce's *Ulysses* three years later came under the jurisdiction of the U.S. District Court and thus, as we've seen, to the sophisticated and humane assessment by Judge John M. Woolsey, who had (unlike Senator Smoot) read the book in question "in its entirety" from cover to cover.

It's easy to think of these blocking figures who rail against the danger of reading as quaint survivors of an earlier, less enlightened age. On the one hand, that age is very much with us in the persistent attempts, for example, to ban *The Catcher in the Rye* (offensive language), *The Bluest*

Eye (sexually explicit content), or the Harry Potter books (witchcraft) from classrooms and libraries;[35] on the other hand, they are in some ways right: reading *is* dangerous, which is why it is important. If literary works (as well as scientific treatises—ask Galileo) did not shake up the world we think we live in, they would indeed be trivial, inconsequential, "entertaining." It is precisely because a book can enrich the mind, challenge, disturb, and change one's thinking, that it may after all—whatever its specific content—possess that curiously elusive quality called "redeeming social value."

Dear Diary . . .

Some forms that, as forms, remain typically outside of literature nonetheless generate examples that have become recognized literary works. Take the example of the diary. Certainly the published diaries of writers like Virginia Woolf have enjoyed and merited publication and study, but what I have in mind is something more like Samuel Pepys's *Diary*, a daily record kept for almost ten years by an English naval administrator, member of Parliament, and fellow of the Royal Society that chronicled his activities, personal, professional, political, and sexual, from 1660 to 1669. In the course of this period, Pepys recorded such epochal events as the Great Plague of 1665, the Great Fire of London in 1665, and the Second Anglo-Dutch War of 1665–67, while also meticulously transcribing descriptions of plays, concerts, meals, and sexual encounters with women other than his wife, often in the same day's account. The diary was written in a shorthand code. After his death, it was decoded with great labor by a scholar who was unaware that the key to the shorthand had been filed quite nearby, in Pepys's library. Other transcriptions and editions followed, and the *Diary* (by turns perceptive, scurrilous, indiscreet, and wise) became a canonical work.

Robert Louis Stevenson called it "a work of art" and observed with admiration that "his is the true prose of poetry—prose because the spirit of the man was narrow and earthly, but poetry because he was delightedly alive . . . you would no more change it than you would change a

sublimity of Shakespeare's [or] a homily of Bunyan's." Stevenson's praise
was affectionate, not hyperbolic: "There never was a man nearer being
an artist, who yet was not one," he wrote, saying that Pepys was comparable to the poet Shelley in "quality" but not in "degree"—"in his
sphere, Pepys felt as keenly."[36] Virginia Woolf, who knew the *Diary* well
enough to mention it regularly in her essays, considered Pepys to have a
rare gift: "in the whole of literature, how many people have succeeded in
drawing themselves with a pen? Only Montaigne and Pepys and Rousseau perhaps."[37] For Woolf, there was no question but that Pepys's *Diary*
was literature. Is it still literature today? Certainly it has been read over
the years with literary attention.

At the other end of this spectrum, consider the vicissitudes of the
work we have come to know as *The Diary of Anne Frank*. Pepys was a
grown man of the world who went many places and saw many things.
Frank was a young girl confined to a hiding place on the upper floors
of an Amsterdam house because of the Nazi persecution of Jews. Pepys
discontinued his diary after almost ten years when it became physically
uncomfortable to write and politically uncomfortable to record. Frank's
diary, begun on her thirteenth birthday, came to an abrupt end a little
more than two years later, when her family was betrayed, discovered,
captured, and sent to a concentration camp.

After Anne Frank's death in Bergen-Belsen, the diary was given to
her father by a family friend. Hoping for publication, Anne had already
revised her diary, with one version containing real names and the other
pseudonyms. Otto Frank restored the names of family members to the
edited account, cut some sections that were critical of Anne's mother or
revealing about the daughter's adolescent sexual feelings, and the diary
was then published in Germany and France in 1950, in the United Kingdom two years later, and—under the title *Anne Frank: The Diary of a
Young Girl*—in the United States in 1952. A play based on the diary won
the Pulitzer Prize in 1955, and a 1959 film, *The Diary of Anne Frank*, was
both a critical and a commercial success. The diary began to be regularly
taught in schools and colleges, even as some scholars began to criticize
the softening and romanticizing of Anne's character in these popular
adaptations. Humanitarians and writers like Eleanor Roosevelt, Nelson

Mandela, and Václav Havel (himself a playwright) commended it for its example and inspiration.

But the transformation of Anne Frank's *Diary* into a ubiquitous work of art was not a seamless development. In a front-page panegyric in *The New York Times Book Review* in 1952, on the occasion of the diary's first publication in the U.S., Meyer Levin called Anne a "born writer" and the book a "classic" that "becomes the voice of six million vanished Jewish souls."[38] The diary immediately skyrocketed from its five-thousand-copy first printing into a nationwide best seller. But Levin never told the *Times* that he had a personal and financial interest in the book: he had asked Otto Frank if he could write a play based on the diary. When his version was rejected in favor of the one written by Frances Goodrich and Albert Hackett (who had worked on the screenplay of *It's a Wonderful Life*), Levin criticized the choice as a way of removing Jews and Jewishness from the Anne Frank story in the service of making it a "universal" tale of heroism and the human spirit, and he sued Otto Frank, accusing him and others of depriving Levin of his opportunity for fame and fortune. Levin's suit failed, and his own reputation suffered, yet some of his incidental observations about the mythologizing of Anne Frank have been sustained.

The play and the film showcased Anne's observation "In spite of everything, I still believe that people are really good at heart," making this uplifting sentiment the last line of the play, although it was written before she was arrested and taken to the camps. The diary actually goes on to discuss "the suffering of millions" for several pages. The result, as many critics have noted, was the production of individual pathos and heroism rather than the story of a terrible, unthinkable event. In Germany at the end of the 1950s, Theodor Adorno reported "the story of a woman who, upset after seeing a dramatization of *The Diary of Anne Frank*, said: 'Yes, but *that* girl at least should have been allowed to live.'"[39] Allowing that it was "good as a first step toward understanding," Adorno added, "the individual case, which should stand for, and raise awareness about, the terrifying totality, by its very individuation became an alibi for the totality the woman forgot."

Hannah Arendt commented in 1962 that the romanticization of Anne

Frank was a form of "cheap sentimentality at the expense of great catastrophe," and the historian Lawrence Langer observed, on the occasion of the publication of a "definitive" critical edition of the diary in
1986, that the young author's "journey via Westerbork and Auschwitz
to Bergen-Belsen, where she died miserably of typhus and malnutri-
tion, would have led her to regret writing the single sentimental line
by which she is most remembered, even by admirers who have never
read the diary." Cynthia Ozick, writing in *The New Yorker* a decade
later, was so critical of the "funny, hopeful, happy" Anne created by the
stage play—and by the elimination of almost all Jewish references in
favor of "universal" ones—that she suggested it might have been better
for the diary to have been burned. Among other things, she noted, the
"bowdlerized, distorted, transmuted, traduced, reduced . . . infantilized,
Americanized, homogenized, sentimentalized, falsified, kitchified, and,
in fact, blatantly and arrogantly denied" diary gave aid and comfort to
the Germans by softening the story and avoiding any reference to the
Holocaust—a view that had been earlier expressed by Bruno Bettelheim
in the pages of *Harper's*.[40] In the classroom, according to recent pedagogical studies, this has been somewhat borne out, as eighth-graders
have tended to read the diary as "hopeful," even a tale of adolescent
romance, resisting the unwelcome information about the family's fate
and Anne's death at Bergen-Belsen. At least one student said that piece
of knowledge had contributed to "ruining" the story.[41]

   This complicated, imbricated, and passionate set of histories surrounding the diary of Anne Frank poses an especially interesting problem for the overarching question about what is, or isn't, literature. Many
of those most perturbed by the softening of the story and the omission of
specific mentions of Jewish identity and the Holocaust are writing from
the perspective of historical accuracy and responsibility. Meyer Levin
felt personally aggrieved, not only as an author but as a Jew; Bettelheim
deplored the effect the altered diary had on readers, especially children,
who were led to think that Anne survived the war. Ozick felt strongly
that sentimental versions erased both death and Jewishness.

   Audiences and readers, whether they are self-exculpating midcentury
Germans, as in Adorno's anecdote, or twenty-first-century schoolchil-

dren, respond to the dramatic, streamlined, "universalized" arc of a narrative culled from the work of the young girl Levin called a born writer—a story shaped (or "distorted") for the times, the book market, and the magnified focus of stage and screen. Those who praise the text do so on grounds they often call explicitly "literary"[42]—as Meyer Levin did in that first review in *The New York Times*. And Ozick's litany of things the diary had become were all, starting with "bowdlerized," descriptions of editorial, aesthetic, and commercial interventions.[43]

Whether *Anne Frank: The Diary of a Young Girl* or any of its spin-offs (the Broadway play, the Hollywood film) is literature may not be quite the right question.[44] When considered in a literary context, it has generated a certain set of responses: the diary is sometimes dismissed or critiqued as naive or sentimental, sometimes lauded as universal and profound. Viewed as cultural history or as historical record, the "same" diary has produced both anger and sorrow, together with a desire, personal and professional, to correct the record, or at least to tell the rest of the story—the part deemed missing from the text as it has been read (or underread) for literary purposes. The frame, the context, will determine how the text is read, assessed, regarded, appropriated, and understood.

What is to be said, then, about the diary of a young girl, preserved against the odds while its author and her family perished? Without the translations into play and film, would the diary, however edited, have attained legendary status? If the process of universalization had not involved, as so many critics complained, the eclipse or erasure of both the specifically Jewish and the catastrophically genocidal frames of the story, would there still have been resistance to the process of making Anne Frank into a timeless and universal heroine?

Words like *timeless* and *universal* are always problematic because they seem to belong to the world of religion rather than the world of literary interpretation and analysis. Such terms indicate a stoppage of time rather than the inevitable changes that come with time's passage. In the case of the diary of Anne Frank, we have a striking example of what happens when reading something as literature in the context of recent and tragic history underscores the tension between literature and history. If it is history, can it be changed in the service of (someone's idea of) art? Does treating the diary as literature inevitably create a climate that is conducive to underreading, to stereotyping of a heroic kind that is in its own way as destructive as the negative stereotypes generated by social prejudice and ignorance?

If so, I think it is because we have forgotten the power of literary reading. When what isn't literature becomes literature, its power is not diminished but augmented. There is no guarantee that reading such a text as literature will produce a historically faithful or politically agreeable assessment. We might place the text in the context of genres other than tragedy or children's literature, the two most familiar categories through which the *Diary* has been read. Other literary options abound, from the historical (the fact that the diary is a mode with its own conventions, one similar to the early epistolary novel) to, for example, the saint's life, the locked-room mystery, the noir thriller, the captivity narrative. Anne's diary is also available for Freudian readings, feminist readings, or readings about the paradoxical functions of language.

Anne Frank was a reader, and she wanted to be a published author. Many of her admirers felt, with Meyer Levin, that she was a born writer, and her diary has been prized by writers for being literary. She describes at great length the act of writing (another good genre for this text, which is all about scenes of instruction). If we give the text the credit for being literary, we cannot at the same time so diminish it to the point that we assume it has only one meaning. We need to allow the activity of *becoming literature* to go where it goes, to understand that literary patterns sometimes write through their authors even as authors think themselves to be controlling the scene.

I understand the desire of some critics to keep the diary as part of the historical record of the period, and I see the way in which Anne's literary celebrity—from the time of the publication of the diary in the United States but especially since the success of the play called *The Diary of Anne Frank*—undercut or usurped the place of more difficult, complex, painful, and necessary information about the Holocaust. In such contexts, human suffering is the topic, and human inhumanity a vital theme. But when a text, in this case the diary, is part of a *literary* investigation, such issues of morality, ethics, and lessons about life are not the whole story. The power of the literary is always divorced from the typical, however much it may be appropriated to support the idea of the type. Once more, it is *how* the story means, rather than *what* it means, that is the literary question. Anne Frank produced her diary in two versions, one with pseudonyms and other literary devices, the other supposedly without them, which is to say that the devices lay beneath the surface, at the level of the text's unconscious. Even without the intervention of her father, who omitted some things and changed others—and the subsequent textual history that produced a critical edition—this mode of literary production opens the diary to the possibility of a sophisticated reading and analysis that is entirely respectful of the text while also reading it against the grain. The protests against such readings would presumably come from the side of the supposed supporters of the literary, not from the side of historians and philosophers. For what multiple literary readings of the diary will surely produce is not a single story but many. Some of these readings will speak of the indomitability of the human spirit, and some, inevitably, will not.

Lost and Found

Another way of investigating the question of what is or isn't literature might be to look not only at the history of taste but also at the way authors and texts are lost and found. This is not as symmetrical a process as the phrase implies. The publication of Herbert Grierson's *Metaphysical Lyrics and Poems of the Seventeenth Century: Donne to Butler,* described as "Selected and edited, with an Essay," occasioned one of the most influential reviews of the early twentieth century, T. S. Eliot's "The Metaphysical Poets," which first appeared in the *Times Literary Supplement* in October 1921. Reviews in the *TLS,* we might note, were unsigned until 1974, when critical anonymity, once the rule rather than the exception, began to seem outdated. "The Metaphysical Poets" explained, contextualized, and offered strong readings of poems by such poets as John

Donne, Lord Herbert of Cherbury, and Abraham Cowley (not to mention the modern French poets to whom Eliot compared them). At the same time, it also began to articulate various critical terms, like "unified experience," "dissociation of sensibility," and the value of difficulty, that would influence both the writing and the teaching of poetry (and literature) for much of the ensuing century. "[I]t appears likely," the review announced calmly, "that poets in our civilization, as it exists at present, must be *difficult*. Our civilization comprehends great variety and complexity, and this variety and complexity, playing upon a refined sensibility, must produce various and complex results. The poet must become more and more comprehensive, more allusive, more indirect, in order to force, to dislocate if necessary, language into his meaning."[45]

The poems of John Donne had been in and out of print since their initial publication in the 1630s, but it was hardly the case that his works were deemed essential to the emerging curriculum of English departments in the early years of their development. Shakespeare, Spenser, and Milton were the Renaissance poets everyone read. For centuries Donne had been regarded as "knotty" (full of intellectual difficulties; difficult to explain or unravel), a word still used to describe his verse. (It's arguable that some also considered them naughty, especially when they were the work of a poet who went on to be an Anglican preacher.) Some nineteenth-century poets, notably Coleridge and Browning, read Donne and admired him. Browning's dramatic monologues are strongly indebted to Donne for their abrupt, direct address to the reader and their use of colloquial speech rhythms. But for the most part Donne was an interesting sidebar rather than a central figure for poets and readers of this period. The taste for knotty, witty, intellectual poetry in English had waned. Then came the one-two punch of Grierson's edition and Eliot's review, and within a few years, Donne's poems were the featured centerpieces of some of the most striking and influential works of literary criticism by the teacher-scholars who came to be known as New Critics.

One indication of the midcentury canonization of Donne is the proliferation of titles of works of fiction and memoir taken from his works. Thomas Merton's *No Man Is an Island*, Ernest Hemingway's *For Whom the Bell Tolls* (both allusions to the same work, Donne's "Meditation XVI"), John Gunther's memoir of his son's early death from cancer, *Death Be Not Proud*—all of these have become classics in their genres. Like Shakespeare, and unlike Spenser and Dryden, Donne crossed over into the allusive mainstream with not even a pair of quotation marks needed to distinguish his seventeenth-century phrases from the lingua franca of modern culture.

I've instanced the fluctuating critical fortunes of Donne's poetry as one example of lost and found. Another, equally canonical, might be the forgetting and the subsequent remembering or re-creating of Chaucer's metrics and scansion. For many years, poets, critics, and readers misunderstood the verse of *The Canterbury Tales, Troilus and Criseyde,* and other major poems by this foundational English author. Signally, readers like Dryden failed to understand that the "final *e*" was sounded ("Whan that Aprill with his shoures soote / The droghte of March hath perced to the roote"), until the scholar Thomas Tyrwhitt (1720–86) identified what one literary history of the period called "the strange delusion of nearly three centuries."[46] Thus Dryden could write, famously (and erroneously):

equality of numbers in every verse which we call *heroic,* was either not known, or not always practiced in Chaucer's age. It were an easy matter to produce some thousands of his verses, which are lame for want of half a foot, and sometimes a whole one, and which no pronunciation can make otherwise. We can only say, that he lived in the infancy of our poetry, and that nothing is brought to perfection at first. We must be children before we grow men.[47]

This passage from the preface to Dryden's *Fables Ancient and Modern,* suggesting that the history of literature is a "progress narrative," starting with the primitive past and progressing to a more sophisticated or grown-up present (that category in motion called modernity), will ultimately be proved a fable. Not that Dryden thought Chaucer wasn't literature—quite the contrary, he was "the father of English poetry," to be regarded in the same honorific light "as the Grecians held Homer, or the Romans Virgil." Nonetheless, Dryden undertook to translate Chaucer, turning his tales "into modern English," despite the objections of some that Chaucer was "dry, old-fashioned wit" not worth the effort, and the complaints of others that much of the beauty of the text would be lost. To the latter, he replied roundly that "not only their beauty, but their being is lost, where they are no longer understood, which is the present case. I grant that something must be lost in all transfusion, that is, in all translations; but the sense will remain, which would otherwise be lost, or, at least, be maimed, when it is scarce intelligible, and that but to a few. How few are there who can read Chaucer so as to understand him perfectly? And if imperfectly, then with less profit, and no pleasure."[48] Dryden accused the purists, who argued that one should read Chaucer in the original or not at all, of being like misers who hoard up their treasures rather than spending or sharing them. He was pleased, though, to note that "Mademoiselle de Scudéry" was at the same time translating Chaucer into modern French (though he speculated that she must be using an old Provençal translation, "for how she should come to understand old English, I know not"). Still, the moment seemed fated: "that, after certain periods of time, the fame and memory of great Wits should be renewed."[49]

The example of Donne is one kind of rediscovery of a lost or neglected text, and the example of Chaucer's metrics, another. But what happens when the text supposedly lost from one era and found in another is discovered to be a new creation? One striking example took place at the end of the eighteenth century, when a teenage boy living in Bristol, England, produced (on parchment or vellum), circulated, and published poems supposedly written by a fifteenth-century priest—poems that, even after the imposture was detected, attracted the attention and admiration of several major Romantic poets.

The young poet was Thomas Chatterton, whose tragic early death—he poisoned himself with arsenic at the age of seventeen, despairing of success in London, starving, and unwilling to return in defeat to Bristol—was surely part of his romantic appeal. Chatterton's "Rowley" poems, attributed to the fifteenth-century personage Thomas Rowley, were much superior, critics have agreed, to the modern poems written in his own voice and name. He had access to a number of old pieces of parchment and to a mysterious chest of documents in the Bristol church of St. Mary Redcliffe, and in his early teens, he set about, imaginatively and industriously, creating for himself a history and a lexicon for Rowley's ancient writings. Interestingly, his Rowley dictionary was based to a significant extent on the glossary to the same edition of Chaucer (edited by Thomas Speght in 1598) that had led John Dryden to conclude that Chaucer's metrics were irregular and deficient. Another of Chatterton's sources, apparently, was the old spelling in Percy's *Reliques,* a repository of early ballads from England and Scotland and which was published in 1765, just as Chatterton began to work on his Rowley project.

Chatterton committed suicide in 1770. Debates about the authenticity of the Rowley poems continued throughout the next decade, with almost all scholars and editors of the period attributing them to Chatterton. Horace Walpole jokingly called the poems Chatterton's "trouvaille" in a conversation at the Royal Academy in 1771—though Oliver Goldsmith maintained that the poems were genuine and that Rowley was their author.[50] Dr. Samuel Johnson, also present at this gathering, was "a stout unbeliever in Rowley, as he had been in Ossian,"[51] the supposed author of a cycle of early Gaelic poems that the Scottish poet James Macpherson claimed to have discovered in the Highlands of Scotland in the same years, and translated into English.

In 1776 Johnson and his biographer, James Boswell, traveled to Bristol; Boswell's lively account of his learned friend's investigations is worth quoting in some detail:

> I was entertained with seeing him enquire upon the spot, into the authenticity of "Rowley's Poetry," as I had seen him enquire upon the spot into the authenticity of "Ossian's Poetry." George Catcot, the pewterer, who was as zealous for Rowley as Dr. Hugh Blair was for Ossian, (I trust my Reverend friend will excuse the comparison,) attended us at our inn, and with a triumphant air of lively simplicity called out, "I'll make Dr. Johnson a convert." Dr. Johnson, at his desire, read aloud some of Chatterton's fabricated verses, while Catcot stood at the back of his chair, moving himself like a pendulum, and beating time with his feet, and now and then looking into Dr.

Johnson's face, wondering that he was not yet convinced. We called on Mr. Barret, the surgeon, and saw some of the *originals* as they were called, which were executed very artificially; but from a careful inspection of them, and a consideration of the circumstances with which they were attended, we were quite satisfied of the imposture, which, indeed, has been clearly demonstrated by several able criticks.

Honest Catcot seemed to pay no attention whatever to any objections, but insisted, as an end of all controversy, that we should go with him to the tower of the church of St. Mary, Redcliff, and *view with our own eyes* the ancient chest in which the manuscripts were found. To this, Dr. Johnson good-naturedly agreed; and though troubled with a shortness of breathing, laboured up a long flight of steps, till we came to the place where the wondrous chest stood. *"There,* (said Catcot, with a bouncing confident credulity,) *there* is the very chest itself." After this *ocular demonstration,* there was no more to be said. He brought to my recollection a Scotch Highlander, a man of learning too, and who had seen the world, attesting, and at the same time giving his reasons for the authenticity of Fingal:—"I have heard all that poem when I was young."—"Have you, Sir? Pray what have you heard?"—"I have heard Ossian, Oscar, and *every one of them."*

Johnson said of Chatterton, "This is the most extraordinary young man that has encountered my knowledge. It is wonderful how the whelp has written such things."[52]

Notice that the "ocular demonstration" of the supposed provenance of the poems is viewed, by both Boswell and Johnson, with the scorn it deserves. The chest is no more evidence of the authenticity of the documents than is the floor jabbed repeatedly by the tourists of Shakespeare's birthplace in Henry James's short story ("'And is this really'—when they jam their umbrellas into the floor—'the very *spot* where He was born?'"[53]). What was required was textual evidence of authenticity, one way or another, which was shortly to be provided, as it happened, by the same Thomas Tyrwhitt who had edited Chaucer and corrected earlier impressions about the pronunciation of his verse. In 1777 Tyrwhitt produced an edition of *Poems, supposed to have been written at Bristol, by Thomas Rowley, and others, in the fifteenth century.* In the third edition, published a year later, he added—and issued as a separate publication—an *Appendix: containing some observations upon the language of the poems attributed to Rowley; tending to prove that they were written, not by any ancient author, but entirely by Thomas Chatterton.*

At the same time, though, we might note that Johnson, whatever his incredulity about Rowley, was quite willing to praise Chatterton, the poet Wordsworth would later call "the marvelous boy"[54] to whom Keats would dedicate his "Endymion," whose modern poems were so unsuccessful, became a sensation, beloved of the early Romantics, and a herald of the new medievalism that would interest Lamb, Hazlitt, Rossetti, and William Morris. Undoubtedly, his tragic death had something to do with it—Wordsworth describes him as "The sleepless soul that perished in his pride"—but Keats's friend Benjamin Bailey stressed the fact that Keats was taken with Chatterton's poetry:

> Methinks I now hear him recite, or *chant*, in his peculiar manner, the following stanza of the "Roundelay sung by the minstrels of Ella":
>
> > "Come with acorn cup & thorn,
> > Drain my hertys blood away;
> > Life & all its goods I scorn,
> > Dance by night or feast by day."
>
> The first line to his ear possessed the great charm. Indeed his sense of melody was quite exquisite, as is apparent in his own verses; & in none more than in numerous passages of his Endymion.[55]

The issue of the authorship and authenticity of the Rowley poems continued to be debated in some circles at least until W. W. Skeat's edition in 1871, a hundred and one years after Chatterton's death. But we should note that by that time, the context was a volume called *The Poetical Works of Thomas Chatterton, with an essay on the Rowley poems.* The "trouvaille" about which Walpole had jested, the "found" poems and "found" poet of the fifteenth century, were now proudly repackaged as the works of Chatterton. Somewhat ironically, we may think, Skeat's introduction noted that the spelling in the longest and most important of the Rowley poems had been modernized, an improvement he thought long overdue, "so as to render them at last, after the lapse of a century, accessible *for the first time* to the general public."[56] The inventive orthography that had distinguished these poems as "authentically" of the fifteenth century, painstakingly gleaned by Chatterton from a Chaucer glossary, from the ballads collected by Bishop Percy, and from the words marked *obsolete* in two etymological dictionaries, was now, by an editorial decision about accessibility to the general public, made to disappear.

As for the fictional Ossian (the same Celtic hero Yeats would write of as Oisin), James Macpherson had claimed that he translated authentic documents written by a third-century Irish bard. No manuscripts were ever produced or found, and Dr. Johnson, never a fan of Scots or Scotland, famously (and accurately) accused Macpherson of "imposture."[57] Chatterton died a spectacular death and become a celebrity; Macpherson lived almost till the end of the eighteenth century, traveled briefly to Florida, worked for Lord North's government, wrote history, and ended as a member of Parliament, buried in Westminster Abbey a short distance from his detractor, Dr. Johnson. But *The Poems of Ossian, the Son of Fingal,* purportedly translated and edited by Macpherson, would continue to appear from 1765 through the end of the following century, usually reprinted with an essay by Hugh Blair, a celebrated professor of rhetoric at the University of Edinburgh, defending the authenticity of the works.[58]

Ossian's other admirers included Walter Scott, the young J. W. von Goethe (who translated sections of it for *The Sorrows of Young Werther*), Johann Gottfried von Herder, and the emperor Napoleon (who read the works in Italian translation). The enthusiastic Napoleon forthwith commissioned Ingres to paint a canvas called *The Dream of Ossian,* and many other painters found inspiration in the topic in the early years of the nineteenth century, producing representations of *Ossian on the Bank of the Lora, Invoking the Gods to the Strains of a Harp,* and *Ossian Receiving Napoleonic Officers.* Not only had Ossian become literature, his work produced other literature; indeed, it produced or generated national literatures. Lost or found? Imposture though Ossian might be, this "found" poet had a huge effect on the spread of European romantic nationalism. The fame and influence of his poetry extended from Scotland to France, Germany, and Hungary. Oscar Fingal O'Flahertie Wills Wilde owes his first two names to the heroes of Ossianic poems—and in his own compelling fiction about forgery and poetry, "The Portrait of Mr. W. H.," he cites both Chatterton and Macpherson.

When it comes to literature, these two ideas are not always symmetrical. Where Donne was "lost" for a while because he was seldom reprinted and even more seldom read, and Chaucer was "lost" because his language and metrics were not understood, both were "found"—restored to the canon and the literary tradition—through the work of subsequent editors and critics.

Does intention matter? Does inadvertence?

In what would prove to be an amusing and instructive pedagogical improvisation, the critic Stanley Fish once invited his students of a 1971 summer course in seventeenth-century religious poetry to interpret a poem they found on the blackboard when they entered the class. The poem was a list of names left over from Fish's previous class in the same room— a class in contemporary theories of linguistics and literary criticism. Predictably, the students leaped imaginatively to their task, finding religious allegories, symbols, doctrines, and holy puns, as well as an underlying structure that disclosed both a Hebrew and a Christian subtext. "As soon as my students were aware that it was poetry they were seeing," Fish wrote, "they began to look with poetry-seeing eyes, that is, with eyes that saw everything in relation to the properties they knew poems to possess." For Fish, this was not a discouraging but an intriguing event, as was the explanation he offered: "Interpretation is not the art of construing but the art of constructing. Interpreters do not decode poems: they make them."[59] In subsequent books and articles, he would go on to develop his reader-response theory of "interpretive communities"—a theory that Fish, who began his career as a Miltonist, demonstrated most signally through a reading, not of ephemera on a blackboard, but of the *Variorum Commentary* on the works of John Milton.[60]

Fish's pedagogical stunt did not make the names on the blackboard literature. What it did do—and what an early experiment by I. A. Richards also did, although Richards used published poems rather than found text—was to demonstrate that there are literary ways of reading. (Richards's book chronicling the process, *Practical Criticism*, was subtitled *A Study of Literary Judgment*.)[61] Not all of these ways are successful or pertinent. But let us imagine for a moment that Fish's students, in that long-ago classroom at the University of Buffalo, had had recourse to instant Internet searches or had determined that their task was to historicize the set of words (all proper names) on the board, or to seek out the ethical, moral, or political connections among them. They would have avoided the excessive critical ingenuity that Fish both admits and admires, and that he does not call misplaced, though others might. They might even have correctly identified the individuals listed, although each was represented only by a surname, so there was plenty of room for error. And they might have constructed a narrative about the connections between Jacobs-Rosenbaum, the coauthors of linguistic textbooks, and Levin and Thorne, who were each then working on a possible relationship between transformational grammar and literary texts. By dint of investigation, the students might have discovered that Fish himself was teaching a linguistics course during the previous period. This would have been, no doubt, a more accurate and demystifying explanation of the names. But it would have had nothing to do with literature. Or with what appears, from the evidence presented in Fish's essay, to have been an admiringly rigorous training in seventeenth-century poetics.

As Literature

One final way we might track the "what is / what isn't literature" question is via the use of *as* in the title of a college course or a program in reading. Take, for instance, the familiar and apparently innocent phrase "the Bible as literature." What is the implication of that little word *as*? Well, for one thing, it implies that there is another way of reading (the Bible as revealed truth; the Bible as moral philosophy). For the Bible, this is arguably a loaded question. Which Bible? Which translation? The Hebrew Bible plus the New Testament?

Many significant works of English and American poetry and prose allude to verses or persons mentioned in the Bible, so it makes sense that the English Bible or some other way of describing the Bible as literature should be offered as a course at schools and colleges. But the same can be said of Greek and Roman mythology, which, if taught, is not usually tagged with *as literature*. "The Bible as literature" is both an inclusion and an exclusion, an acknowledgment of literary influence and literary style, and a bracketing of the question of belief. None of which is completely satisfying, either to believers or to nonbelievers. Reading the Bible as literature, teachers of such courses explain, may involve using reading strategies drawn from such diverse interpretive practices as formalism, post-structuralism, cultural hermeneutics, etc. As one instructor wrote in a memo for prospective students, "Studying the Bible as Literature does not mean that we insist the text (Old Testament) is a series of fables or that it is patently false. Similarly, this way of reading the Bible does not insist that the Old Testament is a document that is historically true in the scientific, strict sense of the phrase. Rather, we are seeking a literary understanding of 'truth.' "[62]

Perhaps predictably, Allan Bloom singled out "the Bible as literature" in *The Closing of the American Mind* as an indication of "the impotence of the humanities," suggesting that to "to include [the Bible] in the humanities is already a blasphemy, a denial of its own claims," and that teaching the Bible as literature rather than "as Revelation" makes it possible for it to be read as a secular document, "as we read, for example, *Pride and Prejudice*." For Bloom, the professors who taught classic texts, among which he includes the Bible, were not interested in the "truth" of those texts.[63] Presumably, the idea of "a literary understanding of 'truth'" would have struck him as fallacious.

The phrase *as literature* has also been used in other contexts, like, for example, "film as literature," once a legitimating move that explained or justified why courses on film were included in the curricula of literature departments. When methods of film analysis moved away from this paradigm and closer to visual, historical, and philosophical analysis—

and as film studies established itself as a humanities discipline in its own right—*as literature* tended to drop away, sometimes replaced by the more anodyne *and,* which often denoted a comparison between specific works of literature and specific films or film genres. On the other hand, "Freud as literature" or "Marx as literature" or "Darwin as literature" suggests that a body of work associated with another discipline or subject area will be read according to protocols designed for, and effective in analyzing, literary works. In the case of Marx and Freud, at least, it sometimes comes with an unspoken subtext, implying that *as literature* is a fallback or secondary framework, and that the analysis of these writers has come under the aegis of literary scholars because they are no longer influential in the fields of psychology or economics.

In his classic essay on the "author-function," Michel Foucault described Freud and Marx as belonging to a class he called "initiators of discursive practices":

> The distinctive contribution of these authors is that they produced not only their own work, but the possibility and the rules of formation of other texts. In this sense, their role differs entirely from that of a novelist, for example, who is basically never more than the author of his own text. Freud is not simply the author of *The Interpretation of Dreams* or of *Wit and Its Relation to the Unconscious* and Marx is not simply the author of the *Communist Manifesto* or *Capital;* they both established the endless possibility of discourse.[64]

Foucault is quick to anticipate objections to his placement of such authors in a more influential position than that of novelists: "The author of a novel may be responsible for more than his own text; if he acquires some 'importance' in the literary world, his influence can have significant ramifications."

But his main point is to try to distinguish between a writing practice that spawns imitators and one that generates productive thought and resistance. "Marx and Freud, as 'initiators of discursive practices,' not only made possible a certain number of analogies that could be adopted by future texts, but, as importantly, they also made possible a certain number of differences. They cleared a space for the introduction of elements other than their own, which, nevertheless, remain within the field of discourse they initiated."[65] These writers have begun a conversation that would have not been possible without them. Thus, the twentieth century saw the popularization of adjectives like *Freudian* and *Marxist*. Given the blurring that often comes with cultural transmission, such terms were almost guaranteed to be caricatured and misunderstood. Nonetheless, their prominence in popular media is a telling indication of the role these writers have played in literary criticism and interpretation, as well as in the way modern thinkers think. "There are," Foucault says provocatively, "no 'false' statements in the work of these initiators," because the issue is not false or true or right or wrong but what he called the possibility of discourse. This drives unsympathetic critics crazy. For some, the flat claim that "Freud was wrong" or that "Marx was wrong" becomes an article of faith and one that definitively halts any possibility of discourse. But Foucault's contention is that such initiators teach a new way of thinking, not a set of prescribed (or proscribed) thoughts. "A person can be the author of much more than a book— of a theory, for instance, of a tradition or a discipline within which new books and authors can proliferate."[66]

So are Marx and Freud literary authors? Are *Capital* and *Civilization and Its Discontents* works of literature? I'd say yes, and not only because these authors write so well, though it is important to me that they do. The moves that they make in setting up an argument, in offering detours and counterexamples, in not being afraid to contradict and reverse themselves, are *literary* in the most complimentary sense of that elastic term. The literary critic Peter Brooks wrote an essay called "Freud's Masterplot," about the argument and stylistic development of *Beyond the Pleasure Principle*, that became a centerpiece for Brooks's book about narrative fiction, *Reading for the Plot*.[67] Freud, Marx, Darwin, and other major intellectual and cultural theorists provided a range of plots and languages for creative writers and critics who came after them.

What isn't literature? It might make sense to adapt the saying about New England weather and suggest that if something isn't literature now, we just need to wait five minutes—or five years, or fifty, or even five hundred. The process takes time (often centuries or decades) to change Thomas Bodley's "riffe-raffe" into the masterpieces of Elizabethan and Jacobean drama, or the actionable obscenity of *Lolita* or *Ulysses* into the most honored of twentieth-century novels. Becoming literature, as we saw in the case of the ballad, isn't always an unreflectively positive transition—there are perceived losses as well as gains with the change in status. For *literature* is a status rather than a quality. To say that a text or a body of work is *literature* means that it is regarded, studied, read, and analyzed in a literary way.

FOUR

What's Love Got to Do with It?

To say you love literature would seem to be a prerequisite for life as a teacher and critic. But it's also the case that when students, buffs, and fans profess that they love Shakespeare or they love Jane Austen—the two most frequently mentioned love objects, in my experience—the teacher often worries as much as she rejoices. Love is not a critical stance; it does not necessarily welcome interpretations, especially multiple interpretations. What Freud accurately called "the overestimation of the object"—the idea that the loved one is imbued with extra value, with superlatives, even with perfection, as a way of ensuring that the lover stays in love—is sometimes a way of avoiding analysis and critique rather than pursuing them.

Like many other people who teach and write about literature for a living (the biographer R. W. B. Lewis once memorably said to me that "teaching Shakespeare was taking money for jam"), I've often encountered undergraduate and graduate students who were concerned that literary criticism, literary analysis, and literary theory would take away their pleasure in reading rather than making it richer and fuller. Happily, that tends to be a brief moment rather than a lasting one, since the delights of literary immersion, whether through an examination of imagery, symbolism, prosody, rhetoric and syntax, historical context, and/or performance, tend almost always to produce new ways of loving familiar texts as well as encounters with new texts to love. Still, there are moments of evasion, avoidance, disavowal: "I don't want to *spoil* it for myself." But there is no cause for concern. Poems, plays, novels, critical essays, aphorisms—these are all vivid, vigorous, healthy, tough, resistant: they will survive. Dismembering them through analysis and interpretation is one of many ways of engaging with and remembering them. Works of literature are not soap bubbles or daylilies or meteors or mirages: they will last, indeed much longer than any reader or critic.

Before "English"

The idea of an "English major" is a fairly recent development, as institutional histories go, dating from the last decades of the nineteenth century. When he was an undergraduate at Yale in the 1850s, wrote Andrew Dickson White, later the cofounder and first president of Cornell University, "there was never a single lecture on any subject in literature, either ancient or modern . . . As regards the great field of modern literature, nothing whatever was done. In the English literature and language, every man was left to his own devices."[1] Frederick Barnard, who would later become president of Columbia College, reported that he gained what literary training he could, not in Yale's courses, but in the literary societies.[2] The novelist Henry James, who spent a brief time at Harvard Law School (but took no degree), said, "A student might read the literature of our own language privately, but it was not a subject of instruction . . . Professor [Francis James] Child provided an introduction to the reading of Anglo-Saxon and Chaucer. There, so far as English literature was to be considered, the College stopped."[3] Child was then the Boylston Professor of Rhetoric and Oratory; it was not until 1876 that he was appointed the first, and at that time the only, professor of English at Harvard. From 1834 to 1854, Henry Wadsworth Longfellow was the Smith Professor of Modern Languages and of Belles Lettres, where, in addition to teaching English, he supervised students in Italian, Spanish, French, and German, as well as offering, or being prepared to offer, Swedish, Danish, and Icelandic.

When English was taught in the university, it was often in the form of historical surveys ("without reference, necessarily, to the texts of the classics themselves"[4]) or the study of philology and rhetoric. The first real courses in English were not offered at Harvard until 1872–73 (long after Henry James was a student), and even then two of the three courses were in Anglo-Saxon and in the history and grammar of the English language. Shakespeare, a popular subject for undergraduates, became a Harvard course in 1876, but even so, the reading and discussion of English poetry and of Shakespeare continued to be largely relegated either to family training at home (or through tutors) or to social clubs on college campuses. Love of literature, when it existed—as manifestly it did, since the period produced numerous writers and poets of distinction—was a personal pleasure, not an academic goal. Was literature useful—or useless? For Emerson, Longfellow, and Henry James, it was invaluable; they lived it and breathed it. Longfellow retired from teaching and devoted himself to writing once his income from publishing permitted him to do so. James decided he did not want to study law (and as we've seen, he couldn't have studied English or literature in the sense we understand those fields today). Instead, he traveled in Europe, wrote fiction, and began to contribute to magazines like *The Nation* and *The Atlantic Monthly.*

In the novels of Jane Austen, both women and men read aloud for their own pleasure and for the pleasure of their listeners. In *Mansfield Park* (1814), Fanny Price is inclined to resist the too easy manner of Henry Crawford, but she has to acknowledge his skill as a performer when he takes up the "volume of Shakespeare" she herself had been reading aloud to entertain the indolent and demanding Lady Bertram.

> [H]is reading was capital, and her pleasure in good reading extreme. To good reading, however, she had been long used; her uncle read well—her cousins all—Edmund very well; but in Mr. Crawford's reading there was a variety of excellence beyond what she had ever met with. The King, the Queen, Buckingham, Wolsey, Cromwell, all were given in turn; for with the happiest knack, the happiest power of jumping and guessing, he could always light, at will, on the best scene, or the best speeches of each; and whether it were dignity or pride, or tenderness or remorse, or whatever were to be expressed, he could do it with equal beauty.[5]

Even more striking is the way in which courtship is accomplished through reading aloud in the posthumously published *Persuasion* (1818), where

the flighty Louisa Musgrove, confined to a sickbed because of an accident, is wooed, and won, by the widower Captain Benwick, described as
"a clever man, a reading man," who sits by her bed and reads her poetry.
However dissimilar they might be, muses the heroine, Anne Elliot, they
would become more alike over time. Louisa "would learn to be an enthu-
siast for Scott and Lord Byron; nay, that was probably learnt already; of
course they had fallen in love over poetry."[6]

Reading aloud, taking books from the public library, participating
in book clubs and reading groups—these were not only modes of self-
improvement but also opportunities for pleasure and sometimes for
romance. As they are still today. Oprah's Book Club and thousands of
individually organized book groups invite lovers of literature (or "lovers of books") to participate in weekly or monthly discussions. Some of
these groups read best sellers; others read classics or books chosen to
reflect on a central theme. Special-topic areas, like African-American
women's reading groups and gay men's reading groups, have formed,
and are flourishing, around the country and the world. Lists of book-
group favorites are posted, and authors of popular novels and self-help
books periodically make themselves available to attend sessions. Dozens
of Shakespeare reading groups advertise online and by personal invitation offering an opportunity to read the plays aloud. And many successful adult professionals, having made careers in fields like law, medicine,
economics, and technology, return to extension and continuing education courses, in person or online, to pursue their interest in, and love of,
literature.

The number of American college students graduating with B.A. degrees
in English, which in 1950 was about 17,000, or 4 for every 100 bachelor's
degrees, increased in the next decade, peaking in 1971 (when there were
more than 64,000 English graduates nationwide, or 7.66 per hundred
total bachelor's degrees). From that point it began to decline, with a
minor uptick in the early nineties. By the beginning of the twenty-first
century, the percentages had returned to the level of fifty years previously, 4 in 100.[7] (Meantime, other humanities fields were experiencing

even more serious declines.) By 2006–7 the number had decreased further, to 3.62 of every 100 bachelor's degrees.

A variety of reasons for this decline can be offered or guessed at, including the economy, information technology, the lure of lucrative careers in the financial sector, the great expansion of academic fields beyond the basic subject areas of midcentury, the national push for science education, and so on. Many English (and other modern literature) majors always planned to go on to law school or other kinds of professional training after college, but the old truism—that a degree in English made you seem literate and well grounded in general education—was gradually replaced by a new truism, that the English major was useless. It was only a short step to thinking that perhaps this made it somehow self-indulgent, whereas ambitious young students ought to be networking, laying the groundwork for a legitimate career, developing marketable skills—in short, thinking ahead. If they thought far enough ahead, they might envisage themselves enrolling in evening courses or cultural tour groups in an attempt to get back in touch with their interests in literature.

It's always been difficult to explain to administrators and fund-raisers why criticism and theory are research. Undergraduate education in the literary classics is considered a part of general education, but specialization, while normative for intellectual advancement in the social sciences and the sciences, has often been looked upon with skepticism or suspicion when conducted in the humanities. Epithets like *political* or *ideological* (terms that are, incidentally, perfectly acceptable categories of analysis in other areas) have been hurled at literary scholars as if such interests somehow undermine or make less pure their interest in works of poetry, fiction, and drama. Robert Alter's 1989 book *The Pleasures of Reading in an Ideological Age* argued that pleasure and love of literature was the proper province of literary study. If literary scholarship were to become too professional, the elusive but crucial element of love might drop out. You can see that this is a kind of double bind: if literary study is centered on love of literature, it is regarded as basic but not advanced, general but not specialized, ancillary and pleasurable but not essential. But when literary study moves into the realm of theory, or editorial practice, or material culture, or any other of its myriad edges, left or right, up or down, it runs the risk of abandoning its main mission to give pleasure, inspire love, and be, in effect, its own reward.

If a scientist were to tell us he or she loved science (as scientists frequently do), we probably would not consider such a remark tantamount to saying that science was not professional, or did not involve research or specialization, or that the speaker was a fan or a dilettante rather than a working scientist. Love of politics does not mean that the lover is not also a potential scholar, or candidate, or bureau chief. But love of literature (or love of art or music) often is taken to indicate a set of recreational interests or a level of social—rather than intellectual—sophistication.

So literary criticism and literary studies, which were once considered the accoutrements of a gentleman's or a lady's social education, or alternatively, in the spirit of Matthew Arnold, a bootstrapping opportunity for the achievement of meritocracy without the advantages of inherited wealth or position, or, in the spirit of the Great Books movement and James Conant's *General Education in a Free Society,* the necessary preparation for productive citizenship in a democracy, are now again—for slightly different reasons and with a different populace—an "extra," an elective, an enhancement rather than either a necessity or a power position.

What used to be called "appreciation" (and, at the advanced or professional or donor level, "connoisseurship") is now sometimes folded into aesthetics or into the history of affect or taste. It was partly in resistance to this idea of literary culture, and the accomplishments of the gentlemanly art of belles-lettres (literally, beautiful or fine writing), that some early-twentieth-century scholars turned to history or to philology as more scientific, archival research fields. What was at issue, sometimes explicitly, was the status of literature as an amateur or a professional pursuit. As time has gone by and the difference between amateurs (who, etymologically at least, are in it for love) and professionals (who do it as their profession and expect to be paid for their work) has continued to erode in fields like sports, music, or politics, literary studies has continued to worry, and to worry about, the distinction. There are, I think, a number of reasons for this. One key reason, certainly the one most pertinent to this discussion, is the belief that literature and love have a special relationship to each other: that loving literature is, after all, what literary study is all about.

Amo, Amas, Amat

The poet and literary critic R. P. Blackmur began a justly celebrated essay called "The Critic's Job of Work" with a declaration that was also a gauntlet deftly thrown down: "Criticism, I take it, is the formal discourse of an amateur."[8] We might notice, admiringly, the seeming casualness of "I take it"—and the rhythm that this personal aside imparts to the utterance. Without it, the statement would be flat, prescriptive, far less interesting: "Criticism is the formal discourse of an amateur"—an example of the very kind of "doctrine" he will go on to critique in his next few pages. Blackmur is not, however, doctrinaire when he comes to the question of the use of concepts that may be "propitious and helpful in getting over gaps," so long as that use remains "consciously provisional, speculative, and dramatic." Writing in 1935, he observed that the "classic contemporary example of use and misuse" was "attached to the name of Freud."

> Freud himself has constantly emphasized the provisional, dramatic character of his speculations; they are employed as imaginative illumination, to be relied on no more and no less than the sailor relies upon his buoys and beacons. But the impetus of Freud was so great that a school of literalists arose with all the mad consequence of schism and heresy and fundamentalism which have no more honorable place in the scientific than the artistic imagination.[9]

The little word *has* here tells part of the story: Freud was still alive when this essay was written, but his work had already begun to be literalized and turned into doctrine. Yet Blackmur was a perceptive reader (and user) of Freud, as he demonstrates in this elegant peroration in the penultimate paragraph: "Art is the looking-glass of the preconscious, and when it is deepest seems to participate in it sensibly"—by which he means with the senses. And what of criticism? What is its nature and role? "Criticism may have as an object the establishment and evaluation (comparison and analysis) of the modes of making the preconscious *consciously* available."[10] To make the preconscious consciously available is the task of the critic. But what does he mean by "the formal discourse of an amateur"?

Blackmur himself was an amateur only in a technical sense. He had no higher degrees, and from 1928 to 1940, he was a freelance poet and critic, until he began an affiliation with Princeton University and became a professor of English. He unpacked the notion of love at the beginning of his essay: criticism "names and arranges what it knows and loves, and searches endlessly with every fresh impulse or impression for better names and more orderly arrangements."[11] Those names and arrangements are the formal aspects of the work. The discourse is the mode of communication: the presentation of the critic's ideas as a connected series of utterances so they provide a unit and a model for analysis. And amateur? Does it mean lover or reader? Critic rather than textual editor or historical scholar? A close reader of the text rather than the context?

Because Blackmur begins with this wonderfully tendentious phrase about an amateur, it might be easy to mistake his meaning—until the reader plunges into the heart of his essay. "A Critic's Job of Work" (the appealingly homely title is a bit misleading) speaks out in favor of Plato and Montaigne, of "imaginative skepticism and dramatic irony" that "keep the mind athletic and the spirit on the stretch," and, wittily, of the "juvenescence of *The Tempest,*" and the "air almost of precocity of [G. B. Shaw's] *Back to Methuselah,*"[12] venerable texts about age that remain forever young. What Blackmur objects to is contemporary criticism that is "primarily concerned with the *ulterior purposes of literature,*" and here he cites three texts, all well reputed, that he thinks are pointing in the wrong direction for literary study: George Santayana's essay on Lucretius, Van Wyck Brooks's *The Pilgrimage of Henry James,* and Granville Hicks's *The Great Tradition.* The problem with all three, however different they may seem, is that they are "concerned with the *separable content of literature*, with what may be said without consideration of its specific setting and apparition in a form; which is why, perhaps, all three *leave literature so soon behind.*"[13]

Remember that this is an essay from 1935. Its own juvenescence, if we may put it that way, seems considerable: "the ulterior purposes of literature," "the separable content of literature," and "leav[ing] . . . literature behind" are very contemporary concerns, as timely now as they were then.

"A Professional Writer"

Several years ago I wrote an essay about "The Amateur Professional and the Professional Amateur."[14] What I meant by "amateur professional" was someone who did not have specific training in a field but nonetheless had become a respected practitioner in it, like C. P. Snow, a scientist who wrote novels and cultural criticism, or Carl Djerassi, a chemist who writes plays, or Judge Richard Posner, who has written on law and literature. What I meant by "professional amateur" was someone who disavowed the status of professional in favor of the preferred role of amateur, gaining points by *not* being a professional: the book reviewer, the belletrist, the polymath, and the public intellectual. Two examples I cited from this category were Kenneth Burke and Edmund Wilson, both of whom wielded enormous critical clout and had a great influence on the literary field in the twentieth century.[15] Wilson went to Princeton, became a highly regarded critic, and wrote books that influenced literary taste and judgment (several of which became classics on academic course curricula). Burke dropped out of Columbia to be a writer, became the editor of a little magazine, *The Dial,* and wrote highly influential works of literary criticism and philosophy. Neither was a traditional college professor.

Over time Edmund Wilson developed contempt for what he regarded as "academic pedantry," and for the "PhD system" that produced and depended upon it—a system he thought ought to have been scrapped after World War I as a "German atrocity."[16] His gleeful animadversions against academia and the Modern Language Association, occasioned by a book series whose editorial practices he disapproved, were published in an article in *The New York Review of Books* (later republished as a separate booklet) and elicited a strong response from scholars, of which the following, from Gordon N. Ray, the president of the John Simon Guggenheim Foundation, is worth quoting in full:

> The recent attack in *The New York Review of Books* on the Center for Editions of American Authors of the Modern Language Association of America raises complex questions of taste and emphasis. It must be obvious at the same time, however, that this attack derives in part from the alarm of amateurs at seeing rigorous professional standards applied to a subject in which they have a vested interest. Here, at least, the issue is not in doubt. As the American learned world has come to full maturity since the Second World War, a similar animus has shown itself and been discredited in field after field from botany to folklore. In the long run professional standards always prevail.[17]

Ray's own scholarship was focused on the life and work of William Makepeace Thackeray, whose letters and private papers he edited (in four volumes) and about whom he wrote a two-volume biography. His reply to Wilson, which stands as the epigraph to an MLA pamphlet called *Professional Standards and American Editions,* is clearly both personal and professional, since his was apparently the kind of scholarship Wilson thought the world would be better off without. But Ray's riposte, and the prominent place given it in the pamphlet, is symptomatic of a particular time in intellectual and professional history. The quarrel of the amateurs and the professionals seems at that moment to have erupted in a way both vivid and virulent. What was at stake? Ray mentions "the alarm of amateurs" at the arrival of "rigorous professional standards," and the newly achieved maturity of the "American learned world." After World War II, with the expansion of the state universities and the G.I. Bill, a wave of comparative democratization hit the U.S. academy, together— not altogether paradoxically—with a growth in graduate programs, a sophistication of editorial practices, and (as Wilson notes dismissively) the need for more, and more varied, projects for dissertation students to undertake. What he calls the "boondoggling of the MLA editions"[18] and what Gordon Ray calls "professional standards" are two sides of the same coin.

The tension felt, the challenge detected and resisted, was not only between amateurs and professionals, between self-made critics and PhD-bearing scholars, but also between the New York world of books, magazines, and intellectual life and the rest of the country. The corridor traversed by the old Pennsylvania Railroad, with all paths leading to or from New York, had long tacitly, and sometimes explicitly, been the province of arbiters of taste and intellectual leadership. In *The Fruits of the MLA*, Wilson had begun by mildly mocking a letter from an unnamed correspondent, the editor of one of the MLA volumes, which presumes to say something about the climate of the East Coast, where Wilson spent his summer vacations: "he professes to envy me my enjoyment of spring on Cape Cod—which is actually rather bleak—since the part of the Middle West to which he is at present condemned cannot be said to have a spring."[19] Gordon Ray, though by then the head of a New York–based foundation, was a graduate of the University of Indiana and had been an administrator at the University of Illinois. The other contributors to *Professional Standards and American Editions* (which bore the subtitle *A Response to Edmund Wilson*) included two scholars based in Iowa and one from Berkeley, California.

The original idea for what became the MLA editions had been generated by the American Literature Group of the MLA, headed by a Princeton professor, Willard Thorp, in 1947–48. But by the time of these editions, produced by a team of five Emerson scholars, appeared from Harvard University Press (to be immediately lambasted by the critic and journal editor Lewis Mumford in an article called "Emerson Behind Barbed Wire")[20], the series had garnered financial support from the National Endowment on the Arts and Humanities and smaller grants from the U.S. Office of Education. It had become a national project.

Edmund Wilson had other ideas, not about the national scope of such a series but about what form it should take. "I myself," he wrote, "had had a project for publishing these classics in an easily accessible form such as that of the French Pléiade series." His target, he said, was "the ordinary reader." He included in his article the full text of a letter he had sent to Jason Epstein, then an editor at Random House (and one of the founders of *The New York Review of Books*), in which he described the Éditions de la Pléiade at greater length as a series that had "included many of the French classics, ancient and modern, in beautifully produced and admirably printed thin-paper volumes, ranging from 800 to 1500 pages." Copies of the letter to Epstein, Wilson noted, had been sent to a group of other people whom he thought might be supportive: "W. H. Auden, Marius Bewley, R. P. Blackmur, Van Wyck Brooks, Alfred Kazin, President Kennedy, Robert Lowell, Perry Miller, Norman Holmes Pearson, John Crowe Ransom, Allen Tate, Lionel Trilling, Mark Van Doren, and Robert Penn Warren."

Poets, literati, public intellectuals, and men of letters: these recipients could also presumably be counted on to know what Cape Cod weather was like in the spring. Of these, Wilson reports, only Perry Miller, "a Professor of American literature at Harvard," raised any question about the problem of preparing authoritative texts, and even Miller, he said, admitted that "the project on Hawthorne, to cite only this one, being undertaken by the University of Ohio is perhaps more 'academic' than the average reader needs."[21]

The ordinary reader and the average reader were to be the ideal clientele for Wilson's American Pléiade edition, which he and Epstein cofounded in 1982 as the Library of America. Back in 1968, when he wrote *Fruits of the MLA*, Wilson was convinced that money intended to come from the National Humanities Endowment to support his project had been "whisked away, and my project 'tabled'—that is, set aside, dismissed. The Modern Language Association had, it seemed, had a project of its own for reprinting the American classics and had apparently had ours suppressed."[22] "Whisked," "dismissed," "suppressed": this is hard language; bitter, even (one would be tempted to say, were the source not so eminent) paranoid language; and Wilson goes on, in his inimitable fashion, to explain to the "ordinary reader" of *The New York Review of*

Books what the MLA is, or was, and what, by inference, it was not. The Modern Language Association, we learn, "publishes a periodical . . . which contains for the most part unreadable articles on literary problems and discoveries of very minute or no interest." To underscore this point Wilson had recourse to a practice that, though it still can be found in journalistic accounts of academic conferences, was as unprofessional then as it is now: the citation of the *titles* of various academic papers as apparently self-evident indications of their worthlessness, indeed their risibility, without the writer taking the trouble to hear or read them. In this case, Wilson was quite sure he would be better off skipping papers on topics like "Flowers, Women, and Song in the Poetry of William Carlos Williams" and "The Unity of George Peele's *The Old Wives' Tale*."

Edmund Wilson's critical essays and other writings were formative for my own thinking about European and American literature. I am not sure, though, that it wouldn't be possible to joke about the titles of essays called "Uncomfortable Casanova" or "Justice to Edith Wharton" or "The Kipling That Nobody Read," all to be found in his collection *The Wound and the Bow*. The tactic of mocking what one has not read is overused and seldom precise. The problem is not that it is unfair but that it is lazy and contemptuous.

However, as we've noted, Wilson felt aggrieved. His proposal had been whisked and dismissed. Persons of no fame, many of whom lived far away, some of whom— especially since they were "teachers of American literature"—might never even have *heard* of the Pléiade series, had prevailed over the publishers, writers, and others to whom Wilson had copied his letter. "I knew," he says, "that the MLA had a strong and determined lobby to further its own designs and that representatives of the MLA had attempted to discourage our project and had, it seems, very soon succeeded."[23] The three damning initials appear over and over, as if they were CIA or FBI or KGB. "Representatives" of this "determined group" were busy furthering "the designs" of the organization: what could a lover of literature do?

Although I don't like Wilson's dismissive tone, I understand his publishing dreams. Still, I have some difference of opinion about the results. I own several Library of America editions; they may be classics, and printed on acid-free paper to ensure their longevity, but they are also bulky, cumbersome, and lacking in the kind of preface and contextual information that I, even as a non–"teacher of American literature," would have found helpful. (The LOA's single slender green-ribbon book mark, a presumptive sign of elegance and leisurely perusal by the ordinary reader, is always supplemented in my copies by a myriad of decidedly inelegant Post-its, each indicating a passage to which I want to return.) Wilson posited a schism between the concerns of the scholar-pedants he caricatured and the ordinary reader. "What on earth is the interest of all of this?" he asks, when discussing some of William Dean Howells's early travel articles and a diary of his travels with his wife, both of which Howells used as source material for his book *The Wedding Journey.* "Every writer knows how diaries and articles are utilized as material for books, and no ordinary reader knows or cares. What is important is the finished work by which the author wishes to stand."[24] Echoing Mumford, he calls source materials "literary garbage,"[25] and he does not hide his contempt for the clueless academics who undertake their scholarship without lucrative contracts with publishers that would provide for advances and royalties. "A professional writer is astounded by the terms accepted by academic persons for work that may take many years. It seems incredible that, in the case of university presses, they sometimes have no contracts at all. They think in terms of academic prestige, and it is time that some solid achievement in this line should be given some more solid compensation. To examine an MLA contract gives a professional writer the shudders."[26] Notice the repetition of the phrase "a professional writer" at the beginning and the end of this supposedly altruistic piece of advice. Where the pamphlet is never shy about mobilizing the first-person-singular pronoun, now we have twice, instead of the word *I,* "a professional writer"—like Edmund Wilson.

Gordon Ray's tart reply, in a publication conspicuously called *Professional Standards,* lumps Wilson with the amateurs who see that their time is passing. But Wilson himself proudly claimed to be a professional writer in comparison with the academic pedants, penniless but sifting the garbage of major authors, who exemplified to him the "ineptitude of [the MLA's] pretensions to reprint the American classics."[27]

We might ask why, in a diatribe so deeply concerned with discrediting professional scholars as drudges who distance themselves from ordinary reading, Wilson should take this determined swerve at just about the last moment (the final page of his piece as it appeared in *The New York Review*) away from being the champion of the ordinary reader and toward the mantle of professionalism. He damns the eminent bibliographer Fredson Bowers with faint praise: "I am on friendly terms with Mr. Bowers, and I know that he is an impassioned bibliographer as well as an expert on Elizabethan texts . . . [b]ut I have found no reason to believe that he is . . . much interested in literature. It has been said, in fact, I believe, by someone in the academic world that, in editing *Leaves of Grass,* he has done everything for it but read it."[28] (Would a professional journalist be satisfied with "it has been said . . . I believe . . . by someone"?)

Wilson is covering all his bases: he will be the true lover of literature—rescuing it from what he elsewhere calls "the very small group of monomaniac bibliographers"[29] who are "[not] much interested in literature"—and also the true professional, who could laugh at the ineptitude of scholars so dim they will work for years on a literary project without any assurance that they will get paid for it. Wilson quite plausibly equates "professional" with "writes for money." The unnamed academics, while they draw salaries, are writing for "prestige," which might translate itself into a new job or a promotion but is also, like the "esteem" of *succès d'éstime*—or the esteem of self-esteem—a kind of love. But Gordon Ray's claim, also plausible, is that the resistance to footnotes, sources, explanatory information, and other "literary garbage" is itself an amateur move. As another of the contributors to *Professional Standards* argues, "where a major author is concerned, there is very little literary garbage."[30]

Which is the amateur and which is the professional? Do any of these persons, or any of these institutions, from publishers to universities, love literature? It seems most reasonable to say that they all do, in their fashion. Reason and love, as Bottom so well observed, keep little company together nowadays. In the upshot, Wilson got his archival series of uniformly bound classics, and scholars got their annotated editions, and the world moved on. This was a contretemps—perhaps it would be just as accurate to call it a spat—that predates the Internet, hypertext editions, and an expansion (and professionalization) of the American academic scene well beyond what was imagined or caricatured in the late sixties. But one thing I'd venture to say is that it never works to accuse someone else of lacking the capacity to love.

Love Stories

What's love got to do with the use and abuse of literature? For one thing, love—as news stories remind us every day, and as classic novels, poems, and plays have told us for centuries, is often about use and abuse. And as with literature, it is sometimes not easy to tell the difference. Consider Hamlet and Ophelia, Elizabeth Bennett and Mr. Darcy, Achilles and Patroclus, Humbert Humbert and Lolita. (Adepts of *The Faerie Queene* will recall that in Book 3 of Spenser's poem, the enchanter Busirane briefly captures the maiden Amoret.) Even, or perhaps especially, in religious poetry, this intrinsic doubling occurs, from Herbert's "Jordan" poems to Donne's Holy Sonnets ("Batter my heart") to "Sir Gawain" and the quests of Spenser's knights. That love is one of literature's favorite, indeed obsessive, topics creates a certain kind of feedback loop, or what is sometimes called, in literary study, a textual effect, which means that something *in* the text is shaping, often without the conscious awareness of the reader or critic, how the text is being read.

Consider John Donne's lyric "The Canonization," which uses as one of its master tropes the coincidence of sacred and profane love to make the earthly lovers also saints, "us canonized for love." The direct, intemperate, and colloquial address of the first line, "For God's sake hold your tongue and let me love," once revisited at the end of the poem, turns out to have more than one connotation, since the poem suggests that their love is "for God's sake" as well as for their own. Donne's poem, a favorite of the New Critics and therefore often taught and studied in introductory English courses, became foundational in the mid-twentieth century to what was described as the English literary canon. In effect, then, the poem, as well as its fictional legendary lovers, was *canonized*—we might even say *canonized for love.*

Scenes of reading in literature are often sites of seduction (for literary characters) as well as seductive (for the reader). We've already noticed this in the case of Jane Austen's *Persuasion,* where the unlikely couple of Louisa Musgrove and Captain Benwick are said to have "fallen in love over poetry." One of the most famous scenes of reading is found in Dante's *Inferno,* where Paolo and Francesca are seduced by reading the story of Lancelot and Guinevere and become, themselves, adulterous lovers:

> One day, to pass the time away, we read
> of Lancelot—how love had overcome him.
> We were alone, and we suspected nothing.
>
> And time and time again that reading led
> our eyes to meet, and made our faces pale,
> and yet one point alone defeated us.
>
> When we had read how the desired smile
> was kissed by one who was so true a lover,
> this one, who never shall be parted from me,
>
> while all his body trembled, kissed my mouth.
> A Gallehault indeed, that book and he
> Who wrote it, too; that day we read no more.
>
> Dante, *Inferno,* 127–138[31]

Gallehault, or Galeott, was the go-between who brought together Lancelot and Guinevere. His name became a synonym for *pander,* which is, as the poem suggests, what the book they were reading became for Paolo and Francesca—and what this passage has become for other poets and other readers: a go-between linking literature and life.

But if the topic of love is in a way not only as old as literature but also coterminous and coextensive with it—if, to stretch the point only a little, all literature is about love, whether it's human love, divine love, disappointed love, love of nature, love of art, love of country, or self-love—then to ask how we should feel about love of literature is to ask the question less precisely than we might. To accuse someone of lacking a love for literature is to say he or she doesn't love literature in the same way we do. What we might rather want to propose is that (1) loving literature is the beginning rather than the end (or the use) of a relationship with it, and (2) like all loves, love of literature is risky, sometimes dangerous, and occasionally disappointing in part precisely because of "the overestimation of the object."

Uncommon Readers

Two examples from Virginia Woolf may helpfully complicate this question of love and what it might have to do with the use (or use and abuse) of literature. The first is from her essay "How Should One Read a Book?," which we've already noticed as the locus of some of her thoughts on the contemporaneity of literature. In this case, Woolf's subject might be called the overprofessionalization of book reviewing, "when books pass in review like the procession of animals in a shooting gallery, and the critic has only one second in which to load and aim and shoot," and thus may miss the mark as frequently as he or she hit it.

> If behind the erratic gunfire of the press the author felt that there was another kind of criticism, the opinion of people reading for the love of reading, slowly and unprofessionally, and judging with great sympathy and yet with great severity, might this not improve the quality of his work?[32]

People reading for the love of reading may, she speculates, make books "stronger, richer, and more varied." This pleasant fantasy—Woolf herself was a book reviewer as well as a novelist and essayist, and she depended upon published critics and criticism—is succeeded by another, equally fanciful: she imagines readers coming to the gate of heaven at the Day of Judgment "with our books under our arms," to be told they need no further reward: "We have nothing to give them here," Woolf's version of the Almighty says to her version of Saint Peter. "They have loved reading."[33]

However uncharacteristically warm and fuzzy this may seem to us (the original version of "How Should One Read a Book?" was delivered at a private school for girls), it echoes the theme begun with the title of Woolf's essay collections *The Common Reader,* a phrase she borrows, with full attribution, from Samuel Johnson's "Life of Gray." By choosing Johnson's phrase as the title of her book of collected and "refurbished" essays and reviews, Woolf raises an interesting problem of identification. The sophisticated writing published under this seemingly modest title was hardly the work of a common reader as described by Johnson or Woolf. Originally described in her diary as a "Reading book" and then under the provisional title "Reading and Writing,"[34] *The Common Reader* included knowledgeable, opinionated essays on major and lesser-known literary figures from the Paston letters and Chaucer to Montaigne, Elizabethan drama, John Evelyn, Daniel Defoe, Joseph Addison, Jane Austen, the Brontës, George Eliot, and Joseph Conrad, and the second volume in the series would continue and expand this range. Though Woolf surely did read for her own pleasure, her essays continually, and often brilliantly, do both "impart knowledge" and "correct the opinions of others."

Moreover, if we were to look at the *context* of Dr. Johnson's famous paragraph, we would discover that it runs quite counter to most of what he has to say about the poet in his "Life of Gray." Having devoted several pages to biography, Johnson now turns to his work.

Gray's poetry is now to be considered [Johnson writes, having devoted several pages to biography] and I hope not to be looked on as an enemy to his name, if I confess that I contemplate it with less pleasure than his life.

The poem *On the Cat* was doubtless by its author considered as a trifle, but it is not a happy trifle.

The *Prospect of Eton College* suggests nothing to Gray which every beholder does not equally think and feel. His supplication to

Father Thames, to tell him who drives the hoop or tosses the ball, is useless and puerile. Father Thames has no better means of knowing than himself.[35]

And so on, through the entire corpus of Gray's poetry, often stanza by stanza and word by word, culminating in a general assessment of his work before the paragraph on Gray's "Elegy Written in a Country Churchyard" that, coming at the end of the "Life," contains the phrase that Woolf uses in the preface to her book.

In the character of his Elegy I rejoice to concur with the common reader; for by the common sense of readers uncorrupted with literary prejudices, after all the refinements of subtilty and the dogmatism of learning, must be finally decided all claims to poetical honours. The *Churchyard* abounds with images which find a mirror in every mind, and with sentiments to which every bosom returns an echo. The four stanzas beginning "Yet even these bones" are to me original: I have never seen the notions in any other place; yet he that reads them here, persuades himself that he has always felt them. Had Gray written often thus, it had been vain to blame, and useless to praise him.[36]

The sentiments of the common reader are thus invoked only at the end of a long and detailed assessment of Gray's poetry, which, in the main, finds his successes intermittent at best, and some of his work incomprehensible or overrated. This is the *only* moment in the "Life of Gray" when Johnson concurs with the common reader, and he does so in a graceful, concessive spirit that leads up to his superbly crafted, quietly devastating final sentence: "Had Gray written often thus, it had been vain to blame, and useless to praise him." We might linger for a moment on Johnson's phrase "useless to praise," which carries the notion that the poetry speaks for itself (and thus that the common reader's views would prevail without any intercession on the part of the critic). This is clearly a condition contrary to fact. The existence of *The Lives of the Poets* likewise contradicts the utopian notion that in an aesthetically just world, quality always prevails. If love of literature is linked to the judgment of the common reader rather than that of the professional critic or scholar, the practice of these two meticulous and learned arbiters of literary taste, Samuel Johnson and Virginia Woolf, puts that connection in question even as it seems, or is taken, to uphold it. Neither critic defers to the common reader, though both imagine him or her as a crucial ancillary part of the world of readers. Each in fact demonstrates an *uncommon* love of literature precisely by combining it with learning—as well as with a strongly urged, felicitously phrased, hard-won, and often infectious set of literary prejudices.

The second example I'd offer from Woolf on the question of literature and love is her intriguing set of observations on the English romantic essayist William Hazlitt. A hundred years after Hazlitt wrote, he was for her an important figure, and from her account of him, his work was, at least among her contemporaries, a familiar voice: "The famous passages about reading *Love for Love* and drinking coffee from a silver pot and reading *La Nouvelle Héloïse* and eating a cold chicken, are known to all."[37] She admires his energy, his intelligence, his vivacity, and his prose style. "Hazlitt strode through the greater part of English literature and delivered his opinion of the majority of famous books." Never mind that he had decided, for one reason or another, not to read some of them:

> Hazlitt is one of those rare critics who have thought so much that they can dispense with reading. It matters very little that Hazlitt had read only one poem by Donne; that he found Shakespeare's sonnets unintelligible; that he never read a book through after he was thirty; that he came indeed to dislike reading altogether. What he had read he had read with fervour.[38]

Woolf quotes a long passage from a Hazlitt essay on old English writers that begins, "It is delightful to repose on the wisdom of the ancients; to have some great name at hand, besides one's own initials always staring one in the face; to travel out of one's self into the Chaldee, Hebrew, and Egyptian characters, to have the palm-trees waving mystically in the margin of the page," and offers this response:

> Needless to say that is not criticism. It is sitting in an armchair and gazing into the fire, and building up image after image of what one has seen in a book. It is loving and taking the liberties of a lover. It is being Hazlitt.[39]

What is "not criticism" to Virginia Woolf? In this specific case, it is what we might call free association—or rather, because nothing is really free (of context, of motivation, of effect), associative thinking. From "Egyptian" and "Hebrew," presumably, Hazlitt's mind moves not only to palm trees in the margins but also to "camels moving slowly on in the distance of three thousand years," to "the dry desert of learning," the "insatiable thirst of knowledge," the "ruined monuments of antiquity," "the fragments of buried cities (under which the adder lurks)," and so on. No piece of poetry, no historic fact, no detail from the text of an old author is cited—what the reader gets instead is the mind of the essayist, dreaming, or, as Woolf says, "taking the liberties of a lover." In Hazlitt, we may say, if we like, that this is delightful or, if we like, that it is romantic or, if we like, that the essayist has earned the right to be fanciful—or, if we prefer, that this is indeed "not criticism" and that we wish he would return to the critical task at hand. For Hazlitt, presumably, all such attitudes are plausible. But what if a critic today undertook such a set of associations, "taking the liberty of a lover"? With a published critic, readers are likely to find it of some interest—if, for example, such a reverie were to appear as a back-page essay in *The New York Times Book Review*. But would we allow such liberties to a sophomore English major? What is the relationship of this kind of love, that permits itself to wander far from the textual starting point and the study of literature?

Woolf's piece on Hazlitt was itself a piece of criticism: she was reviewing his collected works, first for the *New York Herald Tribune*, and then, in a slightly revised form, for *The Times Literary Supplement*.[40] But what is also striking, and typically witty, is Woolf's iteration of the idea of love in connection with Hazlitt, an author celebrated for having written an essay "On the Pleasure of Hating"[41]—an essay Woolf never mentions in her review, but that seems to inform it nonetheless. Hazlitt contended that love and hate were closely allied in literature and in life. He suggested that the popularity of the Scottish novel in his time was related to its harking back to old feuds, while part of tragedy's appeal is that it permits the resurgence of primal feelings that refinement has compelled society to repress. "As we read, we throw aside the trammels of civilization, the flimsy veil of humanity: 'Off, you lendings!' The wild beast resumes its sway within us."[42]

The pleasure of hating in this sense was a *literary* pleasure, however it might also function in politics or in social life. As such, it was also, arguably, a *useful* pleasure, in that it allowed for vicarious action, strong emotion without visible repercussion, the spontaneous overflow of powerful feelings diverted, (almost) harmlessly, into the activity of reading—and into the development, without conscious awareness of its psychic utility, of a best-seller list and a literary canon.

Sigmund Freud made a similar argument when he came to describe the difference between Sophocles's *Oedipus Rex* and Shakespeare's *Hamlet*. Oedipus acts, however unwittingly, in killing his father and marrying his mother. Hamlet, famously, delays, contemplating the killing of the king (and, in Freud's reading, having incestuous feelings for his mother), but failing to act. Inaction, mental conflict, delay; these were evidence of "the secular advance of repression in the emotional life of mankind."[43] Discomforting as these conflicts might be for the patient, their results when it came to literature were more ambiguously interesting. Repression produces neurosis; neurosis produces a compellingly conflicted modern character, torn between desire and inhibition—and so, by implication, becomes instrumental in the development of modern literature.

But this is an argument about the tensions *within a literary character*. What possible relevance can it have to the question of pleasure and unpleasure, or love and hate, when it comes to the writer and the reader? What's love got to do with *that*? This, too, was a topic that Freud took up, notably in an essay called "Creative Writers and Day-Dreaming," first delivered as a lecture in the rooms of a Viennese bookseller and publisher and later printed in a literary magazine.[44] If a daydreamer were to communicate his fantasies directly, Freud suggests, "he could give us no pleasure by his disclosures"—indeed his fantasies (wrote the analyst in a pretabloid, pre–Jerry Springer age) would "repel us or at least leave us cold."

> But when a creative writer presents his plays to us or tells us what we are inclined to take to be his personal day-dreams, we experience a great pleasure . . . The writer softens the character of his egoistic day-dreams by altering and disguising it, and he bribes us by the purely formal—that is, aesthetic—yield of pleasure which he offers us in the presentation of his phantasies. We give the name of an *incentive bonus*, or a *fore-pleasure*, to a yield of pleasure such as this, which is offered to us so as to make possible the release of still greater pleasure arising from deeper psychical sources. All the aesthetic pleasure which a creative writer affords us has the character of a fore-pleasure of this kind, and our actual enjoyment of an imaginative work proceeds from a liberation of tensions in our minds.[45]

This displacement of personal fantasies into an author's imaginative writing speaks to the popularity of what is sometimes called personal writing—the appeal of memoirs, confessions, inspirational stories, survivor's tales, and other self-revealing narratives that collectively constitute a genre of literary schadenfreude omnipresent in today's tabloid journalism. At the same time, Freud's erotic theory of literary enjoyment, the idea that "the purely formal—that is, aesthetic—yield of pleasure" which a writer offers us in the presentation provides a kind of *fore-pleasure* prior to a "release of still greater pleasure arising from deeper psychological sources," proposes yet another kind of answer to the question of literature as love.

FIVE

So You Want to Read a Poem

In the middle years of the twentieth century, the methods of New Criticism (close textual analysis, attention to word choice, verse forms, etc.) were the common pedagogy of college and university English departments, and the standard mode of instruction in grade, middle, and secondary schools. Poems were analyzed as poems, and more often than not, as reflexive objects that had poetry as their not so hidden topic. A good short example of this is Ben Jonson's "On My First Son":

> Farewell, thou child of my right hand, and joy;
> My sin was too much hope of thee, loved boy:
> Seven years thou wert lent to me, and I thee pay,
> Exacted by thy fate, on the just day.
> O, could I lose all father now! For why
> Will man lament the state he should envy?
> To have so soon 'scaped world's and flesh's rage,
> And, if no other misery, yet age?
> Rest in soft peace, and asked, say, "Here doth lie
> Ben Jonson his best piece of poetry."
> For whose sake henceforth all his vows be such,
> As what he loves may never like too much.

The son's name, like the father's, was Benjamin, which means, in Hebrew, *son of the right hand*. But the right hand is, by implication, also Jonson's writing hand, and the word *poetry* comes from the Greek word that means making. So the making of the son and the making of the poem are parallel acts, and in this case, the one substitutes for the other. The embedded inscription, "Here doth lie / Ben Jonson his best piece of poetry," gestures, in a way that is technically called *deixis,* pointing or indicating, to the fact that the poem itself functions like a funeral monument. ("Here" is the sign, often found on actual monuments.) The enjambed line ("Here doth lie / Ben Jonson") suggests both a colon and a question *(who lies here?),* while the use of "his," in what is now an archaic form ("Ben Jonson his best piece of poetry," rather than "Ben Jonson's best piece of poetry"), allows for a double meaning: what lies "here" is both the poet's "best piece of poetry," or making, and also Ben Jonson, the father and the son. The personal adjectives and personal pronouns in the lines that follow ("for whose sake"; "all his vows"; "what he loves") continue the willed conflation or confusion of father and son. "On My First Son" becomes the monument; the word "on," typical of epigrams, essays, and other short pieces in the period, is also a pointer gesturing toward the poem. (This is what rhetoricians call deictis.)

This kind of analysis will be familiar to any reader of midcentury critical classics like W. K. Wimsatt's *The Verbal Icon* or Cleanth Brooks's *The Well-Wrought Urn,* the titles of which provide examples of the phenomenon they describe. (Brooks's title comes from John Donne's "The Canonization." Two other "urn" poems, Keats's "Ode on a Grecian Urn" and Wallace Stevens's "Anecdote of the Jar," became similar iconic touchstones for close readers of poems about poetry.) I'd like to point out a number of corollaries to this method of reading, which is the one in which I was trained and which I still find deeply satisfying: first, the method validates those works that fit its methodology. Thus, poems about poetry, or poems that could be read as poems about poetry, including most so-called metaphysical verse, gained high status, including the poems of Andrew Marvell, many Romantic lyrics and Wordsworth's "Prelude," Shakespeare's sonnets and "Phoenix and Turtle," and a good deal of modern poetry, from Yeats to Wallace Stevens.

Conversely, poems that seemed to resist or to deny the validity of this reading method—like, for example, Cavalier lyrics or Byron's *Don Juan*—tended at the time to be rated lower on the scale. And poems that were either narrative (Chaucer's *Canterbury Tales,* Crabbe's *The Village*) or epic (Spenser's *Faerie Queene,* Milton's *Paradise Lost,* Pope's *Dunciad* or *Rape of the Lock*) were either quarried for verbal gems that could be explicated as if they were lyrics, or else subjected to a different regime of criticism, one that treated them like works of fiction (plot, character, etc.) or works of "influence" (Milton echoes and rewrites Spenser, who echoes and rewrites Virgil; Wordsworth and all the Romantics echo and rewrite Milton; Stevens rewrites Wordsworth, etc.).

A sense of boredom—the New Critical reading, while elegant, was at the same time predictable—and limitation led to the resuscitation and reinvigoration of other critical modes, often versions of the same modes so strongly repudiated by the New Critics: historical, contextual, biographical, editorial, and overtly political or overtly religious readings, that depended as much upon context or history as the actual language on the page. No orthodoxy of reading is without its blind spots. New Criticism's rigorous pointing toward the text needed to be corrected or at least was augmented when the next generation of readers and critics readmitted history to the realm of possible literary evidence. Deconstruction, an extension of rather than a replacement for New Criticism, looked precisely for the blind spots, the apparent discordances, opacities, or unresolvabilities of the literary text, rather than the moments of concord or pleasurable but controllable ambiguity. The deconstructive *aporia*—not a new or fanciful coinage but an old and honored word from the history of rhetoric ("Aporia, or the Doubtfull, [so] called . . . because oftentimes we will seem to cast perils, and make doubt of things when by a plaine manner of speech wee might affirme or deny him"[1])—was, in fact, the counterpart of the New Critic's ambiguity, the desirable goal and end point of a literary analysis. Aporia, as perplexing difficulty, has a long history of usage and has only recently—and unhistorically—been reclassified as critical jargon. This blind spot, or aporia, is analogous to Freud's description of the "navel of the dream," the place where "it reaches down into the unknown."[2]

Literature produces, and is in turn produced by, modes of critical analysis. Literature reads us as much as we read literature. As certain kinds of critical or social thinking become popular, the kind of literature they are effective in analyzing become the kind of literature we recognize as good or even great.

But What Is the Use of Literary Reading?

It is potentially risky to paraphrase any critic's words on the subject of paraphrasing. Nonetheless, it's a risk worth taking, both because Cleanth Brooks's essay "The Heresy of Paraphrase" poses a deft and cogent argument well worth revisiting, and also because Brooks twice goes out of his way to discuss, in signifying quotation marks, the "uses of poetry." Poetry, says Brooks—and here he does not wish to distinguish poetry from other imaginative writing, like novels or plays—cannot be reduced to, or summed up in, a statement, proposition, or message. "What the poem 'says'" is not only not equivalent to the poem or its value; it is also ultimately undeterminable because of vital issues of tone, style, and irony. "The paraphrase is not the real core of meaning which constitutes the essence of the poem."[3] "The 'prose-sense' of the poem is not a rack on which the stuff of the poem is hung . . . it does not represent the 'inner' structure or the 'essential' structure or the 'real' structure of the poem."[4] In fact, he suggests, "one may sum up by saying that most of the distempers of criticism come about from yielding to the temptation to take certain remarks which we make *about* the poem—statements about what it says or about what truth it gives or about what formulations it illustrates—for the essential core of the poem itself."

For Brooks, poems are not received truth but "parables"[5] about poetry. It is this self-referential element to his formalism that has led some successors to feel that his readings have a certain family similarity, that they all wind up in a similar place, affirming the value of poetry and gesturing toward the iconicity of the poem itself, the "well-wrought urn" of Donne's "Canonization" that provides Brooks with the title of his essay collection. But Brooks goes out of his way in this essay and elsewhere to insist that he is not interested in a "special 'use of poetry'— some therapeutic value for the sake of which poetry is to be cultivated."[6] In a short manifesto in *The Kenyon Review*, originally entitled "My Credo," he insists that "literature is not a surrogate for religion" and "the purpose of literature is not to point a moral."[7] Formalists, he says, assume an ideal reader because, in taking into account "a lowest common denominator" of possible readings, "we frankly move from literary criticism into socio-psychology."[8] And while Brooks acknowledges that different critics may have different goals, from editing texts to writing book reviews to presenting papers to the Modern Language Association, he is genially dismissive of both "applied" readings and the supposedly less "drab," "brighter, more amateur, and more 'human' criticism" that flourishes "in the classroom presided over by the college lecturer of infectious enthusiasm, in the gossipy Book-of-the-Month-Club bulletins, and in the columns of the *Saturday Review of Literature*."[9] Brooks doesn't think these versions do much harm, but nor do they do much good. "The reduction of a work of literature to its causes does not constitute literary criticism; nor does an estimate of its effects. Good literature is more than effective rhetoric applied to true ideas."[10] "Literature is not inimical to ideas. It thrives upon ideas but it does not present ideas patly and neatly."[11] Insofar as literature has "uses," it is the task of the critic to analyze the ways that ideas *perform* in literary works, not how works "exemplify" or "produce" them.

Everything Old Is New Again

After many years of being old-fashioned, close reading is again fashionable, although, like all revived fashions, it wears its retrospection with a difference. Suddenly—or not so suddenly—students, graduate and undergraduate, are alight with excitement about this category of analysis, for so long relegated to the supposedly naive past, the heyday of I. A. Richards and practical criticism, and of "new" critics like Cleanth Brooks, Robert Penn Warren, John Crowe Ransom, and William Empson, to name only a few of the literary luminaries of that era. While they continue to resist some of the basic tenets of New Criticism, like the Intentional Fallacy described by William K. Wimsatt and Monroe Beardsley and the Affective Fallacy proposed by Wimsatt, young scholars and critics, for so long immersed in historicism and context, are again intrigued by the idea of close reading a work of literature. Reading, that is to say, not for what the work says about the time when it was produced, or about the author or the reading public, but about how its language functions.

Here it may be useful to say a word about those famous fallacies, and about the genealogy and lineage of close reading, to try to see how the practice (which I would prefer to call simply *reading*) has become both so controversial and so out of fashion that it is once again new.

The intentional fallacy says that the intention of the author has no ultimate control over the meaning of the work. If we were to discover, for example, a letter from William Shakespeare to one of his fellow actors, saying that in *Hamlet* he intended to express his dismay about the corrupt state of contemporary politics, or the parlous economic situation of actors, or his Christian faith, or his loss of faith in marriage, or his belief in providence, or his worry about political succession—this would have no definitive effect on our readings of *Hamlet*. It would be another piece of evidence, but it would not trump or sideline other readings of the play, even readings that run counter to whatever the author's letter asserted. The author, in other words, is entitled to his opinion. But what he intends, even assuming that we could know what that is, is just one point of view among many. (Imagine another letter, written at the same time, to his wife, contradicting the assertions he made in the letter to his fellow actor: the play is about his idealization of love, his loss of Christian faith, his doubts about providence, his confidence in the political system.) The work of literature has a life of its own; it takes on meanings, in the plural, as it is read and performed and discussed.

Discounting intention does not suggest that all meanings are equally persuasive or valid. When Hamlet says in a letter to the king that he is "set naked on your kingdom" (4.2), he does not mean that he is wearing no clothes but that he has no weapon; when Mercutio and Romeo exchange witticisms about Romeo's "pump," they are talking about his shoe style, not about a mechanical device for retrieving water—although as their jesting continues, a wide range of other meanings may attach to this word. So some readings can be "wrong" because of what might be called underreading—not giving enough credit to the historical meanings of modern words. But sometimes even the wrong reading can be right, if defended or presented in a convincing way. Baz Luhrmann's film *Romeo + Juliet* makes much erotic sport of the idea of pumping, and even though this seems in part either a resistance to or a failure to understand, the idea of a pump as a kind of shoe (for men as well as for women, in Shakespeare's time) the scene can be made to work.

The belief in intention belongs to a historicist moment, or to at least two historicist moments: the one against which the New Critics were actively reacting, and the one that inevitably came to react against them. Both historicisms (the second, called "new historicism," and the other—rather unfairly—dubbed in a species of back-formation "old historicism") put strong value in biography, context, "the archive," and a kind of allegorical reading of historical events. But intention—as we will see in relation to questions of biography and truth—can get in the way of close reading, since it forecloses some interpretive options as inappropriate, untimely, unsuitable, not what the author could have meant.

The affective fallacy warned against feeling, or feeling too much, or being carried away by the rightness of a feeling. When W. K. Wimsatt wrote about it in the 1940s, it was a response to the excesses of belletrism and impressionistic criticism. The inevitable bounce-back against the too stringent enforcement of such a fallacy led to reader-response criticism, the idea of interpretive communities, and most recently, an explicitly affective criticism that is all about feelings, whether negative or positive, encompassing the poles of infatuation and disgust. Sometimes, in this era of fact and science, the affective emotions are tied to the hardwiring of the brain, which produces smells, colors, sounds, synesthesia (the blending of the senses), etc. Whatever we may think about affect, I think it is fair to say that it marks a *response* to the work, rather than a *reading* of it. However closely affective arguments are tied to language, there is always a hypothetical suture (a word, phrase, or image "makes me feel like" this or that or, less convincingly, "produces the effect of" this or that). As with polling data, there are outliers, responses that don't seem to fit the prevailing pattern as urged or detected by the critic. But rather than sparking an exciting argument based upon this divergence, such dissent seems to push against the very idea of a community, so that what is occasionally sought is an alternative community that does, or would, or might have, responded in the way that the minority or disaffected reading suggested. In any case, one object of affective criticism ("old" or "new," impressionistic or scientific) would seem to be an explanation of why the feeling was right for the reader.

Although they have sometimes been dubbed critical fallacies, intention and affect (the intention of the author, the response of the reader) remain central to the curiosity and desire of many scholars, critics, and ordinary readers of literature. What did the author have in mind, and what led him or her to write? How does what I feel when I read a poem or a passage derive from the language and imagery on the page? Do other readers feel the same, and if not, is one of us right and another, wrong? Indeed, the provocation for calling such ideas fallacious was that they were so widespread. Wimsatt and Beardsley argued that such questions were not literary, and that they led the reader instead into regions of historical research and individual psychology. One of the persistent goals of scholarship and criticism has been to try to reframe these desires (to know and to feel) within the language of literary investigation: to pose these questions, exactly, as *literary* questions.

Subway Reading

Let's consider one of the most anthologized and analyzed of all twentieth-century poems in English, Ezra Pound's "In a Station of the Metro." The poem is very brief—two lines—which makes it ideal for close reading. But as will be immediately evident, not every reading is *close* in the sense of attention to form.

Take, for example, the question of the text of the poem, which you might think would be, if not an easy, then at least a resolvable question. But in fact that is not the case. In its earliest printing, in *Poetry* magazine on June 6, 1913, the poem was printed this way:

The apparition   of these faces   in the crowd
Petals   on a wet, black   bough.

Shortly thereafter, in *T.P.'s Weekly* for June 1913, Pound published another version of the poem:

The apparition of these faces in the crowd:
Petals on a wet, black bough.

And in his collection of poetry called *Lustra* (1916), the poem appears in a similar form, except the colon at the end of the first line has been changed to a semicolon.

The apparition of these faces in the crowd;
Petals on a wet, black bough.

This is how the poem is almost always printed today. Pound commented extensively on its genesis and offered detailed (and changing) instructions for its proper punctuation.[12] The existence of these varied versions, each with its printing provenance and with the attached explanatory comments of the poet, constitute a good example of what is now known as genetic criticism, the history of drafts and versions or, as its proponents call them, avant-textes or pre-texts.[13] Pretty clearly, the difference in spacing and punctuation will influence both the performative reading of the poem (how is it spoken aloud? with what pauses and emphases?) and also, potentially, its meaning. But we have begun with the problem of establishing the text, and the text here is already, even in a demonstrably modern era, one of many variants, each sanctioned by the author, with an explanation, in some cases, of his intentions and of the effect, or affect, he expects the poem to produce. The first version of the poem was thirty lines long; later the two-line text modeled on the Japanese haiku derived from it.

Almost every account of this short and brilliant poem alludes, at some point, to Pound's evolutionary description of how he came to write it:

Three years ago in Paris I got out of a "metro" train at La Concorde, and saw suddenly a beautiful face, and then another and another, and then a beautiful child's face, and then another beautiful woman, and I tried all day to find words for what this had meant to me, and I could not find any words that seemed to me worthy, or as lovely as that sudden emotion. And that evening, as I went home along the Rue Raynouard, I was still trying and I found, suddenly, the expression. I do not mean that I found words, but there came an equation . . . not in speech, but in little splotches of color . . .

Any mind that is worth calling a mind must have needs beyond the existing categories of language, just as a painter must have pigments or shades more numerous than the existing names of the colors.

Perhaps this is enough to explain the words in my "Vortex":—

"Every concept, every emotion, presents itself to the vivid consciousness in some primary form. It belongs to the art of this form."

In these ruminations published in 1916, Pound went on to discuss the haiku (spelled *hokku* in his text):

The "one-image poem" is a form of super-position, that is to say, it is one idea set on top of another. I found it useful in getting out of the impasse in which I had been left by my metro emotion. I wrote a thirty-line poem, and destroyed it because it was what we call work "of second intensity." Six months later I made a poem half that length; a year later I made the following *hokku*-like sentence:—

"The apparition of these faces in the crowd:
Petals, on a wet, black bough."

I dare say it is meaningless unless one has drifted into a certain vein of thought. In a poem of this sort one is trying to record the precise instant when a thing outward and objective transforms itself, or darts into a thing inward and subjective.[14]

Here is the author, front and center, naming his poem's genre (*hokku*-like; "one-image poem"), explaining its moment of origin, its visual inspiration, its title, its poetic progress from thirty lines to fifteen to two.

To read the poem, must one read this account or know of it? And if so, do we have to believe it? What authority does the author have?

Many critics, contemplating "In a Station of the Metro," have zeroed in on the word *apparition,* which stands out from all the others in that it is multisyllabic, Latinate, abstract, conceptual as well as visual. Several have detected a mythological substrate, indebted to classical literature's descents to the underworld ("apparition" + "faces in the crowd" = shades of the dead, whether experienced by Orpheus, Odysseus, or Aeneas). Some recent commentators have singled out the poem's ethnopoetics,[15] and at least one, close reading Pound's account of the poem's origin, has seen the "foundational cluster beauty / woman / child / lovely / [poetry]" as posing a feminist conundrum: "One idea is that beauty / the feminine matters in the construction of poetry; the other is that it does not."[16]

If one did not have in hand Pound's autobiographical account, would it be tempting to imagine that the faces were flashing by on a moving train, rather than being glimpsed on the station platform, as he seems to describe them? And if one had never heard of haiku, would it matter? What if this were the first one-image poem the reader encountered? How much background or generic context is necessary to read a poem? And if we wanted, for any reason, to read *against* Pound's authority rather than in obedience to it, what might that mean?

Pound calls it a one-image poem, but arguably, it is a *two*-image poem, if one counts the title. Suppose we did not have the title phrase— or if he had excised the title in a further editorial moment? Without that situational marker, which anchors the perception in modernity and in urban space, the two lines might be read quite differently. If we were to compare the poem to, for example, some fragments of ancient verse, recognized as fragmentary, unrecoverable as wholes, what would that do to the poem? Pound famously collaborated with T. S. Eliot in assembling *The Waste Land,* with its paradigmatic assertion that "These fragments I have shored against my ruins." In his account of the genesis of the "Metro" poem, Pound claims that "the image is itself the speech"—that images are not "ornaments." But is the title part of the image? Or is it an ornament?

Another well-known modern instance of an author severely cutting a poem for a similar tightening effect is Marianne Moore's decision to reduce her poem "Poetry" from five stanzas to three lines—a distilled version of the three lines that began the original poem.

> I, too, dislike it.
> Reading it, however, with a perfect contempt for it, one discovers in
> it, after all, a place for the genuine.

These revisions were accepted as canonical—i.e., as the author's version of the poem—when Moore's collected poetry was published in 1967, but when facsimiles of the (out-of-print) 1924 volume *Observations* came under review by scholars, debates ensued about whether the editorial changes Moore introduced should be regarded as improvements. In any case, the two poems called "Poetry" are formally and textually quite different, and the shorter of the two does not contain one of Moore's most famous and most quoted phrases, "imaginary gardens with real toads in them."

It is not uncommon for works of literature, whether in verse or in prose, to exist in more than one version. I mention it here because the question of reading may be thought, naturally enough, to involve reading a particular something, and that something (usually called the *work* or the *text*) is increasingly, in these sophisticated editorial days, a *plural* something—like, for example, the two different, "authentic" versions of *King Lear* that are now regularly printed by editors of that play, or what used to be called the "Bad" Quarto of *Hamlet*.

The First Quarto of *Hamlet* included this version of a speech that would become celebrated in a very different form:

> To be, or not to be, I, there's the point,
> To Die, to sleepe, is that all? I all:
> No, to sleepe, to dreame, I mary there it goes,
> For in that dreame of death, when wee awake,
> And borne before an euerlasting Iudge,
> From whence no passenger euer retur'nd,

The vndiscovered country, at whose sight
The happy smile, and the accursed damn'd. (7.114–121)

Will any non-academic reader claim that this is the "real" (since apparently "original") "To be or not to be," or ask whether it has been effectively superseded by the more familiar text? For an increasing number of Shakespeare scholars, the First Quarto (no longer dubbed "the Bad Quarto," as if it had a moral flaw) has a legitimacy all its own, regardless of the wider admiration accorded the Second Quarto and Folio. Actors have performed the first version with considerable success, unhampered by the overfamiliarity that breeds not contempt but its affectively positive equivalent, stultifying adoration. The total effect is often that of an aria performed, applauded, and experienced as a whole. The experience of the First Quarto is both disorienting and refreshing—the pleasure of encountering the energies of this astonishing play anew. If it sends us back to the more familiar version, all the better—but this passage seems to suggest a set of rhythms, and an acting style, that show us something powerful and strong.

Coleridge described prose as "words in their best order" and poetry as "the best words in their best order."[17] Close readers in the middle of the twentieth century tended to use *poem* in an extended sense—to refer, for example, to plays in verse, especially the plays of Shakespeare, and by extension, other Elizabethan and Jacobean playwrights. "Hamlet, the Prince or the Poem" was the title of an essay by the critic C. S. Lewis,[18] and the use of *poem* here is indicative. Teachers of fiction, and especially of long novels, used close reading to direct attention, for example, to the opening sentences or first paragraphs of these works. This pedagogical technique had a strategic as well as an aesthetic and intellectual payoff, since even those students who had not read the work in question—or had not read far into it—could be brought into a conversation about artistry, word choice, tone, voice, irony, and foreshadowing. A classic instance is the beginning of Jane Austen's *Pride and Prejudice:*

It is a truth universally acknowledged, that a single man in possession of a good fortune must be in want of a wife.

A skilled teacher can elicit discussion of this single sentence for an
extended period before turning to the second sentence, which not
only superbly undercuts the first but makes the reader reread and re-
consider it:

However little known the feelings or views of such a man may be on
his first entering a neighborhood, this truth is so well fixed in the
minds of the surrounding families, that he is considered the rightful
property of some one or other of their daughters.

Again, a whole discussion might well be devoted to the single word
property, which has major resonances throughout the novel and through
Austen's work more generally. Bear in mind that the single man with
the good (not great) fortune alluded to in this first sentence is the amiable and pliable Mr. Bingley, not the far wealthier and more complex
Mr. Darcy. The novel sidles into the narrative of its central love affair
through this delectably wicked glance at local customs, town gossip, and
the neat slide from high-toned philosophical bromide ("it is a truth universally acknowledged") to the bathetically domestic, or the domesti-
cally bathetic, "must be in want of a wife." Think for a second about how
else the sentence might have concluded: "should put his money in a safe
place"; "should consider the welfare of others before his own comfort";
"should be grateful for the prudence of his forebears and the providence
of a beneficent deity," etc.

The reading tactic deployed here is, as I've noted, what has been variously called close reading or slow reading or reading in slow motion. The
latter phrase is that of Reuben Brower, a professor of English at Harvard
in the fifties and sixties and, before that, professor of Greek and English
at Amherst College.[19] Brower was the legendary teacher of an equally

legendary Harvard course, Humanities 6, almost always referred to as Hum 6.

Perhaps the clearest and most eloquent demonstration of how close reading works was offered by one of Brower's former assistants in the course, Paul de Man, who would become one of the most admired literary exponents of deconstruction, and whose own pedagogy produced a roster of critics as accomplished as Brower's. Here is de Man's account, from an essay first published in *The Times Literary Supplement* in 1982. In its clarity and descriptive analysis, it is well worth quoting at length.

My own awareness of the critical, even subversive, power of literary instruction does not stem from philosophical allegiances but from a very specific teaching experience. In the 1950s, [Walter Jackson] Bate's colleague at Harvard, Reuben Brower, taught an undergraduate course in General Education entitled "The Interpretation of Literature" (better known on the Harvard campus and in the profession at large as HUM 6) in which many graduate students in English and Comparative Literature served as teaching assistants. No one could be more remote from high-powered French theory than Reuben Brower. He wrote books on Shakespeare and on Pope that are models of sensitive scholarship but not exactly manifestos for critical terrorism. He was much more interested in Greek and Latin literature than in literary theory. The critics he felt closest to, besides Eliot, were Richards and Leavis, and in both of them he was in sympathy with their emphasis on ethics.

Brower, however, believed in and effectively conveyed what appears to be an entirely innocuous and pragmatic precept, founded on Richards's "practical criticism." Students, as they began to write on the writings of others, were not to say anything that was not derived from the text they were considering. They were not to make any statements that they could not support by a specific use of language that actually occurred in the text. They were asked, in other words, to begin by reading texts closely as texts and not to move at once into the general context of human experience or history. Much more humbly or modestly, they were to start out from the bafflement that such singular turns of tone, phrase, and figure were bound to produce in readers attentive enough to notice them and honest enough not to hide their non-understanding behind the screen of received ideas that often passes, in literary instruction, for humanistic knowledge.

This very simple rule, surprisingly enough, had far-reaching didactic consequences. I have never known a course by which students were so transformed. Some never saw the point of thus restricting their attention to the matter at hand and of concentrating on the way meaning is conveyed rather than on the meaning itself. Others, however, caught on very quickly and, henceforth, they would never be the same. The papers they handed in at the end of the course bore little resemblance to what they produced at the beginning. What they lost in generality, they more than made up for in precision and in the closer proximity of their writing to the original mode. It did not make writing easier for them for they no longer felt free to indulge in any thought that came into their head or to paraphrase any idea they happened to encounter.

At the end of this account of the surprising effects of Reuben Brower's pedagogical method, de Man offers an analysis that may seem even more surprising.

Mere reading, it turns out, prior to any theory, is able to transform critical discourse in a manner that would appear deeply subversive to those who think of the teaching of literature as a substitute for the teaching of theology, ethics, psychology, or intellectual history. Close reading accomplishes this often in spite of itself because it cannot fail to respond to structures of language which it is the more or less secret aim of literary teaching to keep hidden.[20]

It's worth doing a close reading of the last sentence, the topic of which is close reading. De Man's elegant formulation is built on a series of negations and reversals: "in spite of itself"; "it cannot fail"; "the more or less secret aim . . . to keep hidden." When it is coupled with "deeply subversive" in the previous sentence, we have what might be described as a critical language of reluctant but persistent uncovering. The concept of literary teaching here is explicated immediately above: the methods of "those who think of the teaching of literature as a substitute for the teaching of theology, ethics, psychology, or intellectual history." Language, in all its waywardness, slows down and diverts the goal of identifying a "meaning"—meaning that the text will then be said to express. This is why close reading is "subversive": what it subverts is a rush to a corresponding meaning outside the text. Reading in slow motion, frame by frame—does not allow for the "general impression," which is so often an imprecise paraphrase of what the reader thinks the poem, or novel, or story, or play, *ought* to be saying. What it actually says may get in the way of that confident appropriation. Details emerge that may derail the express.

We might draw an analogy with what was known in my childhood as "look-say" reading as opposed to phonics or "sounding it out." Confronted with the image of an equine quadruped and the letters H-O-R-S-E, the eager reader cried out "Pony!"

De Man's essay was called "The Return to Philology," and the quiet irony is evident. Philology, that supposedly old-fashioned discipline, was the most radical way of reading. Radical in the sense of word roots, and radical in the sense of destabilizing common sense when it conflicted with what the words on the page were saying and doing. Writing in the early 1980s, de Man saw the analogy between Brower's course and what came to be called "theory."

> The personal experience of Reuben Brower's Humanities 6 was not so different from the impact of theory on the teaching of literature over the past ten or fifteen years. The motives may have been more revolutionary and the terminology was certainly more intimidating. But, in practice, the turn to theory occurred as a return to philology, to an examination of the structure of language prior to the meaning it produces.[21]

Had this essay been written a few years later, it might have observed not only the turn to theory (what, in other fields, like history and anthropology, became known as "the linguistic turn") but also a kind of inevitable response (I hesitate to call it a backlash) in the turn—or return—to history. History, rather than theology or psychology, became, for many readers and teachers, the anterior "meaning" of literary texts.[22]

When historicism emerged as a central defining practice in English departments in the later twentieth century, one of its core practices was to do powerful close readings of historical texts in the context of the readings of works of literature. The elements of surprise, consternation, and arrest were introduced into the reading of what had previously been described as secondary texts for literary study: a treatise on witchcraft, say, or an instruction manual on swordsmanship or mathematics, or a conduct book for young ladies or young gentlemen. Work of this kind was invaluable in returning to prominence questions of historical reference in literary texts that had sometimes been ignored, or consigned to footnotes, by formalist practices of close reading.

The importance of the Gunpowder Plot of 1605 as a reference for Shakespeare's *Macbeth*, or the changes in domestic fiction brought about by the Married Women's Property Act of 1882, or the observations of the early modern astronomer, ethnographer, and translator Thomas Harriot when he traveled to the Americas with Walter Raleigh in 1585–86— all of these became focal points for important scholarship in English and American literature and culture. But every practice is prone to its own excesses, and over time it has occasionally been the case that the historical fact took preeminence over the literary work. When history is regarded as the "real" of which the poem, play, or novel is (merely or largely) a reflection, something crucial is lost, and that something is *literature*.

The Poetry Cure

Some early examples of English poetry exhibit a striking kind of fictive usefulness, embedded in the artifice of poem-making. In these cases, the poem—or the rhyme, or the perfect word—comes to the poet as inspiration, whether from God or from the muse of poetry, supplying words where they were lacking, and changing or healing the speaker. These stories are legendary and exemplary. Here are three examples, one from the earliest-known English poem, another from a religious lyric, and a third from a love sonnet.

The story of "Caedmon's Hymn" is told, movingly, by the monk and scholar known as the Venerable Bede. Caedmon was a lay brother who worked as a herdsman at the monastery. Once, when the monks were feasting and singing, he retreated to sleep with the animals because— says Bede—he knew no songs. He dreamed that "someone" came to him and told him to sing a song of the beginning of creation. At first he demurred but then began to sing the short—and beautiful—poem known as "Caedmon's Hymn." The next day he reported these events to the monastery, was asked to write another poem, and, having complied, was invited to take monastic vows. He became—again according to Bede—a prolific poet of religious verse, all composed, like the hymn, in the vernacular—that is to say, in Old English, not in Latin. Bede's *Historia Ecclesiastica*, which reports this, is, however, written in Latin.

Like all foundation myths, this one can, if we choose, be regarded as an invention, a fiction, an allegory, an embellishment of fact, or any other species of instructive story. But the hymn exists in a number of dialect versions, and what it records is a story of literary inspiration. "Sing," the command given to Caedmon, remains throughout much of the history of English—and earlier—literature the figure inviting or initiating poetic performance (Virgil's *Aeneid* famously begins "Arms and the man I sing"). The moment of inspiration (after a period of mute or stumbling incapacity) is not infrequently restaged in later poems as a birth, or rebirth, of song and creative fluency.

Consider, for example, George Herbert's poem "Denial," which begins

When my devotions could not pierce
    Thy silent ears,
Then was my heart broken, as was my verse:
    My breast was full of fears
        And disorder.

and ends

O cheer and tune my heartless breast,
    Defer no time;
That so thy favors granting my request,
    They and my mind may chime,
            And mend my rhyme.

The mended rhyme comes with the word "rhyme," which accords with "chime" and "time," and repairs the loss of rhyme in the previous stanza, which ends in "disorder." Herbert expertly deploys the final lines and stanzas of his poems to perform this kind of mind-mending, in poems like "The Collar," "Love (III)," and the "Jordan" poems, among others. As with Caedmon, the literary fiction—whatever the spiritual reality— is that of divine assistance, inspiration, collaboration.

A more secular version of this trope—for it is a trope, a figure of speech—is on display in the first of Philip Sidney's *Astrophil and Stella* sonnets, where the lover, seeking words to describe his passion, turns dramatically from rhetoric to spontaneous feeling:

Loving in truth, and fain in verse my love to show,
    That she dear she might take some pleasure of my pain:
    Pleasure might cause her read, reading might make her know,
    Knowledge might pity win, and pity grace obtain,
I sought fit words to paint the blackest face of woe,
    Studying inventions fine, her wits to entertain:
    Oft turning others' leaves, to see if thence would flow
    Some fresh and fruitful showers upon my sunburned brain.
But words came halting forth, wanting Invention's stay;
    Invention, Nature's child, fled stepdame Study's blows;
    And others' feet still seemed but strangers in my way.

Thus, great with child to speak, and helpless in my throes,
　Biting my truant pen, beating myself for spite:
　"Fool," said my Muse to me, "look in thy heart and write."

(1–14)

This great sonnet is deeply—and deliberately—disingenuous in its ingenuity. Disclaiming artifice, study, and literary device, it deploys them with consummate artistry. The poem is a primer in literary figures, from anadiplosis, the repetition of the last word from a previous clause or phrase at the beginning of the next, to the vivified pun on "feet" (anatomical and poetical), and finally to the professions of incapacity "helpless in my throes"; "truant pen") and the triumphant breakthrough when the Muse dictates the manner of plain speech ("look in thy heart and write"). Significantly, it is the Muse's speech, not the poet's, that comes to end (and mend) the sonnet—although the Muse herself is, like Invention and stepdame Study, one of the invented personae of the poet's text.

　The naive voice in such a poem is achieved *through* learning, not despite it. Elizabethan and Jacobean poets were skilled in the use of rhetorical devices, having learned them in school and through the examples found in numerous rhetorical textbooks, like Henry Peacham's *The Garden of Eloquence Conteyning the Figures of Grammer and Rhetorick* (1577), Thomas Wilson's *The Arte of Rhetorique, for the use of all suche as are studious of Eloquence, sette forth in English* (1553), and George Puttenham's *The Art of English Poesy* (1589). Modern students may be familiar with metaphor, simile, personification, and a handful of other figures of speech, but the poetic toolbox of earlier poets contained dozens, indeed hundreds, of tropes. Recognizing them, and the twists and turns that made them new, was one of the manifold pleasures of reading. For a modern reader, the reverse is the case: the identification of tropes and figures often comes after the first and second readings of the poem, if at all, and is often associated with the classroom rather than with the immediacy of aesthetic or intellectual response.

　These rhetorical treatises directly address the question of use. The poet, equipped with skills in language and style, is enabled to move in courtly circles and to affect both language and politics.[23] The idea of material advancement through poetry was not an exaggeration. It was possible to overcome the disadvantages of low birth through education. Archbishop Cranmer (himself not born to the aristocracy) contended that "poor men's children are many times endued with more singular gifts of nature . . . eloquence, memory, apt pronunciation, sobriety, and such like, and also commonly more apt to apply their study, than is the gentleman's son delicately educated."[24]

Puttenham's title, *The Art of English Poesy*, should be inflected with a stress on the word *English:* he took for granted the effectiveness, importance, and art (in the largest sense, encompassing rhetorical skill, craft, politics, and eloquence) of earlier poets, both historical and divine. What he set out to do, by tracing the role of the poet through Western cultural history and "Englishing" the names of some classical literary tropes, was to define the potential use of poetry, poetics, and poets for the emerging English nation. The explanatory subtitle of Chapter 2 is "That there may be an art of our English poesy, as well as there is of the Latin and Greek"; the explanatory subtitle of Chapter 3 is "How poets were the first priests, the first prophets, the first legislators and politicians in the world; the explanatory subtitle of Chapter 4 is "How the poets were the first philosophers, the first astronomers, and historiographers, and orators, and musicians of the world," and so on. Taken together with the address to the queen, this framing constitutes a political as well as a social and aesthetic argument. Poets are good for nation-building, and a national literature is good for the nation.

Moreover, the idea of poets as legislators and politicians—a concept that, by the time of Shelley's *Defense of Poetry,* had become rhetorical in the abased sense of that term—was, for the Elizabethans, a practical reality. Shelley would claim that poets were the "unacknowledged legislators of the world," but in ancient Greece and throughout the Renaissance, poets were, in fact, fully acknowledged as political players. "Poet" was not a full-time occupation to the exclusion of other pursuits. Philip Sidney was a diplomat, Walter Raleigh a courtier and explorer, George Herbert a priest.* John Donne was trained as a diplomat and anticipated

---

* He was an orator at Cambridge before he became an Anglican priest.

a career in government until his marriage produced a breach between Donne and his political patrons. Edmund Spenser pursued a political career in Ireland (his prose pamphlet *A View of the Present State of Ireland* recommended aggressive conquest of the Irish native population and the instigation of English language and customs); his prose epic *The Faerie Queene*, one of the masterworks of the English literary canon, was written in hopes of obtaining a place at court—hopes that did not come to fruition for political reasons. As one of Spenser's early-twentieth-century editors wrote, "Poetry was a noble pastime, even a vocation, but for a gentleman it was not a profession. All it could do for him would be to bring his talents to the notice of those who were in the position to better his fortunes."[25]

The argument of *The Faerie Queene*, setting forth its poetic program, was addressed to Spenser's friend Walter Raleigh. Spenser explained that "the generall end" of the book was "to fashion a gentleman or noble person in virtuous and gentle discipline." So this, too, was a use of poetry. The choice of a fictional narrative for what Spenser called his "continued Allegory, or darke conceit," was connected—or so he alleged—to the idea of fashioning the moral character of his gentle or noble readers:

> To some I know this Methode will seeme displeasaunt, which had rather hauve good discipline deliuered plainly in way of precepts, or sermoned at large, as they use, then thus cloudily enwrapped in Allegoricall deuises. But such, me seeme, should be satisfied with the vse of these dayes, seeing all things accounted by their showes, and nothing esteemed of, that is not delightfull and pleasing to commune sense.[26]

Excuse or not—since allegory's "dark conceit" was also, equally usefully, a way of disguising controversial views under the device of fiction—this explanation for why one of the most brilliantly imagined poems in the English language takes the form of poetry and fiction rather than precepts and sermons is a good example of the use of *use*. In Spenser's letter to Raleigh, "the *vse* of these dayes" is customary practice, what people are used to, what they like or prefer—in this case, "showes." A few years later, Ben Jonson would excoriate mere "showes" as the stage design and props provided by his collaborator, Inigo Jones, as contrasted with the greater complexity of poetry: "O showes! Showes! Mighty Showes! / The Eloquence of Masques! / What need of prose /Or Verse, or Sense, t'express Immortal you?"[27] But "showes" for Spenser still seemed to include *literary* exhibitions or fictions.

So the uses of rhetoric, eloquence, "poetical ornament," figures of speech, and fictional examples were, for the poets, scholars, and politicians of the English Renaissance, a way of (1) fashioning gentlemen, (2) inculcating moral virtues as painlessly and pleasurably as possible, (3) concealing or disguising unpopular opinions under the guise of fiction or allegory, and (4) seeking—and sometimes obtaining—political, social, and financial advancement. Literature had uses: it did things, it gained things for the poet, even though—and perhaps because—his profession was not "poet" but something else.

Can Poetry Make "Nothing" Happen?

The combination of poetry and advocacy, we might note, is as vital and necessary today as it was centuries ago. When the poet Robert Bly accepted the National Book Award for poetry in 1969, he invoked the moral authority of the radical intellectuals of the sixties:

> We have some things to be proud of. No one needs to be ashamed of the acts of civil disobedience committed in the tradition of Thoreau. What Dr. Coffin did was magnificent; the fact that Yale University did not do it is what is sad. What Mr. Berrigan did was noble; the fact that the Catholic church did not do it is what is sad. What Mitchell Goodman did here last year was needed and in good taste . . . In an age of gross and savage crimes by legal governments, the institutions will have to learn responsibility, learn to take their part in preserving the nation, and take their risk by committing acts of disobedience. The book companies can find ways to act like Thoreau, whom they publish. Where were the publishing houses when Dr. Spock and Mr. Goodman and Mr. Raskin—all three writers—were indicted? . . .

You have given me an award for a book that has many poems in it against the war. I thank you for the award. As for the thousand-dollar check, I am turning it over to the draft-resistance movement, specifically to the organization called the Resistance . . .[28]

The only dated part of the speech is the amount of the check. Today's National Book Award winners each get ten thousand dollars and a trophy.

But there is something moving about the spectacle of a poet trying to change the world with "many poems against the war" and a thousand-dollar check. Especially when we contrast it to the cancellation of a proposed White House symposium on "Poetry and the American Voice" convened by First Lady Laura Bush for Lincoln's birthday, February 12, 2003. When the poet and editor Sam Hamill responded to the invitation by sending out an e-mail urging invitees to send him poems and statements opposing the invasion of Iraq, he received over 5,300 submissions, from poets as well known as Adrienne Rich, Lawrence Ferlinghetti, Philip Levine, and Diane di Prima. The symposium was postponed indefinitely, and the White House put out the following statement: "While Mrs. Bush understands the right of all Americans to express their political views, this event was designed to celebrate poetry."

Slam Dunk

Outside of the classroom poetry is often a specialized interest, what consumer guides call a niche product. But in recent years audiences have been drawn to two kinds of in-person cultural performances: the poetry reading and the poetry slam. The former typically takes place in a bookstore, café, or college auditorium. The speaker is a well-known poet or several—often, but not always, appearing in connection with the publication of a new book. The slam features individuals or teams who speak within a strict time limit (three minutes) and are awarded points by a judge for their performance. Participants in poetry slams are usually young, often influenced by hip-hop or dub poetry, and sometimes connected to youth poetry organizations. Although in both formats—the reading and the slam—poets occasionally recite works by others, the characteristic mode is personal performance of one's own work.

Responses to slam culture have, predictably, been varied. *The New York Times* reported that Harold Bloom called poetry slams "the death of art."[29] Still, it's undeniable that poetry has attracted new enthusiasts, younger participants, and high energy in recent years, in part through this medium of performance.* The Renaissance lyric gained popularity through the performances of troubadours and the global phenomenon of Petrarchism, so it's not so unlikely that a new generation, for whom downloading songs on iPods and other MP3 players is second nature, should make the connection between song and poem. The word *lyric* dates back etymologically to a time when a poem was sung to the accompaniment of a lyre, and has, since the end of the nineteenth century, also meant the words of a popular song—surely the most common use of the term today.

Despite the occasional gloomy prognosis, poems and poetry are alive and well today—in the classroom, the poetry magazine, the writing workshop, the lecture hall, the bookstore, on the Internet, and in the streets. The death of art is always being predicted somewhere, and is perhaps a necessary pronouncement to ensure the tangible edginess, the sense of delighted transgression, that comes with practicing a living and changing art or craft.

---

* and through rappers like Eminem and Jay-Z.

SIX

Why Literature Is Always Contemporary

When the poet and playwright Ben Jonson wrote, in his memorial poem on Shakespeare, that "he was not of an age, but for all time," Jonson was praising the timeless quality of Shakespeare's work, but his words also point toward its uncanny timeliness, its capacity to intersect with the times. "Thou art alive still," he assured his dead friend and rival, "while thy book doth live / And we have wits to read, and praise to give."[1] Although this capacity to live is often regarded as synonymous with the elusive quality we call greatness, it is in fact, as Jonson notes here, also a collaborative effect produced by the relationship between text ("thy book") and reader. In a similar spirit, Virginia Woolf remarked about the Romantic critic William Hazlitt, "He has an extraordinary power of making us contemporary with himself."[2]

No matter how much we historicize works of literature, putting them in the context of the age of the author or his times (the Age of Dante; the Age of Jonson; the Age of Elizabeth, etc.), poems, plays, novels, and other works of literature, whether imaginative or intellectual, are being read right now—and that *now* is always shifting with the time and place of the current reader. So reading any literary work involves a kind of stereo-optical vision: one eye on the image of the past, the other on the present, the two eyes then combining them into a vivid single picture.

Often an author, a genre, or a specific work changes under the scrutiny of time, so that it is impossible to say with certainty that today's valued texts will be regarded as literature tomorrow, or that today's pulp fiction will not ascend to canonical status in the future. It may seem paradoxical to claim that all literature is contemporary. It would appear that the opposite is the case. But this seeming paradox, I want to argue, is intrinsic to the nature and culture of literature, and also—not incidentally—to the pleasures of reading and writing.

On the one hand, the situation is so straightforward: a reader today encounters a work of literature from the perspective of the present. No matter how much the reader tries to project back into the past—into, let us say, a time when Chaucer's works were available only in manuscript form, or when Donne's poems and Shakespeare's sonnets circulated privately among a small group ("his sugared sonnets among his private friends," as one of Shakespeare's contemporaries noted[3],) or when Gertrude Stein hosted writers like Ernest Hemingway, Thornton Wilder, and Ezra Pound in her Paris salon in the twenties—there is always some consciousness, or perhaps we should say some unconsciousness, of the difference between that "now" and the "now" of the present day. Not only are methods of printing, dissemination, and reading different; so are other essential categories like dress, politics, hygiene, transportation, and the availability of electric power. The change in reading habits from public and collective to private, solitary reading, has been commented upon by many critics, and we have only to look at some of the latest technologies, like the iPad, the Nook, the Kindle, and the Sony Reader, to remember that there is no timeless and universal reading practice. Not only for those with photographic memories, who remember passages from their placement on the page, the typeface, and the quality of the paper, but indeed for everyone who reads, sees, hears, or hears *about* a work of literature, the situation of the encounter is part of the reading experience.

Up Close and Personal

A few years ago I was invited to address the Jane Austen Society of North America at a Boston hotel. When I arrived, I found a ballroom filled with a large and enthusiastic group of self-professed "Janeites," men and women, older and younger, who had gathered from around the world. By my approximate estimate, about 20 percent were in period costume, wearing the dresses, knee breeches, laces (and in some cases, wigs) of the late eighteenth century. None of them were, I presume, time travelers, though all were having a good time celebrating their favorite author. As with other popular modes of historical reconstruction, the dressing up was part of the fun, and also part of the learning process. Visitors to Austen's Chawton Cottage are likewise welcomed to the property by a young man stationed at the door in period dress, but the gift shops at such historical properties, with their postcards, aprons, and calendars for the current year, are as determinedly of the present day as the costumed greeter is of the "past."

Such re-created environments, commemorating literary personages, their ancestral homes, and the artifacts surrounding them—what is now generally called "cultural tourism"—are one striking aspect of contemporary life. They range from "Shakespeare's Birthplace" in Stratford, so memorably described in a delectable short story by Henry James, to cultural pilgrimage sites like the Brontë Parsonage Museum in Haworth, Yorkshire, and the Keats-Shelley house in Rome. Often the goal is to give visitors some sense of the imminent presence of the author, as if he or she has only momentarily stepped out of the room. When I visited the Brecht House in Augsburg, Germany, some years ago, the playwright's cyeglasses lay beguilingly on a table, as if he had just set them aside. Like the historical reenactment of famous battles, or the frozen-in-time colonial sites and living museums (Plimoth Plantation, Old Sturbridge Village, Colonial Williamsburg) where modern people in period clothing churn butter and tend livestock, these cultural sites are places where readers, fans, and buffs enjoy a touch of the faux real. As such, they are monuments at once to nostalgia and to commerce, the twin engines of literary flamekeeping. I'm a constant and fascinated visitor to such places, especially the homes of poets and writers. I do want to emphasize, though, that the very phenomenon is itself contemporary: what we are experiencing is not—or not only—the eighteenth century but, rather, the "eighteenth century" in deliberate, detectable quotation marks, the diacritical indicators of the present day.

The literary critic Susan Stewart has some wise things to say about the healthiness of anachronism and the value of change, both of which, resisting a deadly authenticity, produce instead the energy of life. She cites with approval the views of the Scottish poet and novelist James Hogg, who judged a ballad's antiquity by the degree to which it had been modernized: "this must be attributed to its currency, being much liked, and very much sung in the neighborhood."[4] For Stewart, likewise, "the ballad arrested, integral, and impervious, is the ballad as artifact," whereas what she calls, delightedly, "ballads-in-drag," which "find their most exaggerated and exemplary forms in such fabrications as Chatterton's 'Bristowe Tragedie' and Sir Walter Scott's *Lay of the Last Minstrel*," generate an atmosphere of pageant and spectacle in which "performer, audience, and narrative are mutually enfolded in a decorative 'pastness.'"[5]

It's this word, *pastness*, that I want to take up for a moment. Clearly, pastness is not the same as the past. It seems to mean something like *the flavor of the past*. The suffix *-ness* indicates a state or condition. (The stately *Oxford English Dictionary*, in a sportive mood, offers as examples some "distinctive nonce-uses of the suffix since the nineteenth century," including Coleridge's "Sir-Thomas-Browne-ness," George Eliot's "dislike-to-get-up-in-the-morning-ness," and Percy Grainger's "love-child-ness.") On this model, pastness is an *effect*, something between an idea and a sensation. It is not merely a concept, nor yet a temporality, but a feeling imparted to, or by, something—in Stewart's example, the audience and performers of a ballad that evokes the past by using devices of the present. Pastness in this sense is not fakery. It does not pretend to *be* the past, nor is it designed to deceive. It is instead a kind of form—let's call it, for the moment, literary—that assertively has things both ways: the past as a creation of the present.

Presentism and Its Discontents

Reading from the present has come in for rather a lot of bashing lately, from historians and literary scholars, who decry presentism as an anachronistic application of contemporary attitudes or standards to the events or the literature of the past. Despite the trendy suffix *-ism*, the term is about a century old. Accusations of presentism were, for a while, a kind of academic gotcha, with the implication that the presentist had not done his or her historical homework or was not committed to interpreting the literary text in the context of its original time and place. Attacks on presentism have come from outside, as well as within, the university. The Pulitzer Prize–winning book critic Jonathan Yardley, citing Gordon S. Wood's essay collection *The Purpose of the Past,* lamented that "this practice of 'presentism' is now so widespread in academia that it threatens to become standard and accepted practice." In this case, it was the professional scholars who were being accused of presentism because of their interest in categories like race, class, and gender. Yardley rued the "complaints by professional historians about abuses of history, by politicians and other amateur malefactors," when, in his view, it was not the writers of popular history but the academics, members of departments of history, who needed to resist the "trend" of viewing the past "through whatever contemporary lens they find congenial."[6]

Some celebrated instances may make clear the way in which critics, for better or worse, can make a work contemporary. When Samuel Taylor Coleridge says, "I have a smack of Hamlet myself, if I may say so,"[7] or when T. S. Eliot writes about Othello's last great speech ("Soft you; a word or two before you go, / I have done the state some service, and they know't—" [5.2.336–354]) that "What Othello seems to me to be doing in making this speech is *cheering himself up,*"[8] they might seem to be bringing the text forward into the present day.[9] But Eliot is scathing in his own response to Coleridge on Hamlet and to a similar appropriation of the play by Goethe: "probably neither of these men in writing about Hamlet remembered that his first business was to study a work of art." The "substitution—of their own Hamlet for Shakespeare's" is something he deplores, and he caps off his paragraph of rueful scorn with a characteristic shot: "We should be thankful that Walter Pater did not fix his attention on this play."[10] Eliot is zeroing in on what is sometimes called identification. He does not regard it as a literary strategy but as an extraliterary, or nonliterary, move, an abandonment of the critic's proper business, "to study a work of art."

It's important to acknowledge that literary professionals, as well as amateurs and book buffs, are sometimes inclined to speak of books—

and works of literature generally—in terms that if not labeled present-ist are nonetheless addressed to contemporary readers. This may not mark any diminution of learning. To the contrary, it is a mode frequently found in the great generalist critics, and in scholars of any period who think of literature as speaking to the modern condition as well as to its "own" time.

The medieval scholar E. Talbot Donaldson, in his edition of Chaucer's poetry (significantly subtitled *An Anthology for the Modern Reader*), offers learned accounts of the historical roles played by various types represented among the Canterbury pilgrims, but adds to that information some insights drawn from modern—or transhistorical—times. Thus, in discussing Chaucer's Prioress, he writes that the poet "describes her in terms borrowed from the stock descriptions of heroines of medieval romance—soft red mouth, gray eyes, well-proportioned nose, and broad forehead—and makes her, inevitably, sincere and demure, 'simple and coy.'" But then without a pause, Donaldson goes on to say, "Such a woman naturally appeals to a man, and the narrator's enthusiasm for her is aroused to so superlative a degree that a superlative modifies almost every one of her qualities. Of course he never does get around to speaking about her conscience . . . the Prioress's charity—a word that in Chaucer's time connoted the whole range of Christian love—gets lost among dogs and mice."[11]

Donaldson's observation "Such a woman naturally appeals to a man" is partly a version of the writing style that in fiction is known as free indirect discourse: he is projecting this thought, as the second half of his sentence makes clear, into the mind of Chaucer's narrator, a personage often called "Chaucer the pilgrim," since the poet deftly gives the intermittently naive figure a name identical to his own. It's nominally the enthusiastic narrator who develops a crush on the Prioress, enough so that he overlooks her failings in charity to focus on her adorable ways. But there remains some residue in "Such a woman naturally appeals to a man" (notice, again, the present tense) that allows a twinkling suggestion that the scholar, too, is not immune to the Prioress's charms. And if any readers bridle at "naturally" (or, indeed, at "to a man"), that is part of the tone achieved by this urbane account—an account that dares to transgress into the realm of the almost personal, and that, in doing so, makes the appeal of the Prioress, a fourteenth-century figure, both historical and contemporary. I should note that by "contemporary," I mean the date of Donaldson's text, originally published in 1958. Fifty years later, such an observation seems either bold, dated, or, charmingly, a little of both.

Now and Then

The word *now* is what linguists call a shifter: *now* in 1920 meant 1920; *now* in 2019 will, presumably, mean 2019. To put the case in literary-historical terms, Shakespeare's *Henry V* exists in at least three time zones—the time in which it was written (the end of the sixteenth century), the time in which it is set (the medieval kingship of Henry V, 1413–22), and the time in which it is being read, interpreted, or performed. Moreover (and this will come as no surprise to anyone who follows the sinuous ins and outs of academic scholarship), the epithet *presentist* has now become a proud badge of identity. Titles of essays and essay collections now display the once disfavored term as an affirmative critical stance.[12] After some intense years of historicizing, critics began to say that the "present moment had been obliterated" by some of the techniques used to focus attention on the past.[13] "As what must be excluded from critical awareness to sustain historical contact," wrote one scholar of English Renaissance literature, "the present may be considered the unconscious of new historicism."[14] Where the pejorative use pointed toward what was presumed to be an unbridgeable cultural gap between that time and this, the presentist critic asserts that older literature continues to shape ideas about identity, politics, gender, and power.

In fact, presentism, minus the *-ism*—indeed, minus any label at all—is what many, perhaps most, readers do when they pick up a book and read it. If Flaubert the author could say about the main character of his novel, "Madame Bovary, c'est moi!," so indeed do many readers. Whether the book in question is *Pride and Prejudice*, *Huckleberry Finn*, *The Bostonians*, or *Catch-22*, readers tend to identify with the major characters and to measure their actions and thoughts by the degree to which they imagine themselves in similar situations or with similar choices.

One symptom of this tendency to experience older texts as works of the present is the renewed commercial popularity of novels that have been made into films. These are not novelizations but repackagings. Typically they will replace a traditional book or cover with a still from the movie or the mention of an actor who played a starring role, in the same way the novels made popular by Oprah's Book Club, republished with that information clearly marked, have brought a wider new readership to works like *Anna Karenina* or the novels by William Faulkner. An *Oprah* producer shared her thoughts on a current selection, George Eliot's *Middlemarch,* by citing on her blog the following description of the novel, credited to Vintage Classics: "Bright, beautiful, and rebellious Dorothea has married the wrong man, and Lydgate—the ambitious new doctor in town—has married the wrong woman. Both of them long to make a positive difference in the world, but their lives do not proceed as expected. Along with the other inhabitants of Middlemarch, they must struggle to reconcile themselves to their fates and find their places in the world." This is a presentist summary, since it gives no indication of a time period other than the present—though *Middlemarch* is elsewhere clearly described as a "classic novel." Married to the wrong person, longing to make a positive difference in the world—these are dilemmas with which the reader is tacitly invited to identify. The book is not presented as self-help or as anything other than a major novel (though there is no information given on George Eliot or any date of publication other than the honorific "classic," which means, among other things, "not new").

"The Poet Is Always Our Contemporary"

Needless to say, the word *present* is as much a shifter as the word *now,* and there have been presentists in all periods, not just in the *present* present. The Bloomsbury art critic Roger Fry used the term to describe himself at a time when the focus of art historians was largely on the past:

"I've never been a Passéist," he wrote to his friend Helen Anrep, "—I was a Futurist but I have gradually trained myself to be a Presentist, which is the most difficult."[15] It was Fry's friend and biographer Virginia Woolf—the critic who admired Hazlitt for his "compelling power of making us contemporary with himself"—who set out for book readers, and book lovers, a compelling vision of the continuing presentness of literature. "The poet is always our contemporary," Woolf wrote in the essay called "How Should One Read a Book?" "[T]he illusion of fiction is gradual, its effects are prepared," she wrote, but "who when they read [lines of verse] stops to ask who wrote them, or conjures up the thought of Donne's house or Sidney's secretary; or enmeshes them in the intricacy of the past and the succession of generations? The poet is always our contemporary. Our being for a moment is centred and constricted, as in any violent shock of personal emotion."[16]

In support of her claim about immediacy and the "immense range of emotion" evoked by poetry, Woolf offered five passages, none of which she identifies for her readers, and several of which, I am guessing, would be difficult for today's "common reader" to recognize. The editor of the annotated edition, published in 1986, footnotes four of them: passages from Beaumont and Fletcher's *Maid's Tragedy,* John Ford's *Lover's Melancholy,* Wordsworth's *Prelude,* and Coleridge's *Rime of the Ancient Mariner* The fifth passage, described by Woolf as a "splendid fantasy," reads as follows:

> And the woodland haunter
> Shall not cease to saunter
>   When, far down some glade
> Of the great world's burning,
> One soft flame upturning
> Seems, to his discerning,
>   Crocus in the shade . . .

To this passage, the editor's footnote reads, "These lines remain unidentified." Certainly I myself did not recognize them, but in the age of the Internet, it took me under a minute to find the author, Ebenezer Jones, a minor poet of the nineteenth century. The poem ("When the World Is Burning") was included in Arthur Quiller-Couch's *Oxford Book of English Verse: 1250–1900,* so at the time of that collection's publication, 1919, it was canonical and respected enough to merit selection and inclusion. We might consider this an example of the *non*-contemporaneity of literature (who today reads Ebenezer Jones or would cite him as an example in a general discussion of the poet as "always our contemporary"?), but Woolf's tone is confident: Jones's poetry, like that of the Jacobean playwrights and the Romantic poets, offers the reader an opportunity "to bethink us of the varied art of the poet; his power to make us at once actors and spectators; his power to run his hand into characters as if it were a glove, and be Falstaff and Lear; his power to condense, to widen, to state, once and for ever."[17]

Once and forever. This treads perilously close to "timeless and universal," and yet Woolf's invitation and injunction to the reader is to *compare* these passages, not merely to respond to them. Taste, she says, can be trained and developed, allowing the reader to find commonalities—she suggests—between, for example, *Lear* and the *Agamemnon:* "Thus with our taste to guide us, we shall venture beyond the particular book in search of qualities that group books together; we shall give them names and thus frame a rule that brings order into our perceptions. We shall gain a further and a rarer pleasure from that discrimination." And so on to the reading of critics as well as writers, critics like Coleridge and Dryden and Johnson, whose own "rules" and taste may challenge that of the reader but whose views should not turn readers into sheep who lie down under their authority. "They are only able to help us if we come to them laden with questions and suggestions won honestly in the course of our own reading."[18] It is the act of questioning, of finding questions, rather than the determination of rules or answers, that is the real literary activity. But as Woolf is at some pains to point out, this is, again, not the same thing as "I know what I like" or "Anything goes." The further and rarer pleasure is the pleasure of discrimination, distinction, comparison, analysis, interpretation.

The last paragraph of Woolf's essay directly addresses the central preoccupation of this book, the use of literature. "Yet who reads to bring about an end, however desirable?" she asks, not entirely rhetorically. "Are there not some pursuits that we practice because they are good in themselves, and some pleasures that are final? And is not this among them?"[19] Both "pursuit" and "practice" seem important concepts here. A pursuit is both an occupation and a pastime; to practice is, similarly, both a method and a regimen.

Deliberate Anachronism

Every great author, wrote Wordsworth, has the "task of creating the taste by which he is to be enjoyed; so it has been, so will it continue to be."[20] This utterance immediately became so famous that it was regularly parodied. Thomas de Quincey, for example, begins his essay "On Murder Considered as One of the Fine Arts" with a satirical praise of the murderer John Williams, whose attention "to the composition of a fine murder" had, "as Mr. Wordsworth observes, 'created the taste by which he is to be enjoyed.'"[21] But the sentiment had staying power—for the art of murder as depicted in subsequent crime fiction, indeed, as well as for more conventional poetry, plays, and novels—and if it seems a truism, that does not mean it is not a truth.

We might compare this to a remark made over a century later by Jorge Luis Borges. "The fact is that each writer *creates* his precursors. His work modifies our conception of the past, as it will modify the future."[22] Where Wordsworth looked ahead to successor generations, Borges describes something more uncanny: the alteration of the past. Long before Photoshop, image manipulation, or *Zelig*, literature had developed techniques, theories, and practices that transformed and rewrote past works by the act of reading them.

Borges's short story "Pierre Menard, the Author of the *Quixote*," describes, in the voice of a (fictional) bibliographical scholar, the attempt of a (fictional) French novelist to write Cervantes's *Don Quixote*. "He did not want to compose another *Quixote*—which is easy—but the *Quixote itself.* Needless to say, he never contemplated a mechanical transcription of the original; he did not propose to copy it. His admirable intention was to produce a few pages which would coincide—word for word and line for line—with those of Miguel de Cervantes."[23] The scholar-narrator quotes from a long letter he received from his friend Menard: "To compose the *Quixote* at the beginning of the seventeenth century was a reasonable undertaking, necessary and perhaps even unavoidable; at the beginning of the twentieth, it is almost impossible. It is not in vain that three hundred years have gone by, filled with exceedingly complex events. Amongst them, to mention only one, is the *Quixote* itself."[24] Nevertheless—or perhaps we should say *therefore*—the critical admirer asserts that "Menard's fragmentary *Quixote* is more subtle than Cervantes'." He thus sees artful irony in certain details of the text, like Don Quixote's preference of arms over letters: "Cervantes was a former soldier: his verdict is understandable. But that Pierre Menard's Don Quixote—a contemporary of *La trahison des clercs* and Bertrand Russell—should fall prey to such nebulous sophistries!" Where other critics have tried to explain this away, as, for example, "(not at all perspicaciously) a *transcription* of the *Quixote*" the scholar suggests that a more plausible explanation "(which I judge to be irrefutable)" was "the influence of Nietzsche," to which he adds one further suggestion: Menard's modesty led him, whether by irony or by resignation, to propagate ideas that were the opposite of the ones he believed.[25]

It's easy to see what fun Borges had, especially when he produced (still in the persona of the scholar-friend) what is claimed to be a devastating comparison between the two texts—texts that, on the page, look (to the uninitiated) exactly alike:

It is a revelation to compare Menard's *Don Quixote* with Cervantes'. The latter, for example, wrote (part one, chapter nine):

. . . truth, whose mother is history, rival of time, depository of deeds, witness of the past, exemplar and adviser to the present, and the future's counselor.

Written in the seventeenth century, written by the "lay genius" Cervantes, this enumeration is a mere rhetorical praise of history. Menard, on the other hand, writes:

> . . . truth, whose mother is history, rival of time, depository of deeds, witness of the past, exemplar and adviser to the present, and the future's counselor.

History, the *mother* of truth: the idea is astounding. Menard, a contemporary of William James, does not define history as an inquiry into reality but as its origin. Historical truth, for him, is not what has happened; it is what we judge to have happened. The final phrases—*exemplar and adviser to the present, and the future's counselor*—are brazenly pragmatic.

The contrast in style is also vivid. The archaic style of Menard—quite foreign, after all—suffers from a certain affectation. Not so that of his forerunner, who handles with ease the current Spanish of his time.[26]

This is brilliant as well as comical, and speaks directly to the point. Read through the lens of the present, labeled "pragmatic" because James was a pragmatist, the text of version two (Menard) is compared to the text of version one (Cervantes). Knowing that Menard is a twentieth-century French speaker, we see the foreign and affected tinge in language we previously thought graceful and straightforward. Viewed from the vantage point of a Freudian century and anticipating the *mise en abyme* of postmodernism, the phrase "mother of truth" makes history a creator rather than a chronicle. "The text of Cervantes and that of Menard are verbally identical, but the second is almost infinitely richer."[27]

André Maurois, commenting on this last sentence, notes that although apparently absurd, it expresses "a real idea: the *Quixote* that we read is not that of Cervantes, any more than our *Madame Bovary* is that of Flaubert. Each twentieth-century reader involuntarily rewrites in his own way the masterpieces of past centuries."[28] Literature is always contemporary. But is the process always involuntary? Menard's voluntary task contrasted with the involuntary rewriting of the normative reader invoked by Maurois. But Borges, speaking through his deliberately sententious and sometimes fatuous scholar-narrator, concludes his story with a fantasy that both describes the state of the art then, and the spin-offs, adaptations, and appropriations of later decades, from Jane Smiley's *A Thousand Acres* to John Updike's *Claudius and Gertrude:*

> Menard (perhaps without wanting to) has enriched, by means of a new technique, the halting and rudimentary art of reading: this new technique is that of the deliberate anachronism and the erroneous attribution.[29]

That is to say, the technique deployed so inventively and economically in "Pierre Menard, the Author of the *Quixote.*"

Blind Spots

I began this chapter by suggesting that literature is always contemporary because it is read by contemporary readers. Such readers can no more shake off their own time and place, however skillfully and diligently they study the past, than they can change their instinctive body carriage or their habituated sense of fashion and style. The bell-bottom trousers and sideburns of the seventies are different from their modern incarnations, however these styles may be revived and made newly fashionable. Some authors translate readily into multiple time periods, seeming to be timeless by the way they are taken up, appropriated, and understood by successive generations. Shakespeare, Austen, and Dickens are clear examples of this temporal sleight of hand, which may be likened to trains that, moving along parallel tracks at similar speeds, give the illusion of standing still. Other authors and texts, as we've seen previously, are—sometimes deliberately (and often very effectively)—out of synch or out of time with the always moving present, so their archaism or quaintness or otherness is made, at least periodically, into a quality of difference that can itself be valued. And sometimes those difficult or distant texts can coincide with a cultural moment as in the case, perhaps, of the Gothic, which always seems, appropriately for its content, to be a revival or a revenant, disrupting the present, whether the period when it appears is the late eighteenth century of *The Castle of Otranto*, the nineteenth century of Poe, the Brontës, or Robert Louis Stevenson, the Southern Gothic of Faulkner and Harper Lee, or the popular Gothic romances of the mid-twentieth century, or the twenty-first century's revived interest in vampires.

But there is one persistent exception to this capacity on the part of the reader to see with contemporary eyes, and that is when what is being read and judged is the work of the present. Contemporary literature is, apparently paradoxically, the one period of literature that can generate or elicit a critical blind spot. In an odd sense, the literature of today and of recent times is partially blocked from view by our proximity to it. As she did with the immediacy of poetry, Virginia Woolf deftly explored the problem, in this case in an essay first published in *The Times Literary Supplement* titled "How It Strikes a Contemporary."

Woolf's interest, at least initially, is in the unreliability of critics when it comes to contemporary writing.

> In the first place a contemporary can scarcely fail to be struck by the fact that two critics at the same time will pronounce completely different opinions about the same book. Here, on the right, it is declared a masterpiece of English prose; on the left, simultaneously, a mere mass of waste-paper which, if the fire could survive it, should be thrown upon the flames. Yet both critics now are in agreement about Milton and about Keats. They display an exquisite sensibility and have undoubtedly a genuine enthusiasm. It is only when they discuss the work of contemporary writers that they inevitably come to blows. The book in question, which is at once a lasting contribution to English literature and a mere farrago of pretentious mediocrity, was published about two months ago. That is the explanation; that is why they differ.[30]

Readers seek guidance, writers seek appreciation. The inability of critics to offer definitive judgments disconcerts both "the reader who wishes to take his bearings in the chaos of contemporary literature" and "the writer who has a natural desire to know whether his own work, produced with infinite pains and in almost utter darkness, is likely to burn for ever among the fixed luminaries of English letters or, on the contrary, to put out the fire." But even the great critics of the past—Dryden, Johnson, Coleridge, Matthew Arnold—were hardly impeccable in their judgments of new work. "The mistakes of these great men about their own contemporaries are too notorious to be worth recording." Woolf has her own views about her own contemporaries: "Mr. Lawrence, of course, has moments of greatness, but hours of something very different. Mr. Beerbohm, in his way, is perfect, but it is not a big way. Passages of *Far Away and Long Ago* [a memoir of W. H. Hudson's childhood] will undoubtedly go to posterity entire. *Ulysses* was a memorable catastrophe—immense in daring, terrific in disaster."[31]

How have her predictions fared over time? "Mr. Lawrence" is D. H. Lawrence. That memorable catastrophe, Joyce's *Ulysses,* has been subsequently regarded, together with Proust's *À la recherche du temps perdu*—as perhaps the greatest novel of its time. Hudson, the author of *Green Mansions,* is a supporting player rather than a lead actor in the estimation of the period. Woolf, herself both a writer and a critic, hopes that "the critics whose task it is to pass judgment upon the books of the moment, whose work, let us admit, is difficult, dangerous, and often distasteful," will approach their work with generosity, but at the same time be "sparing of those wreaths and coronets which are so apt to get awry, and fade, and make the wearers, in six months' time, look a little ridiculous."[32] She enjoins them to "take a wider, a less personal view of modern literature," and above all, to ignore the tempting byways of historical gossip ("that fascinating topic—whether Byron married his sister") and instead to "say something interesting about literature itself."[33]

Contemporary literature after Woolf's time has continued to pose this same set of dilemmas. At Harvard in the early 1980s undergraduate English majors were not permitted to write their senior theses on writers who were still living. I'm not sure why—perhaps the idea was that the critical verdict had not yet been definitively rendered on these writers, since their careers were still in motion, or that there was not sufficient critical writing (essays, critical books and articles, reviews, etc.) for a young scholar to consult and assess. But times have changed. These days there are so many students who want to write about living or recent authors that the "older" writers are neglected in favor of the new. From an institutional point of view, we might say that contemporary writing, which was in some sense always *literary,* has now become *literature*—the inside rather than the outside, or the boundary or limit case. What is acknowledged, both tacitly (in the lifting of this interdiction, one that no present-day student would imagine as reasonable) and explicitly (through the teaching of the work of living writers and their periodic visits to campus), is that literature itself is a work in progress and in flux. Literature, that is to say, is itself a literary artifact.

Seeing the Mountain Near

"You cannot see the mountain near," wrote Ralph Waldo Emerson about the difficulty of critics' experience in perceiving the stature of a contemporary. "It took a century to make it suspected; and not until two centuries had passed, after his death, did any criticism which we think adequate begin to appear."[34] Emerson's mountain metaphor is wonderfully chosen and immediately persuasive. Distance—a viewpoint, a perspective, an observation perch—is required to bring the invisible, unsuspected neighboring immensity into view. And the mountain, once too close to be seen, is the monumental figure of William Shakespeare, now become "the horizon beyond which, at present, we do not see." Instead of blocking the view, the author, over time, becomes its measure and its module; again paradoxically, his work becomes contemporary. "Now, literature, philosophy, and thought, are Shakspearized." "Our ears are educated to music by his rhythm."

We notice the effect of words like *now* and *at present,* terms we have identified as shifters, words that can be understood only from their context. In such temporal markings—the *now* and *at present* of 1850—we can observe the history of presentism, its own inevitable repositioning as the past. Consider this pair of maxims from Oscar Wilde, both directly relevant to the question of seeing through contemporary eyes: "The nineteenth century dislike of Realism is the rage of Caliban seeing his own face in a glass. The nineteenth century dislike of Romanticism is the rage of Caliban not seeing his own face in a glass."[35] In both cases, an age looks at itself, misrecognizing what it sees, or what it fails to see.

The maxims are part of the preface to Wilde's novel *The Picture of Dorian Gray*—a novel that takes as its central conceit its main character's increasing debauchery and his wish, which is granted, that his portrait should age and become disfigured while he himself remains young and beautiful. After Dorian's death, the portrait reverts to its original beauty, while his body bears all the signs of age and vice. The frame of this modern fable is a conversation between the aesthete Lord Henry Wotton and the portrait painter Basil Hallward, who are both taken with Dorian's beauty. Wilde wrote to a correspondent, "Basil Hallward is what I think I am: Lord Henry what the world thinks of me: Dorian is what I would like to be—in other ages, perhaps."[36]

Wilde's biographer Richard Ellmann points out that in "The Critic as Artist," a critical dialogue written at the same time as the novel, Wilde argued that literature was superior to visual art. Because literature exists in time and not only in space, it can change—or, as Ellmann says, "it involves a psychic response to one's own history." In *Dorian Gray*, Wilde set out to write a fictional narrative that would embody this argument by allowing literature and painting to exchange their roles for a moment: the painting changes, the literary character appears to stop time, until the denouement, where, dramatically, each is restored to its intrinsic form. As he declared in "The Critic as Artist,"

> [T]he secrets of life belong to those, and those only, whom the sequence of time affects, and who possess not merely the present but the future, and can rise or fall from a past of glory or of shame. Movement, that problem of the visual arts, can be truly realized by Literature alone.[37]

The Picture of Dorian Gray engaged the question of whether the present could see itself and whether it could face what it saw. Read variously as a Gothic novel, a fiction of the doppelgänger, an allegory of closeted homosexuality, and a narrative of aestheticism and its discontents, *Dorian Gray* is also the story of modern literature's attempt to read itself reading, to see its own contemporaneity. One face or the other, the portrait or the man, could be seen or shown as it was, or as it seemed to be. The other face was occluded and would be seen only belatedly, after the fact.

We might compare the changing picture of Dorian Gray to another famous artifact embedded within a work of literature: the statue in the last scene of Shakespeare's tragicomic romance *The Winter's Tale*.[38] For in that play, as in Wilde's novel, the audience is confronted with an artifact that seems to have changed—the supposed "statue" that is, in fact, the living Queen Hermione, hidden away from her husband for sixteen years and presented to him as if she were a work of art. The husband, though overjoyed, cannot resist an aesthetic objection: the statue does not accurately represent the woman he remembers. "Hermione was not so much wrinkled, nothing / So aged as this seems." The reply to his critique is swift: "So much the more our carver's excellence, / Which lets go by some sixteen years and makes her / As she liv'd now" (*WT* 5.3.28–32). The word *now* once again makes the moment a shifter, always contemporaneous with the audience, the reader, the spectator. And the play ends, as virtually all Shakespeare's plays do, with a gesture toward inclusion and dialogue, as the characters exit to talk over what they have experienced. Offstage, out of our hearing, they will "leisurely / Each one demand, and answer to his part / Perform'd in this wide gap in time." This gap, whether it is sixteen years or the two hours' traffic of the stage or the intervention of four centuries between 1611 and the present, opens a space for the use of literature: its openness for commentary, debate, wonder, and pleasure is what makes literature always contemporary.

SEVEN

On Truth and Lie in a
Literary Sense

"Human kind / Cannot bear very much reality," T. S. Eliot wrote in the first of his *Four Quartets*.[1] Variously misremembered and misquoted as "Mankind cannot bear very much reality" and—with a deplorable indifference to the rhythms of blank verse—"Mankind cannot bear too much reality," this phrase, lifted from its context, has achieved the status of an aphorism, and—what seems always to follow—a truth. Since this chapter will offer a resistant account of reality as it has come to be valued in the world of literature and writing, we might begin by asking how much is "too much"—or, alternatively, what is it that makes "reality" real or reality "real"? The problem is already apparent.

What is the use of reality in literature? Sometimes contemporary writing is itself referential—pointing toward or running parallel with actual events and persons, as, for example, in novels by E. L. Doctorow or Don DeLillo, or in the genre of the "occasional poem," written to commemorate an event. But what happens when reality becomes a trait, or a criterion, for the success, excellence, or sincerity of a piece of writing?

The brief celebrity of the nonfiction novel in the 1960s, following the publication of Truman Capote's *In Cold Blood*, presented real events narrated in the style and using the techniques of fiction. My interest here, however, is in the converse situation: works that present themselves as true and that disclose themselves, or are forcibly disclosed, to be invented.

The normative distinction on best-seller lists is between fiction and nonfiction. But like all binaries, this one is difficult to sustain. What is interesting about the fiction/nonfiction divide is precisely the formal pretense that these things are opposites, or alternatives, to each other, rather than versions of each other, or aspects of a larger category of writing and reading. There is a certain irony in the fact that we praise works of fiction for being true-to-life, and condemn works of nonfiction when they turn out to be fabrications. I have sometimes found myself sharing the ethical outrage of those who feel duped by false memoirs. But from a critical rather than a moral or ethical standpoint, should these deceptions be telling us something about the nature of writing?

We might also want to consider the curious status of a term like *nonfiction*, which implies that the standard kind of writing—what linguists and anthropologists would call the unmarked term—is *fiction*. Why is the true-story narrative for modern readers defined in terms of a double negative? Is nonfiction the equivalent of "not untrue," and how is that different from "true"?

The documentary filmmaker Errol Morris offered some thoughtful commentary on the vexed question of reenactment in film and television:

> Critics argue that the use of re-enactment in documentaries suggests a callous disregard on the part of a filmmaker for what is true. I don't agree. Some re-enactments serve the truth, others subvert it. There is no mode of expression, no technique of production that will instantly produce truth or falsehood. There is no veritas lens that provides a "truthful" picture of events. There is cinéma vérité and kino Pravda but no cinematic truth.
>
> The engine of uncovering truth is not some special lens or even the unadorned human eye; it is unadorned human reason. It wasn't a cinéma vérité documentary *[The Thin Blue Line]* that got Randall Dale Adams out of prison. It was a film that re-enacted important details of the crime. It was an investigation—part of which was done with a camera. The re-enactments capture the important details of that investigation. It's not re-enactments per se that are wrong or inappropriate. It's the use of them. I use re-enactments to burrow underneath the surface of reality in an attempt to uncover some hidden truth.

Is the problem that we have an unfettered capacity for credulity, for false belief, and hence, we feel the need to protect ourselves from ourselves? If seeing is believing, then we better be careful about what we show people, including ourselves, because regardless of what it is we are likely to uncritically believe it.[2]

This chapter will focus on the memoir boom and its discontents, including a proliferation of hoaxes so numerous, and so successful, as to create what is essentially a new literary genre. I want to explore the complicated relationship of the memoir style not only to the genre called autobiography but also to a certain kind of imagined, artful, or speculative biography, all of which make claims to truth. What interests me is what is called real and what is called literary, and what the two might, or might not, have to do with each other.

On Truth and Lie

Sir Philip Sidney had declared in his *Defence of Poesy* (1595) that "The poet nothing affirmeth, and therefore never lieth."[3] In my edition of the *Defence*, the headers at the top of the page reinforce the point: "The historian captive to truth," reads one, and another says with equal directness, "The poet is least a liar."[4] For Sidney the word *poet*, or maker, meant the writer of imaginative literature, whether in verse or in prose. The goal of poesy was not factual accuracy, but something else, something different, something more like Horace's famous dictum that art should both delight and instruct. Thus, comparing the usefulness of history and poetry, Sidney could assert that "a feigned example hath as much force to teach as a true example."[5]

But today it seems to be the real (or the faux real) that is actively, and avidly, sought. Let's consider an example that is also a cautionary tale—although, as will quickly be evident, it is hard to decide who, or what, is being cautioned. The story of Herman Rosenblat's Holocaust "memoir," *Angel at the Fence,* hit both Oprah Winfrey and the publishing world with dismaying force when the "truth" unraveled in December 2008.

Oprah had welcomed Herman and Roma Rosenblat as guests on her show in 1996, after Herman won a contest sponsored by the *New York Post* for "the best love story sent in by a reader."[6] The story he told was of his internment as a boy in a Nazi concentration camp, and how he was sustained by a young girl who threw apples over the fence to him. Many years later, in Israel, he went on a blind date with the same girl but did not recognize her. Subsequently, they met again in New York and married.

When the Rosenblats returned to *The Oprah Winfrey Show* eleven years later, Winfrey lauded their romance as "the single greatest love story, in twenty-two years of doing this show, we've ever told on the air." The story was picked up in the "couples" volume of *Chicken Soup for the Soul* and was ultimately sold, in book form, to Berkley Books. Then the scandal broke. The story turned out to be a fantasy, an embellishment, or a lie (depending upon who you asked), and Berkley canceled the book before its scheduled release.

Reporter Gabriel Sherman, who raised significant questions about the Holocaust "memoir" in *The New Republic*, noted dryly that the publisher had advertised *Angel at the Fence* (subtitled *The True Story of a Love That Survived*) as "a perfect Valentine's Day gift."[7] Not only the astonishing coincidences, but also the on-the-ground facts, were quickly put in doubt by persons familiar with the geography of Buchenwald. No such fence, it was noted, existed; it would not have been possible for a civilian to gain such access to a prisoner in the camps. The result, as Sherman reported, was—unsettlingly but unsurprisingly—backlash not against Herman Rosenblat, but against those who questioned the verisimilitude of the story, including Deborah Lipstadt, a distinguished professor of history and Holocaust studies and the author of the 1993 book *Denying the Holocaust*. Doubters were lambasted as "going after a Holocaust survivor without any proof."[8] In effect, they were pilloried as *Angel* deniers.

What was the scandal here? What was the crime? Had Rosenblat called his narrative a fiction, would Oprah have been interested in it? Would a publisher have put it under contract? Would the advance have been less?

The excuse given for the support of the book's claims were in some ways more problematic than the claims themselves, since, as the Valentine's Day publication date suggested, the story was supposed to be all about love. Love, it was said, clouded memory and embellished it. Love, Rosenblat himself asserted, made him do it. Why did he invent the story about the girl and the apples? "I wanted to bring happiness to people, to remind them not to hate, but to love and tolerate all people. I brought good feelings to a lot of people and I brought hope to many."[9] Although he and his brothers were in fact interned in the camp, what "brought hope to many" and attracted the attention of an agent, a publisher, and Oprah Winfrey was not the survival but the love story.

The next step seems, in retrospect, inevitable. Within days of these revelations, a publisher began negotiating to issue the book as a work of fiction. What was to be published, though, was not the original text but a version based on a screenplay already in production. The book thus became the secondary partner in a book-and-movie tie-in deal. The publisher, York House Press, issued a statement that tried to explain, as well as to explain away, what had happened:

> Mr. Rosenblat, now age 80, fantasized that his wife of 50 years came as a girl to nourish him by tossing apples to him over the barbed wire at a sub camp of the infamous Buchenwald concentration camp. This is a story he told himself and others repeatedly until it was integrated seamlessly into his otherwise factual account. It is beyond our expertise to know how Holocaust survivors cope with their trauma. Do they deny, rationalize or fantasize and promote fiction along with truth? Perhaps the coping mechanisms are as individual as the survivors themselves. Would, for humanity's sake, that Mr. Rosenblat's fantasy were true and that not just one girl, but a whole crowd, had come to toss apples over the fence, and to liberate those within much sooner than was actually the case.[10]

In this interesting mix of popular psychology ("coping mechanisms"), guilt-trip apologia ("it is beyond our expertise"), and resistance to the facts (all accounts suggest that there was no fence that bordered on public access, so that even "a whole crowd" of apple-tossing empathizers would have been unable to perform the rescue operation as described), the publishers sought to rehabilitate, even to reenoble, the author-fantasist. The problem with the "false memoir," they implied, did not lie with Herman Rosenblat but with the tragic fact of the Holocaust itself, and the refusal of history to make his fantasy retroactively true. "Mr. Rosenblat's motivations were very human, understandable, and forgivable," they wrote. What does *human* mean in such a context? Or *very* human? Fallible? Exculpable? Full of pathos? Compare this to "for humanity's sake," in the paragraph above. Rosenblat is human, all too human. So is his story, whether fictional or factual. It is history that is, and was, inhumane. In fact, it might be the case that it was not love but *history* that made him do it.

And after the apologia, the assertive declaration: "York House Press is in serious discussion to publish a work of fiction in early spring that is based on the screenplay, tentatively called *Flower at the Fence*, about Herman Rosenblat's life and love story, that is grounded in fact and that rises to the proper levels of artistic value, ethical conduct and social responsibility." Here, presumably, is the claim to literary legitimacy, however oblique. Whatever the "proper levels of artistic value" may be construed to be, how do they intersect with ethical conduct (on whose part? author? publisher? screenplay writer?) and social responsibility? What is the social responsibility of a work of fiction? And in what sense is the work to be "grounded in fact"? Pretty clearly, the publishers want to have things both ways: the unutterable truth of the Holocaust and the forgivable fiction of the love story.

Furthermore, the "serious discussion" in which the putative publisher is engaged (presumably a conversation about contractual issues) becomes linked, by a kind of rhetorical slippage or legerdemain, to an implied seriousness of the work. What is being discussed is a "work of fiction" that is also based on "fact." Because if it were not—if, for example, the entire narrative had been invented by a twenty-five-year-old creative-writing student with no personal link to the Holocaust—the commercial possibilities for both the film and the book to be derived from it ("can we now call it a 'novelization'?") would be much more limited. Was the Rosenblat scandal really just a category crisis, readily resolved by resituating the book on a shelf marked *fiction*?

With perhaps predictable regularity, hoax memoirs have returned again and again to the topic and the ground of the Holocaust, the over-determined historical locus of witnessing, testimony, survivors—and deniers. But the tendency persists in all testimonial, confession, autobiographical writing, even in the writing of other lives. The claim of truth invites not only the suspicion but perhaps even the formal inevitability of the lie. "There is no testimony," writes Jacques Derrida, "that does not structurally imply in itself the possibility of fiction, simulacra, dissimulation, lie, and perjury."[11]

Yet another supposed memoir, *Misha: A Memoir of the Holocaust Years*, told the story of a Jewish child who killed a Nazi soldier in self-defense, trekked over a thousand miles through Europe in quest of her deported parents, and was adopted by a pack of wolves. And this entire story, too, it developed, was a fabrication. The author, Misha Levy Defonseca, acknowledged that she was born in Belgium to Roman Catholic parents who were arrested and killed during the resistance; her birth name was Monique De Wael. Despite the revelation that the claims made in the book—which had been translated into eighteen languages and made into a movie in France—were false, De Wael deployed the language of "reality" to justify what she had done. "The story is mine. It is not actually reality, but my reality, my way of surviving," she said in a statement released by her lawyers.[12] She asked forgiveness of "all who felt betrayed" and said she "felt Jewish" and had felt so "since forever."

Daniel Mendelsohn, the author of a book on his quest for the story of his great-uncle and other Jewish victims of the Nazis, dismissed this empathetic banality with brisk contempt: "'Felt Jewish' is repellent; real Jewish children were being murdered however they may have felt."[13] Mendelsohn thus countered De Wael's claim of an alternative reality with his own deployment of *real*, then followed it up with an extended discussion of what it means to say "my reality." "It's not that frauds haven't been perpetrated before," he observed. "What's worrisome is that, maybe for the first time, the question people are raising isn't whether the amazing story is true, but whether it matters if it's true."

Mendelsohn drew attention to the borderline between memoir and fiction and on the differential value that modern readers and writers seemed to place on them as bearers of emotional and historical truth. Why do we feel so outraged and bamboozled when a memoir turns out to be a fake? Is our indignation moral, ethical, aesthetic, stylistic—or, indeed, feigned? Does the *use* of the memoir change or disappear when it is proved not to be true?

The number of hoax memoirs on all topics has been on the increase, with the claims ever more extravagant and exploitative. *Love and Consequences: A Memoir of Hope and Survival* was the title of a "heart-wrenching" memoir of gang life in South Central Los Angeles that turned out to be a fabrication. "Heart-wrenching" was how the book was described by a feature-article writer in a profile of the author, "Margaret B. Jones," later revealed to be the nom de laptop of Margaret Seltzer. Here is how *The New York Times* feature story on the author described the book:

> Her memoir is an intimate, visceral portrait of the gangland drug trade of Los Angeles as seen through the life of one household: a stern but loving black grandmother working two jobs; her two grandsons who quit school and became Bloods at ages 12 and 13; her two granddaughters, both born addicted to crack cocaine; and the author, a mixed-race white and Native American foster child who at age 8 came to live with them in their mostly black community. She ended up following her foster brothers into the gang, and it was only when a high school teacher urged her to apply to college that Ms. Jones even began to consider her future.[14]

The following week this personal biography was exposed as a hoax, the publisher, Riverhead, recalled the book and offered refunds to purchasers, and the editor and publisher said they had never met the author prior to publication, relying instead on the word of a literary agent and the author's signed statement that she was telling the truth.

Margaret Seltzer, it turned out, had grown up with her biological family in the wealthy L.A. neighborhood of Sherman Oaks and attended Campbell Hall, a private Episcopal day school in North Hollywood. When interviewed on the radio in connection with book promotions, Seltzer/Jones had spoken in an African-American vernacular, although she and her family are white. The publisher, editor, agent, and newspaper profiler all faced public criticism, and the press drew the expected comparisons with other hoax authors: James Frey, who fabricated the story of his supposed memoir of drug addiction, *A Million Little Pieces* (powerfully promoted by Oprah Winfrey), and Laura Albert, the real author behind the memoirist "J. T. LeRoy," whose invented personal narrative described him as an addict and the son of a West Virginia prostitute. Albert went to the extreme length of having someone impersonate "LeRoy" in public, confessed to the hoax in a *Paris Review* interview in 2006, and was successfully sued for damages. A movie contract made with "LeRoy" was found by the courts to be null and void.

More than one commentator, including the novelist Anne Bernays, asked why Selzer didn't just forthrightly declare her work fiction. Bernays wrote a letter to the editor of the *Times:*

It's clear that Margaret Seltzer, author of "Love and Consequences," is a gifted writer with a soaring imagination. It seems perverse, then, that she chooses to deny her destiny as a novelist.

Ms. Seltzer's insistence that only nonfiction can "make people understand the conditions that people live in" is way off the mark.

Has she never read Charles Dickens—or even Jane Austen?[15]

It's tempting to reflect on Seltzer's title, since *Love and Consequences* obliquely echoes "Truth or Consequences," the name of a long-running American quiz show. "Love" rather than "truth"; "and" rather than "or." Is this the contemporary fantasy of "having it all," with no repercussions? Or an example of Freud's dictum about dreams: there is no *no* in the unconscious?

Novel Histories

James Frey had written a memoir that turned out to be a fiction. In his op-ed piece for *The New York Times* Daniel Mendelsohn, citing Frey as the standard for contemporary authorial deception, described Frey's book as a "novel—er, memoir."[16] Mendelsohn's phrase may remind us of how oral written speech has become; this slip of the tongue that is not a slip of the tongue playfully performs the act of false naming that, on a far more serious scale, Mendelsohn was determined to expose and condemn.

The early history of the novel in English, interestingly, could be described—if inelegantly—by a reverse formulation as "the memoir—er, novel." The original title of the 1722 Defoe novel we call, for short, *Moll Flanders*, was *The fortunes and misfortunes of the famous Moll Flanders, &c.: who was born in Newgate, and during a life of continu'd variety for threescore years, besides her childhood, was twelve year a whore, five times a wife (whereof once to her own brother) twelve year a thief, eight year a transported felon in Virginia, at last grew rich, liv'd honest, and died a penitent: written from her own memorandums.*[17] In other words, the claim of truth or reality was part of the publishers' apparatus and, presumably, part of the appeal: *written from her own memorandums*. Moll's story of suffering and redemption, even if it does not include cohabiting with wolves, seems to fit in rather nicely with the preferred narrative of the modern best-selling memoir. Yet Moll's first-person narrative was written by a man, and one whose own personal adventures did not resemble hers.

Defoe's *Robinson Crusoe* (more properly *The life and strange surprizing adventures of Robinson Crusoe; of York, mariner: who lived eight and twenty years, all alone in an un-inhabited island on the coast of America, near the mouth of the great river of Oroonoque, having been cast on shore by shipwreck, wherein all the men perished but himself: with an account how he was at last strangely deliver'd by pyrates in two volumes, written by himself,* published in 1719) had likewise presented the author as editor of a "true" account: "The Editor," Defoe wrote in his preface, "believes the thing to be a just History of Fact; neither is there any Appearance of Fiction in it."[18]

The first edition of Samuel Richardson's epistolary novel *Pamela* (1740) credited him as the "editor" of what was presented as an authentic set of letters, with only names and places altered. Nothing else, it was claimed, was done to "disguise the Facts, marr the Reflections, and unnaturalize the Incidents." As a result, what was offered to the public was *"Pamela* as Pamela wrote it, in her own Words, without Amputation, or Addition."[19] Here the claim to historical accuracy, coupled with the immediacy of the letters' apparent composition (Pamela "breaks off" writing when interrupted, her tears fall on the page, etc.), created a form in which it became problematic to separate truth from fiction—or, as Michael McKeon describes it, "the epistemological status of *Pamela* is difficult to disentangle from that of Pamela—from her claims to, and her capacity for, credibility." Since Pamela's story was that of an attempted rape by a wealthy squire ("Mr. B.") of a young female servant in his household, the plot is, and was, sensational enough to elicit accusations of licentiousness. The only side of the story we hear is Pamela's: her account of her employer's initial kindness, the attempted seduction, her imprisonment in his country house, the illegitimate child he had with a former lover. Pamela periodically talks about her writing supplies—her pens, paper, ink, and wax—especially when she is imprisoned and worries that her access to writing will be curtailed.

I don't want to overemphasize the commonalities between the emergent-novel form of the eighteenth century and the resurgent real-life memoir of the twenty-first. But there are some striking connections. Richardson's *Pamela* was modeled on the conduct books of the time, forerunners of today's self-help manuals (and yesterday's etiquette books). Like the memoir, these genres now appear with great regularity among weekly best sellers and are prominent in displays at airport bookstores and chain stores. By combining the risk of personal hazard with notions of virtuous conduct and putting both into the epistolary first person, *Pamela* anticipates some of the hardship tales of privation, suffering, addiction, or rescue that still captivate readers today.

False Memoirs and Literary Truth

The phrase *false memoir* has obvious analogies with the notion of false memories, or false memory syndrome, and repressed or recovered memory. Much has been written on this phenomenon, comparing such false allegations to the witch trials of past centuries and chronicling the capacity for abuse by psychothcrapists and other counselors. Pursuing this analogy may well land us in the murky territory of writing as pathology or writing as therapy. Researchers like James Pennebaker have worked on the problem from the side of psychology;[20] Freud and Breuer long ago called it abreaction, the liberation of repressed ideas by reviving and expressing them.

> The injured person's reaction to the trauma only exercises a completely "cathartic" effect if it is an *adequate* reaction—as, for instance, revenge. But language serves as a substitute for action; by its help, an affect can be "abreacted" almost as effectively. In other cases speaking is itself the adequate reflex, when, for instance, it is a lamentation or giving utterance to a tormenting secret, e.g., a confession. If there is no such reaction, whether in deeds or words, or in the mildest cases in tears, any recollection of the event retains its affective tone.[21]

Catharsis, which means *purgation* in both a medical and a theatrical sense, was used at this foundational moment in psychotherapy as a way of describing a purgation of the emotions. Psychotherapy, in this sense, is theater performed for an audience of one.

When Freud abandoned his so-called seduction theory in favor of the idea that fantasy, not real experience, was at the heart of many patients' accounts of child sexual abuse, he developed the theories about infantile sexuality that became central to psychoanalysis. As he wrote to his friend Wilhelm Fliess in a letter announcing his change of heart ("I no longer believe in my *neurotica*"), this decision was based partly on the unlikelihood that actual abuse was so widespread ("in all cases, the *father*, not excluding my own, had to be accused of being perverse"), but even more importantly, on the impossibility of distinguishing truth from fiction: "there are no indications of reality in the unconscious, so that one cannot distinguish between truth and fiction that has been cathected with affect."[22] Cathected with affect: that is, highly charged with emotion.

The unconscious, Freud says, has "no indications of reality," so when a patient describes past events it is not possible from such internal evidence to distinguish between things that really happened and things that feel as if they happened. Indeed, these events have, we might say, "happened" psychically, even if they have no basis in external fact. This theory was controversial then, and it is certainly not less controversial now. But it is, as you can see, closely related to the phenomenon of the false memoir. And—even more directly—it is related to the larger question of creative writing, the literary imagination, and the use and abuse of literature. Indeed, the coincidental presence of the word *abuse* (borrowed from a celebrated translation of Nietzsche's essay on history writing) offers a convenient hook or hinge. Is literature a use or an abuse? Is it caused by abuse?

Manifestly not all memoirs are alike. Many have become memorable—and indeed have become *literature*—because of their style at least as much as their content. Among these works are, for example, the *Confessions* of St. Augustine and of Jean-Jacques Rousseau but also more recent writing—say, the nonfiction of James Baldwin, Vladimir Nabokov, Maxine Hong Kingston, Tobias Wolff, or Elie Wiesel. But rescuing the baby doesn't mean bottling and selling the bathwater. The fact that something really happened isn't any guarantee of its credibility in a piece of writing. And some of the most famous memoirs, of course, have been fictional, like John Cleland's erotic novel, *Memoirs of a Woman of Pleasure* (1748), better known as *Fanny Hill*.

The word *memoir* only gradually began to mean reminiscences (often in the plural, as in "writing one's memoirs") and then biography or autobiography; the original uses were more legal or official, related to the memo, or written account containing instructions or facts to be judged. So the memoir has moved, perhaps inexorably, from fact to narrative embellishment, from other to self. But what is this addiction for books about addiction—or gang warfare, or child abuse, or deprivation? Not surprisingly, this kind of personal privation and struggle has often had appeal, and not only in the twenty-first century. It is not enough to say we live in hard times. Nor have other literary genres skated lightly over pain, loss, illness, conflict, betrayal, murder, or untimely death: this is a fair catalog of some of the central incidents of Greek tragedy, early modern English drama, and many classic works of nineteenth-century fiction. But the memoir craze, like *American Idol* and reality television, makes everyone a hero. Pathos, once a key ingredient in the response to tragedy and lyric, is now evoked in and by the memoir, the personal story, "my" story even if, in written form, it is occasionally "as told to" someone else.

Cause and Effect

Which comes first, the life or the "life story," the craft of life writing? To what extent is the shape of a life conditioned by our literary expectations about crises, turning points, growth, and change? "We assume that life *produces* the autobiography as an act produces its consequences," wrote Paul de Man, "but can we not suggest, with equal justice, that the auto-biographical project may itself produce and determine the life and that whatever the writer *does* is in fact governed by the technical demands of self-portraiture and thus determined, in all its aspects, by the resources of his medium?"[23]

This is true for "high" or "literary" versions of autobiography (de Man is thinking about Rousseau, St. Augustine, and Wordsworth), but it is equally relevant to popular and celebrity accounts. How did the great man or great woman—or these days the representative, proudly "ordinary" man or woman—become him- or herself? The dramatic or literary arc is already in place: early life, setbacks, signs of genius, prom-ise, or unusual attainment, sundering from fellows or family, the first professional break or breakthrough, a triumph, a tragedy, reflections, recriminations, late style, etc.

The modern autobiography is occasionally written by the subject but more often with (or, functionally, *by*) a writing partner or amanuensis. These partners are sometimes called ghostwriters, but there is a distinction to be made between the invisible ghostwriter and the credited collaborator, and down the line, these attributions of authorship have something to do with that elusive category of reality, or truth, in writing. Here are a few examples.

The New York Times best-seller-list description for *Real Change*, "by Newt Gingrich with Vince Haley and Rick Tyler," included Haley, Gingrich's research director at the American Enterprise Institute, and Tyler, Gingrich's director of media relations, as the book's coauthors. On the Conservative Book Club website and on the book cover, however, *Real Change* is credited entirely to Gingrich, and the accompanying ad copy tells potential readers that in the book Newt Gingrich explains the role of the conservative majority. Whatever things may be real about *Real Change*, the claim of authorship is not prominent among them. *Plus ça change.*

Another book on the *Times* list that week, *I Am America (and So Can You!)*, like the Gingrich book, bore on its cover a large photo of the credited author, Stephen Colbert, as well as a tagline send-up of book-promotion-speak as "From the Author of *I Am America (and So Can You!)*" The *Times* conscientiously listed Colbert's coauthors from his television show, *The Colbert Report*, describing *I Am America* as "by Stephen Colbert, Richard Dahm, Paul Dinello, Allison Silverman et al." But none of these names appears on the book cover. By contrast, the book jacket of another cowritten work on the list, *Send Yourself Roses* "by Kathleen Turner with Gloria Feldt," declares straightforwardly, in reasonable-sized print, that the book, the biography-memoir of the actress, was written "in collaboration with Gloria Feldt."

Authorship may not seem to be one of the key reality principles so much as a matter of truth in packaging. Nonetheless, for the time being, let's note that these nonfiction books are jostling for public favor with books described as memoirs, autobiographies, meditations, or spectacularly—and unexpectedly—posthumous accounts. The attraction of these real-life narratives and their "ripped from the headlines" appeal seems undeniable, a symptom of the times (and the *Times*). Thus, on the same best-seller list, we find:

- *Manic* by Terri Cheney. A memoir of life with bipolar disorder.
- *Hope's Boy* by Andrew Bridge. A memoir of foster care by an advocate for poor children.
- *Lone Survivor* by Marcus Luttrell. The only survivor of a Navy Seals operation in northern Afghanistan describes the battle, his comrades, and his courageous escape.
- *The Thing About Life Is That One Day You'll Be Dead* by David Shields. A meditation on mortality, focused on the author's ninety-seven-year-old father.
- *Reconciliation* by Benazir Bhutto. A posthumous look at Islam, democracy, and the West, by Pakistan's former prime minister and assassinated opposition leader.[24]

Presumably, considerations of space in this last item produced the verbal compression "a posthumous look," suggesting that Bhutto is writing after her own death—a development that would have made her the literal ghostwriter of her own book.

What might be the use of such personal accounts of the self? Let's recall Philip Sidney's dictum: "a feigned example hath as much force to teach as a true example." We might likewise note that a bad example has as much force to teach as a good example. The good example is a model for conduct, in the mode of Plutarch's *Lives* or the lives of the saints, where allegory displaces mimesis and acts are symbolic in the first instance, real only—or preeminently—in their power to induce imitation. In a more modern sense, this is the *Profiles in Courage*, ordinary-hero snapshot, the inspirational feature story writ large. The obverse is schadenfreude, or the bad example. Triumphs over adversity, addiction (drugs, alcohol, sex, fame, chronic lying, you name it). It doesn't take much to see that this is itself a seductive mode. If St. Augustine—or Rousseau—had had nothing to confess, would we read their memoirs?

Under a strict definition of literature, few if any of these memoirs, real or false, would qualify. Conceivably, if any had surpassing literary merit—however we were to determine that elusive criterion—it might somehow transcend the dialectic of truth and lie. But *faked* and *false* and *lie* and *wholesale fabrication* are damning terms when the public is deceived and not delighted.

Fact into Fiction

The best-selling book *Bringing Down the House: The Inside Story of Six MIT Students Who Took Vegas for Millions* (Free Press, 2002) was made into a successful film entitled *21* in 2008. The book, by Ben Mezrich, was listed as a work of nonfiction, and he went on to produce other books in the same vein with similarly explanatory subtitles: *Ugly Americans: The True Story of the Ivy League Cowboys Who Raided the Asian Markets for Millions* (2005), *Busting Vegas: The MIT Whiz Kid Who Brought the Casinos to Their Knees* (2005), and *Rigged: The True Story of an Ivy League Kid Who Changed the World of Oil, from Wall Street to Dubai* (2007).[25] (Are we sensing a pattern here?)

Questions about the truth value of *Bringing Down the House* resurfaced with the opening of the movie and the concurrent revelation of several less than fully truthful memoirs. The public was now on the alert for falsification and in a mood to equate it with deception rather than with the art of fiction. Mezrich had conflated some characters, fabricated others, and invented some significant details in the story. "Every word on the page isn't supposed to be fact-checkable," he told an interviewer. "The idea that the story is true is more important than being able to prove that it's true."[26] But Mezrich's book was published with a disclaimer explaining that the names, locations, and other details had been changed and that some characters were composites. As the *Boston Globe* reporter noted, though, the disclaimer was "in fine print, on the copyright page" and might readily have been missed by readers. Other editors and nonfiction authors, when consulted, expressed skepticism about Mezrich's techniques: "It's lying," said Sebastian Junger, author of *The Perfect Storm*. "Nonfiction is reporting the world as it is, and when you combine characters and change chronology, that's not the world as it is."[27] Gay Talese, often regarded as one of the inventors of the modern nonfiction genre, was similarly emphatic: taking liberties of this kind is "unacceptable" and "dishonest."[28] Mezrich, when asked, invoked the word *literary* to describe the choices he made: "I took literary license to make it readable."[29]

What does *literary* mean in this connection? Is it a version of the more familiar phrase *poetic license*? License in such a context has more to do with giving, or taking, permission than with legal sanction.

A few years later, Mezrich was back with a new book, *The Accidental Billionaires*, subtitled *The Founding of Facebook: A Tale of Sex, Money, Genius and Betrayal,* in which the boundaries of fact and fiction were unapologetically, indeed triumphantly, blurred. As with James Frey, who transformed himself from faux memoirist to fiction writer (and profited by the exchange), so Ben Mezrich declared that he would capitalize on what had been perceived as a transgression of the rules: "I see myself as attempting to break ground. I definitely am trying to create my own genre here," he told an interviewer. "I'm attempting to tell stories in a very new and entertaining way. I see myself as an entertainer."[30] A bookstore owner noted that copies originally piled on a table for new nonfiction, would later be relocated to the business section. Mezrich's book included imagined and re-created scenes, some in the "he might have" mode that has become popular in certain kinds of biography. One review, dryly adopting the book's style of unabashed psychological guesswork, began, "Though we cannot know exactly what went through Ben Mezrich's mind as he wrote *The Accidental Billionaires*, his nonfictionish book about the creation of Facebook, we can perhaps speculate hypothetically about what it possibly might have been like."[31] The film version, called *The Social Network*, told the story of Facebook's founding through the accounts of several characters, never indicating which of them was "true."

Biofeedback

If memoirs often tend to veer in the direction of self-fictionalizing, the venerable practice of biography, literally "life writing," would seem to depend to a certain extent on telling the truth. Thus, biography is often poised somewhere between the categories of literature and history. While in many ways this would seem to increase the prestige of biography as a genre, since these days history is a less suspect, more rational and evidence-based category than literature, it has made for a slightly anomalous role for the modern practitioner of this ancient craft.

Biography, it seems, has been suffering from an inferiority complex of sorts even as its practitioners triumph in the bookstores. The founding of the Leon Levy Center for Biography at the City University of New York was described by its faculty director, David Nasaw, himself a distinguished biographer (*Andrew Carnegie; William Randolph Hearst*), as a way of changing the perception of biography as "the stepchild of the academy."[32] The editor of *The American Historical Review* commented that "increasingly historians are turning to biography," even though in the past they "haven't considered it a kind of legitimate scholarship in some respects."[33] The new center supports biographers working in a wide range of modes, including film, television, and graphic novels, and the executive director, Nancy Milford, author of biographies of Zelda Fitzgerald and Edna St. Vincent Millay, told a reporter that she "insisted that at least half the fellows come from outside the academy."[34] So on the one hand, biographers are seeking credibility and standing within the academy (as non-academicians call the world of universities and colleges). On the other hand, they stand proudly outside it. Where does the readership come from? According to the head of the Leon Levy Foundation, Levy's widow Shelby White, her enthusiasm for the project came from "a love of biography and history and reading about other people's lives. I guess I'm a snoop."[35]

The gratification of snooping, or even of a more seemly curiosity, was not the stated goal for biographers from ancient times through the

Victorian period. Once upon a time, biography was supposed to model character and the conduct of life. Plutarch's *Parallel Lives of the Ancient Greeks and Romans* placed, side by side, biographies of famous men from these two periods. Plutarch announced in the opening sentences of his *Life of Alexander* that his objective was to depict the character of his subjects rather than every detail of their daily existence. "It must be borne in mind," he wrote (in the celebrated translation by John Dryden), "that my design is not to write histories, but lives. And the most glorious exploits do not always furnish us with the clearest discoveries of virtue or vice in men; sometimes a matter of less moment, an expression or a jest, informs us better of their characters and inclinations, than the most famous sieges . . ." Plutarch compared his art to that of the portrait painter, who focuses attention on the lines and features of the face, rather than on other parts of the body, as the most indicative signs of character.[36] This comparison between the biographer and the portrait painter or sculptor would become a favorite in later biographies, and calls attention, tacitly but importantly, to the degree of artifice involved in making something "true to life."[37]

The historian Jill Lepore cites a story told by David Hume in his 1741 essay "Of the Study of History." Having been asked by a "young beauty, for whom I had some passion," to send her some novels and romances to read while she was in the country, Hume sent her, instead, Plutarch's *Lives*, "assuring her, at the same time, that there was not a word of truth in them." She read them with pleasure, apparently, until she came to the lives of Alexander and Caesar, "whose names she had heard of by accident," then indignantly sent the book back to Hume "with many reproaches for deceiving her."[38]

The story is amusing, but it is also condescending, the more so because the writer is conscious of its charm. Both the description of this female reader as a "young beauty" and the fact, so casually dropped, that she had heard of the two famous heroes of antiquity only "by accident" put her firmly in her place, which is quite a different place from that of Hume. The first sentence of the essay sets the tone: "There is nothing which I would recommend more earnestly to my female readers than the study of history, as an occupation, above all others, the best suited both to their sex and education, much more instructive than their ordinary books of amusement, and more entertaining than those serious compositions, which are usually to be found in their closets." Hume playfully deplores the preference of "the fair sex" for fiction: "I am sorry," he says, "to see them have such an aversion to matter of fact, and such an appetite for falsehood." By contrast, "truth," he insists, "is the basis of history." Though he will later change his tone from "raillery" to something more serious (and at that point will introduce as his anticipated readers two male subjects: "a man of business" and "a philosopher"), he maintains that even a witty and well-bred woman can have nothing interesting to say to "men of sense and reflection" unless she is conversant with the history of her own country and of ancient Greece and Rome. Plutarch, for Hume, is history. And history is based on truth.

The concept of "biographical truth," as Judith Anderson argues in a book of that title, could as easily be called "biographical fiction." The relation between fiction and fact in the period raises questions about what is meant by truth, she suggests. Life writing "occupies a middle ground between history and art, chronicle and drama, objective truth and creative invention."[39] Biography "is a mixed form, having always a tendency to merge on the one side with fiction and on the other side with history."[40] Anderson's study covers the Venerable Bede's *Life of Saint Cuthbert*, Cavendish's *Life of Cardinal Wolsey*, Roper's *Life of Sir Thomas More*, More's *History of King Richard III*, Shakespeare's *Richard III* and *Henry VIII* (subtitled *All Is True*), and Bacon's *History of King Henry VII*. All these texts, according to Anderson, are "peripherally or essentially literary."[41]

What do we mean by *literary*, when we are discussing works of biography? Is it an indicator of style, of archetype, of mythic quality, of the felt presence of the writer? Anderson says that each of the authors she examines "employs the techniques of fiction," which include authorial self-consciousness, an awareness of critical interpretation, and an increasing acknowledgment of the writer's "own creative shaping of another's life."[42]

The pleasure evinced by biographers at the founding of the Levy Center is, to a certain extent, recuperative (gaining respect, visibility, and funding), but in another way, it is classificatory and categorical. We may recall that the authorizing body evincing a wary interest in receiving biographers into the fold was made up of historians. Biography for them, and for many present-day biographers, is a species of history writing, whether the topic is a political or historical figure or a person of literary, artistic, or cultural significance. But the conflation of author and subject that is the central trope—and the irresistible lure—of the memoir creates category confusion when it is transposed into the world of biography.

The "Statement of Purpose" of the Society of American Historians explains that its goal is "To promote literary distinction in historical writing" by awarding a number of prestigious prizes. What is gained, I wonder, by adding the word *literary* here? If the society's goal were merely "To promote distinction in historical writing," what element would be lost? Which is another way of asking, what does the Society of American Historians consider literary, and how is that trait importantly different from the other kinds of writing produced by historians?

A number of career paths lead to success in this field, and some of the most commercially successful practitioners are neither historians nor academics—which does not mean, of course, that they are not scholars. One of the most honored biographers in the United States is David McCullough, an English major at Yale, who then became a journalist and editor (*Sports Illustrated;* the U.S. Information Agency; *American Heritage*) before embarking on a career in which he won the Pulitzer Prize (twice) and the National Book Award (twice) for biography. Present-day British biographers like Claire Tomalin (biographies of Thomas Hardy, Samuel Pepys, Jane Austen, Katherine Mansfield, Mary Wollestone-craft, etc.) and Victoria Glendinning (biographies of Elizabeth Bowen, Edith Sitwell, Vita Sackville-West, Rebecca West, Anthony Trollope, Jonathan Swift, and Leonard Woolf) are writers whose other activities include journalism, broadcasting, criticism, and (in the case of Glendinning) fiction writing.

The New York Times annual list of notable nonfiction books is always stocked with biographies and memoirs. In 2007, for example, of the fifty books on the list, there were fifteen biographies and eight memoirs, including biographies of Alexis de Tocqueville, Alice Roosevelt Longworth, Pablo Picasso, Leni Riefenstahl, Henry Morton Stanley, and the cartoonist Charles Schulz. The memoirs covered topics from waiting tables at a posh Manhattan restaurant to growing up with (a) a Haitian family, (b) an orthodox Jewish family, (c) a Catholic family, (d) a minister's family, and (e) an Iowa farm family during the Great Depression.

In 2008 the pattern was similar: biographies of Andrew Jackson, Dick Cheney, Samuel de Champlain, Condoleezza Rice, Sérgio Vieira de Mello, Rudolf Nureyev, and Anne Hathaway (Shakespeare's wife, not the contemporary actress); memoirs of an English childhood, an African childhood, an "appalling upbringing at the hands of . . . catastrophically unfit parents,"[43] and a novelist's memoir-response to the stillbirth of her first child.[44]

In short, biography today is not one thing—and never has been. The crossover between "popular" and "serious" in biographies is probably greater than in many other categories, since airport readers and other adults who choose books as a favorite entertainment option will often buy biographies—in hardcover—if they are attracted by the subject or have seen the book mentioned or blurbed in the media.

There are historian-biographers, literary biographers (which is to say, biographers of literary figures who address the author's works as well as the life), celebrity biographers, and biographical memoirists whose personal memoirs include the narrative history of a parent, partner, or other central personage. (A classic hypothetical example is Bennett Cerf's quip about a book that would be an automatic best seller, "Lincoln's Doctor's Dog.")

Authorized biographies give the writer access to privileged materials but often also assume that the result will be laudatory. Music stars, actors, artists, humanitarians, sports heroes, and other public figures tend to be the subject of authorized biographies, with Pat Robertson, Cecil Beaton, Pope John Paul II, Konrad Adenauer, and Helen, the queen mother of Rumania, also among those whose representatives gave permission to their biographers, in some cases selecting them as fit repositories of information and potential praise.

A *celebrity* biographer like Donald Spoto researches and writes about the lives of film stars, movie directors, playwrights, saints, and glamorous people in the public eye: Audrey Hepburn, Jacqueline Kennedy Onassis, Princess Diana, Ingrid Bergman, Elizabeth Taylor, Marilyn Monroe, Laurence Olivier, Marlene Dietrich, Preston Sturges, Lotte Lenya, Tennessee Williams, Alan Bates, Alfred Hitchcock, Stanley Kramer, St. Joan of Arc, St. Francis of Assisi. Others working in this genre include J. Randy Taraborrelli, chronicler of the lives of Madonna, Michael Jackson, Cher, Diana Ross, Janet Jackson, *Jackie, Ethel, Joan: Women of Camelot*—and Kitty Kelley, author of *Jackie Oh!*, and books on Nancy Reagan, the Bush dynasty, and Frank Sinatra. The subtitles of Kelley's books on Sinatra and Mrs. Reagan frankly call them "unauthorized" biographies, a term that, while once presumably opprobrious, is now a guarantee of high-level gossip.

A *literary biography*, as we've noted, is the account of the life and work of a writer. This term seems as if it contains a misplaced modifier, since while the subject may be a poet, novelist, or playwright, this does not guarantee that the resulting book will be literary. The contrary is quite often the case, despite the idealized early examples of Samuel Johnson's *Lives of the Poets* and of the defining work in the genre, Boswell's *Life of Johnson*.

To a certain degree, these categories are self-evident. But we could make another kind of provisional distinction based upon the presentational nature (and thus the ideology) of the printed text—between those biographies that *display* the research that has gone into them with a proliferation of marked footnotes and endnotes, and those that *hide* the research process, providing either silent footnotes or, in some cases, none at all, just a list of sources at the back of the book. The distinction would suggest something of the book's desire and self-image (or the desire and self-image of the author, publisher, literary agent, or press). But more important, it would say something about how these various makers hope the book would be read. Is the experience to be like that of reading a novel (with the added pleasure of knowing that it is "true")?

Or is it more like what anthropologists, before they, too, became more literary, used to call "writing up" the findings of their fieldwork?

Some twentieth- and twenty-first-century biographers utilize a kind of unmarked endnote which is intended to preserve the smooth unbroken surface of the text, making the book read more like a novel than a piece of scholarship—no intrusive superscript numbers to break the illusion. If a quotation or a fact appears in the text and the reader wants to know where it comes from, he or she can turn to the back of the book, where the page number and a brief citation from the text is followed by an indication of the source.[45] Many skilled practitioners follow this style, including Goodwin, David McCullough, and Meryle Secrest, to name just a few.[46]

This is not a low/high distinction in terms of quality but, rather, a presentational and performative style, with consequent effects upon the reading experience and upon the sense of intimacy and connection developed between reader and biographical subject. Although the author/biographer (some websites even identify these writers as "celebrity biographers") is often recognized as a public intellectual, what is celebrated is his or her knowledge, research, clarity, and what is often called a "magisterial" command of the material. Robert Skidelsky's biography of Keynes, Arnold Rampersad's biography of Ralph Ellison, Robert McCrum's biography of P. G. Wodehouse, Ian Kershaw Smith's biography of Adolf Hitler, Nigel Saul's biography of Richard II, and Jacques Roger's biography of Buffon all were hailed as magisterial by reviewers, and this list could be almost infinitely extended, since *magisterial,* the Latinate version of *masterly,* is the mot juste or the highest accolade for biographical writing. It seems to connote a rising above the fray. The biography is a masterwork; it brings the subject to life; it is definitive and defining; it tells at least one convincing version of the truth. As such, it seems like the opposite of the kind of hoax memoirs we began by discussing. Yet the two genres—the one magisterial, the other often, predictably, unauthorized—have some key elements in common. For one thing, both of these mainstays of the nonfiction best-seller list are, in their own ways, fictions.

"The Fictitious Life"

Virginia Woolf used the subtitle *A Biography* for three of her own works: *Orlando,* a groundbreaking novel written in a series of historical literary styles and inspired by the life of Vita-Sackville West; *Flush,* the life story of Elizabeth Barrett Browning's dog, a brilliant device for telling Browning's story through the eyes and mind of a cocker spaniel; and *Roger Fry,* an impressionistic biography of the art critic, a close friend. All three of these works are literary, no quotation marks needed. Whether Woolf herself felt any "anxiety of influence" with regard to biography is a fair question: she was the daughter of one celebrated biographer (Sir Leslie Stephen, the first editor of the *Dictionary of National Biography*) and a lifelong friend of another (Lytton Strachey, author of *Eminent Victorians; Queen Victoria; Elizabeth and Essex*). In an essay called "The New Biography," Woolf wrote that the task of the biographer was, in part, to combine the "incompatible" truths of fact and of fiction. "For it would seem that the life which is increasingly real to us is the fictitious life."

The term *biography* is a fairly recent one, dating in origin to the end of the seventeenth century; the *OED* traces it back to Dryden, who applied it to Plutarch. Woolf credits the emergence of modern biography to James Boswell's *Life of Johnson:*

> So we hear booming out from Boswell's page the voice of Samuel Johnson: "No, sir; stark insensibility," we hear him say. Once we have heard those words we are aware that there is an incalculable presence among us . . . All the draperies and decencies of biography fall to the ground. We can no longer maintain that life consists in actions only or in works. It consists in personality.[47]

From this height, Woolf suggests, biography fell—becoming more prolix, more prosy, more lengthy, and more tedious:

> [T]he Victorian biography was a parti-coloured, hybrid, monstrous birth. For though truth of fact was observed as scrupulously as Boswell observed it, the personality which Boswell's genius set free was hampered and distorted . . . the Victorian biographer was dominated by the idea of goodness. Noble, upright, chaste, severe: it is thus that the Victorian worthies are presented to us.[48]

And not only the *Victorian* worthies. Some Victorian biographers—Woolf singles out Sir Sidney Lee—contrived to write multivolume biographies, "worthy of all our respect," books that are monumental "piles . . . of hard facts," in effect noble and upright but irretrievably boring to read: "we can only explain the fact that Sir Sidney's life of Shakespeare is dull, and that his life of Edward the Seventh is unreadable, by supposing that both are stuffed with truth, although he failed to choose those truths which transmit personality."[49]

Woolf is here teasing Sidney Lee with a phrase of his own design—"The aim of biography is the truthful transmission of personality"—with which she begins her own essay, only to suggest that the two elements, truth and personality, are extremely difficult to "weld into one seamless whole," which is why "biographers for the most part have failed" to do so.[50] Lee's life of Shakespeare is 776 pages long; his biography of Edward VII ran to two volumes. This scrupulous heft, detail piled on detail in the service of "truth," was increasingly typical, indeed, increasingly expected. "The conscientious biographer may not tell a fine tale with a flourish but must toil through endless labyrinths and embarrass himself with countless documents."[51] The method, however painstaking, strikes her as exhibiting "prodigious waste" and "artistic wrongheadedness." One of the virtues of the "new biography," as Woolf goes on to describe it, is that it is, in contrast, relatively brief, pithy, and lively.

We might pause for a moment to reflect upon Woolf's choice of Sidney Lee as the epitome of the achievements and problems of Victorian biography. Lee, born Solomon Lazarus Lee, was a close friend and associate of Woolf's father and succeeded him in 1891 as the editor of the *Dictionary of National Biography*. Leslie Stephen was not only an editor but a prolific biographer, author of books on Pope, Swift, Hobbes, Samuel Johnson, and George Eliot. He died in 1904; Lee lived until 1926; Woolf's essay was written in 1927. In selecting Sidney Lee as the antitype of the new biography, Woolf both sidesteps and sideswipes her father's work and his demands, upon which she reflected in her diary a year later, on his birthday (November 28): "His life would have entirely ended mine. What would have happened? No writing, no books;—inconceivable."

In writing about the "new biography" Woolf thus resolutely turns a page between the past and the present, the parental generation and her own. "With the twentieth century," she says,

> a change came over biography, as it came over fiction and poetry. The first and most visible sign of it was in the difference in size. In the first twenty years of the new century biographies must have lost half their weight. Mr. Strachey compressed four stout Victorians into one slim volume *[Eminent Victorians];* Mr. Maurois boiled the usual two volumes of a Shelley life into one little book the size of a novel. But the diminution in size was only the outward token of an inward change. The point of view had completely altered. If we open one of the new school of biographies its bareness, its emptiness makes us at once aware that the author's relation to his subject is different. He is no longer the serious and sympathetic companion, toiling even slavishly in the footsteps of his hero. Whether friend or enemy, admiring or critical, he is an equal . . . He chooses; he synthesizes; in short, he has ceased to be the chronicler; he has become an artist.[52]

We might think that this opens the door to the self-fictionalizing abuses of the faux memoir. But Woolf has something different in mind; she is fairly ferocious about the importance of "the substance of fact." Where she wants the biographer to act like a novelist is in the matter of style, not in embroidery or speculation: "the biographer's imagination is always being stimulated to use the novelist's art of arrangement, suggestion, dramatic effect to expound the private life. Yet if he carries the use of fiction too far, so that he disregards the truth, or can only introduce it with incongruity, he loses both worlds; he has neither the freedom of fiction nor the substance of fact." Mixing the worlds "of Bohemia and Hamlet and Macbeth" with the world "of brick and pavement; of birth, marriage, and death; of Acts of Parliament," etc. is "abhorrent."[53]

So what is literary about biography to Virginia Woolf is the complicated freedom of the biographer in the matter of writing. Not in making things up, but in making them vivid and in establishing equality with the subject from the point of view of—point of view. Woolf herself uses an early version of unmarked notes in *Flush*, her biography of Elizabeth Barrett Browning's cocker spaniel. The dramatic (or melodramatic) last line of one chapter reads, "He was stolen."

> . . . suddenly, without a word of warning, in the midst of civilisation, security and friendship—he was in a shop in Vere Street with Miss Barrett and her sister; it was the morning of Tuesday the 1st of September—Flush was tumbled head over heels into darkness. The doors of a dungeon shut on him. He was stolen.[54]

In Woolf's text—unlike, alas, in mine—no superscript note is present to mar the stark drama of the moment. But the event related is verified and qualified by a deadpan unmarked note at the back of the book:

> P. 82: "He was stolen." As a matter of fact, Flush was stolen three times; but the unities seem to require that the three stealings shall be compressed into one. The total sum paid by Miss Barrett to the dog-stealers was £20.[55]

What was new about the new biography, as performed by writers like Lytton Strachey (and by Woolf) was its combination of rigorous scholarship, psychological insight, and wit.

Strachey's narrative style subsumed the scholarship into an apparently seamless narrative. Although there are no identifying notes after each character's utterances or inner thoughts, Strachey follows his sources very closely. Consider this wryly empathetic passage from *Queen*

Victoria (1921), in which Strachey describes the situation of Prince Albert:

> The husband was not so happy as the wife. In spite of the great improvement in his situation, in spite of a growing family and the adoration of Victoria, Albert was still a stranger in a strange land, and the serenity of spiritual satisfaction was denied him. It was something, no doubt, to have dominated his immediate environment; but it was not enough; and besides, in the very completeness of his success, there was a bitterness. Victoria idolized him; but it was understanding that he craved for, not idolatry; and how much did Victoria, filled to the brim though she was with him, understand him? How much does the bucket understand the well? He was lonely. He went to his organ and improvised with learned modulations until the sounds, swelling and subsiding through elaborate cadences, brought some solace to his heart. Then, with the elasticity of youth, he hurried off to play with the babies, or to design a new pigsty, or to read aloud the "Church History of Scotland" to Victoria, or to pirouette before her on one toe, like a ballet-dancer, with a fixed smile, to show her how she ought to behave when she appeared in public places.[56]

The brilliance of this account lies at least in part in its artful use of free indirect discourse, in which the thoughts and even the speech of characters are communicated to the reader in a reportorial mode, so that it remains unclear whether the sentiments are those of the narrator or of the first-person subject. The term derives from the French style *indirect libre,* and one of its pioneering practitioners in France was Flaubert. The effect of this style—a style expertly employed in English by writers like Woolf and Joyce—is to produce ironic disjunction and implicit commentary at the same time that it offers an opportunity for narrative identification with fictional or historical characters. Strachey's delicately ironic empathy with the prince consort, like Woolf's empathy with the dog Flush, slides into and out of Albert's consciousness while always tethering itself to verifiable details. A prefatory note, appearing opposite the dedication page ("To Virginia Woolf"), informs the reader that "Authority for every important statement of fact in the following pages will be found in the footnotes. The full titles of the works to which reference is made are given in the Bibliography at the end of the volume." A footnote to this passage cites three pages from the *Correspondence of Sarah Spencer, Lady Lyttelton.*

Strachey's descriptions and impressions are not speculations, as is often the case in twenty-first-century biography (the subject "might" have thought such-and-such, or he "could" have thought; or, cloaked in the form of a rhetorical question, "Did" he think, or "Might he have" thought . . .). Instead, Strachey draws his dialogue directly from letters and other written accounts. To give some sense of how he does this, I want to quote briefly from these letters. You will see both how close he is to the source, inventing no detail, and how the conversion from a third-person account to free indirect discourse brings the subject (as we so easily say) "to life."

Here, then, is an excerpt from Lady Lyttelton's letter to the Hon. Caroline Lyttelton, Windsor Castle, October 9, 1840:

> Yesterday evening, as I was sitting here comfortably after the drive, reading M. Guizot, suddenly there arose from the rooms beneath oh such sounds! It was Prince Albert—dear Prince Albert—playing on the organ, and with such master skill as it appeared to me, modulating so learnedly, winding through every kind of bass and chord, till he wound up into the most perfect cadence and then off again, louder and softer . . . I ventured at dinner to ask him what I had heard. "Oh, my organ!—a new possession of mine. I am so fond of the organ! It is the first of instruments—the only for expressing one's feelings—and it teaches to plan—for on the organ, a *mistake!* Oh, such a misery!" and he quite shuddered at the thought of the *sostenudo* discord . . . [57]

And there is this, from a letter five years later, September 22, 1845, reporting that Lady Lyttelton had, in "a fit of courage," spoken frankly to the queen and prince about how Victoria was perceived on a recent trip abroad:

The Prince advised her (on her saying, like a good child, "What *am* I to do another time?") to behave like an opera-dancer after a pirouette, and always show all her teeth in a fixed smile. Of course, he accompanied the advice with an immense pirouette and prodigious grin of his own, such as few people could perform after dinner without being sick, ending on one foot and t'other in the air . . .[58]

And finally, from a letter yet another five years later (July 22, 1850), which finds Lady Lyttelton once again musing on her reading, this time from the royal residence at Osborne House on the Isle of Wight, when she is interrupted by the sound of Albert at the organ:

—Last evening *such* a sunset! I was sitting gazing at it and thinking of Lady Charlotte Proby's verses, when from an open window below this floor began suddenly to sound the Prince's *orgue expressif,* played by his masterly hand. Such a modulation, minor and solemn, and ever changing, and never ceasing, from a piano like Jenny Lind's holding note, up to the fullest swell, and still the same "fine vein of melancholy"! And it came in so exactly as an accompaniment to the sunset. How strange he is! He must have been playing just while the Queen was finishing her toilette. And then he went to cut jokes and eat loads at dinner, and nobody but the organ knows what is *in him*— except, indeed, by the look of his eyes sometimes.   [59]

These letters are delicious period pieces, and they show Lady Lyttelton's continuing fondness for "dear Prince Albert." But what is so striking is the way Strachey selects his details from this wealth of correspondence (scrupulously footnoting each) and resists distraction. Lady Lyttelton, so tempting an epistolary subject, disappears; what is retained, pared down, and made significant are the evidences of Albert's musical solace, domestic liveliness, and private melancholy. In a passage of two hundred words, the biographer distills material gleaned from letters that span ten years of the royal marriage.

Strachey made his reputation on two biographies, both Victorian in subject matter though emphatically not in style. *Eminent Victorians,* his brief but telling narratives of the lives of Florence Nightingale, Thomas Arnold, Cardinal Manning, and General Gordon (the "four stout Victorians" wittily described in Woolf's essay) was a bombshell and an instant success. *Queen Victoria*, a few years later, secured both his reputation and his income. As Woolf wrote in her essay "The Art of Biography," "Anger and laughter mixed; and editions multiplied."[60] Here is Strachey's own account of Victorian biography and its discontents, from the preface to *Eminent Victorians:*

> . . . the most delicate and humane of all the branches of the art of writing has been relegated to the journeymen of letters; we do not reflect that it is perhaps as difficult to write a good life as to live one. Those two fat volumes with which it is our custom to commemorate the dead—who does not know them, with their ill-digested panegyric, their lamentable lack of selection, of detachment, of design? They are as familiar as the cortege of the undertaker, and wear the same air of slow, funereal barbarism.[61]

For Strachey, "the first duty of the biographer" is to preserve "a becoming brevity—a brevity which excludes everything that is redundant and nothing that is significant," and the second duty, "no less significant," is "to maintain his own freedom of spirit."[62] He considers his job "to lay bare the facts of the case," not to extrapolate or fantasize. He appends a list of principal sources at the end of each biography in *Eminent Victorians.* His art is in the arrangement of details, and in letting the telling detail speak. Although his book has been described as ironic, he calls it dispassionate and impartial. Often the wit inheres in what he does not say.

After *Eminent Victorians,* aptly described by Virginia Woolf as "short studies with something of the over-emphasis and the foreshortening of caricatures" (we might compare them to modern-day *New Yorker* profiles), Strachey turned to larger projects, and here, as Woolf observes, the challenges of the genre became evident:

> In the lives of the two great Queens, Elizabeth and Victoria, he attempted a far more ambitious task. Biography had never had a

fairer chance of showing what it could do. For it was now being put to the test by a writer who was capable of making use of all the liberties that biography had won: he was fearless; he had proved his brilliance; and he had learned his job. The result throws great light upon the nature of biography. For who can doubt that after reading the two books again, one after the other, that the *Victoria* is a triumphant success, and that the *Elizabeth* by comparison is a failure? But it seems too, as we compare them, that it was not Lytton Strachey who failed; it was the art of biography. In the *Victoria* he treated biography as a craft; he submitted to its limitations. In the *Elizabeth* he treated biography as an art; he flouted its limitations.[63]

About Victoria, much was known, much recorded, much available to the diligent and responsible researcher. "The biographer could not invent her, because at every moment some document was at hand to check his invention." So Strachey "used to the full the biographer's power of selection and relation, but he kept strictly within the world of fact. Every statement was verified; every fact was authenticated." But in the case of Elizabeth, the opposite conditions obtained. "Very little was known about her. The society in which she lived was so remote that the habits, the motives, and even the actions of the people of that age were full of strangeness and obscurity." The opportunity was there for biography to approach the condition of poetry or drama, that "combined the advantages of both worlds," of fact and fiction.

And yet in Woolf's view, the attempt failed. Despite the consummate skill of the biographer, "the combination became unworkable; fact and fiction refused to mix. Elizabeth never became real in the sense that Queen Victoria had been real, yet she never became fictitious in the sense that Cleopatra or Falstaff is fictitious."[64] This is a point on which Woolf, the author of those two masterful fictional "biographies," *Orlando* and *Flush*, clearly feels strongly. "The two kinds of fact will not mix." Her essay is called "The Art of Biography," and she begins by putting that concept in question ("Is biography an art?").

Nonetheless, Woolf foresaw a time when, she thought, biography would evolve to meet changing circumstances in the world. Writing after Strachey's death, and many years after she had hailed "the new biography" in 1927, she looked ahead to a moment when the biographer would revise traditional techniques to meet the opportunities and demands of modern culture. "[S]ince we live in an age when a thousand cameras are pointed, by newspapers, letters, and diaries, at every character from every angle, he must be prepared to admit contradictory versions of the same face. Biography will enlarge its scope by hanging up looking-glasses at odd corners."[65]

Virginia Woolf, who died in 1941, could hardly anticipate the super-saturated media environment in which today's biographies are written, reviewed, and read: a 24/7 bombardment of news cycles, Internet gossip, YouTube, e-mail, and text messaging. What she regarded as frenetic interruptions—newspapers, letters, diaries, even those "thousand cameras," a phrase I think she must have intended as hyperbolic—sound rather leisurely in a paparazzi world. The truth of a life today often involves scandal, confession, and self-exposure. And what has become of the art of biography and its relation to literature?

Larger Than Life

We might think that the days of the Victorian doorstop biography, in many pages or sometimes multiple volumes, has returned in a new guise. The second volume of Robert Skidelsky's 1994 biography of John Maynard Keynes, subtitled *The Economist as Savior, 1920–1937,* covers seventeen years of Keynes's life in 635 pages, plus notes and sources. The third volume, *Fighting for Freedom, 1937–1946,* is 580 pages long. Peter Manso's biography of Marlon Brando, also from 1994, came in at 1,021 pages, not including the notes and sources. These are not atypical numbers: consider Juliet Barker's *The Brontës* (1994, 830 pages plus notes); James R. Mellow's *Hemingway: A Life Without Consequences* (1992, 604 pages plus notes); Harrison Kinney, *James Thurber: His Life and Times* (1994, 1,077 pages plus appendices and notes). I pulled these books from my shelves—this is a random rather than a systematic survey—but the pattern seems fairly consistent. David McCullough's highly regarded book on Harry Truman (1992) was 1,117 pages long, his *John Adams*

(2001), 751 pages. It is hard to think of another trade-publishing genre that is so lengthy and yet is considered commercially viable. In hardcover and paperback, these books sell.

Clearly—leaving aside for the moment the question of style—such biographies are not literary in the sense described by Strachey, dominated by a sense "of selection, of detachment, of design." Modern biographies that chronicle the life of literary figures tend to include in their accounts of the subject's life a description or assessment of the work, including plot summary and analysis, together with some sense of the work's reception, qualifying them for the technical description of literary biography—a genre described by novelist John Updike as liable to abuse (the "Judas biography," containing unflattering portraits from the testimony of a former friend or spouse; the inaccuracies reprinted from previously published, erroneous accounts), as well as the potentially useful work of reacquainting the reader with an author (albeit via what Updike calls a "nether route").[66] Within this genre, there is, again, a wide range of literary expertise and critical objective. The biographies of Sylvia Plath by Diane Middlebrook and Jacqueline Rose, both talented literary scholars, were consequential and important for the analysis of her poetry. Another version of the same life story, Janet Malcolm's biography of Plath and her husband, Ted Hughes, addressed the unreliability of memory and the difficulty, when dealing with interested parties, of separating fact from fiction. "In a work of nonfiction, we almost never know the truth of what happened," Malcolm observed. And with a controversial matter like that of Plath's life and death, she noted, the problems are especially acute. "The pleasure of hearing ill of the dead is not negligible, but it pales before the pleasure of hearing ill of the living."[67]

The technique that Lytton Strachey used in *Queen Victoria*—the judicious quotation from letters and other sources to produce a kind of biographical dialogue—still distinguishes the best modern biographies, like Janet Browne's two-volume biography of Charles Darwin or David McCullough's *John Adams*. Emotional responses, internal thoughts, and other novelistic devices are crafted from the archival information, the "facts" upon which Woolf so strongly insisted. The biographer's gift is one of deploying information, not of inventing it. Thus, describing the arrival of a letter to Adams that dispatched him to the Court of France, McCullough writes,

> Thinking the packet must be urgent business, Abigail opened it and was stunned by what she read. Furious, she wrote straight away to Lovell, demanding to know how he could "contrive to rob me of all my happiness.
>
> "And can I, sir, consent, to be separated from him whom my heart esteems above all earthly things, and for an unlimited time? My life will be one continued scene of anxiety and apprehension, and must I cheerfully comply with the demands of my country?"[68]

Active and emotive terms like "thinking," "stunned," furious," and "demanding" are all inferred, effectively, from the source material, and "straight away" is derived from the date. The dramatic or literary effect (what would, in fact, eventuate in a screenplay) is elicited from within, not imposed from without.

Likewise, Janet Browne describes Darwin's proposal to his future wife:

> . . . on Sunday he spoke about marriage to Emma. Not unexpectedly, the event deflated both of them—Darwin was too exhausted by the nervous strain, with a bad headache, and Emma was "too much bewildered" to feel any overwhelming sense of happiness. To Darwin's astonishment, she accepted him. Even so, the proposal caught her so unprepared that she went straight off to the Maer Sunday school as usual. Darwin's exclamation in his diary that this was "The day of days!" was wildly misleading in its retrospective intensity . . .
>
> "I believe," said Emma afterwards, "we both looked very dismal": An elderly Wedgwood aunt thought something quite the reverse had happened: that Darwin had asked but received a rejection.[69]

Here, too, it is possible to see how the emotional responses of the protagonists and the dramatic arc of the story are derived from source materials: the headache, the bewilderment, the astonishment, the very mood of the day, even the comically erroneous response of an onlooker, misreading the "dismal" expressions of the couple. Reality, in this case, means sutured to a certain kind of evidence.

We might contrast this way of writing a life with the kind of work that resembles the televised docudrama or "dramatic re-creation." In the filmic version, actors perform on-screen as a voice-over offers the play-by-play of a real (but restaged) event. Shadows loom out of the darkness; scenery (a lonely road, a family mansion) offers an atmospheric B-roll boost; flashbacks increase the suspense. The language associated with the voice-over narrations in docudramas is heavy with subjunctives—*would, could, might*—and suppositions masquerading as rhetorical questions: "Did she know?" "Would he attempt?" "What was going through his mind at that moment?"

I have been calling the mode of biography that functions in this manner *speculative,* by which I mean a language heavily laden with subjunctives and similar suppositions: "There is reason to think that if she had"; "Were he to meet her then, as perhaps he did, they might have found"; "Having been to France, he would have known that." Rather than being brought to life by specific textual evidence (Darwin's diary, Abigail Adams's letter), these hypotheticals are presented *instead of* evidence. By a certain authorial sleight of hand, they *become* the evidence whose absence they conceal. Moreover, contemporary culture has increasingly come to accept such fantasy projections as evidence, so eager are we to "know" the characters (historical, modern, famous, or infamous) about whom these real-life stories are told.

Horse Sense

My favorite example of this kind of projection taken to its logical extreme is Laura Hillenbrand's fascinating biography *Seabiscuit: An American Legend,* in which the technique of imagining what is going through the mind of the protagonist is employed to show us the inner thoughts of a racehorse.[70]

The word *celebrity* appears a number of times in Hillenbrand's narrative, and appropriately so. The horse, who, in his racing heyday, liked to pose for photographers, was called "Movie Star" by reporters. As the reader follows the "making of a legend" from obscurity to celebrity to calamity to bittersweet triumph, it becomes clear that the book can be compared to works like *Judy Garland: The Secret Life of an American Legend* (David Shipman), *Marlene Dietrich: Life and Legend* (Steven Bach), or biographies of the Kennedys. But there is one way in which Hillenbrand's *Seabiscuit* differs, of necessity, from the celebrity biography. A staple of the celebrity biography is that curious set of tenses and moods (from optative subjunctive to free indirect discourse) through which the author attempts to project the thoughts, or putative thoughts, of the celebrity subject. "One aspect of pre-production which pleased Garland was the make-up tests."[71] "The visitor was unwelcome, though Marlene realized that one way or another he was as inevitable as history."[72] "As always, when in trouble, Jack turned to his father."[73] A certain genre of horse (or dog) story uses the same kinds of voice and mind projection—think Jack London—or even, as in the case of Anna Sewell's *Black Beauty,* is told in the first-person voice of the subject: "When I was young I lived upon my mother's milk, as I could not eat grass."[74]

In *Seabiscuit,* the central figure's consciousness is never so baldly anthropomorphic. But at the center of the book, surrounded by taciturn trainers and jockeys, is the silence of the equine legend, a silence marked, as if anxiously, by recurrent attention to what was going on in his mind. "Seabiscuit had the misfortune of living in a stable whose managers simply didn't have the time to give his mind the painstaking attention it needed," we are told about the horse's early overraced and undervalued years, while jockey Red Pollard's natural empathy "had given him insight into the minds of ailing, nervous horses."[75] At a turning point in Pollard's career, when he finally guides Seabiscuit to a significant victory, the author's prose can't resist turning toward the psychological projections familiar from a certain mode of celebrity biography:

Seabiscuit stood square under his head-to-toe blanket, posed in the stance of the conqueror, head high, ears pricked, eyes roaming the horizon, nostrils flexing with each breath, jaw rolling the bit around with cool confidence.

He was a new horse.

In the fiftieth start of his life, Seabiscuit finally understood the game.[76]

In its own way, this description is a triumph. It makes the point that the author wants to make, but in order to do so it becomes necessary to project her feelings, or the reader's, into the mind of the horse.

Seabiscuit is meticulously documented, with silent notes placed at the back of the book, so as not to disturb the narrative flow. Given the nature of the story, most of the sources are newspaper articles, features from *Turf & Sport Digest* or the *Daily Racing Form*, audiotapes of race calls, films and newsreels, or previous versions of Seabiscuit's life story. But in none of these is there a viva voce interview with the biographical subject. If Seabiscuit felt that he was "a new horse," if he brimmed with "cool confidence," if he "finally understood the game," it was something said by others, or by the biographer, not (how can one resist this? it is, after all, the point of the cliché) straight from the horse's mouth.

Since the distinctions I am drawing—between the technique of speculation and the style of free indirect discourse—may seem to be minor or evanescent, let me try to make them sharper by saying that what I've called speculative biography imputes motives, intentions, and causes, linking historical events in an arc of character intentionality that is a fictional construct. Why did X do this or that? Perhaps he thought; did she imagine; were they hoping? Here it may be helpful to see how a reviewer described a recent book about the life of the poet Robert Frost:

The book is billed as a novel, but this is only because it is speculative rather than veritable; it is more properly classified a *vie romancée*, a bio enhanced with the loosey-goosey methods of fiction. Variations on this form have become increasingly fashionable in recent years—

so fashionable, in fact, that two fictional portraits of Henry James alone were published in 2004, with another trailing along the next year.[77]

In a work like Colm Tóibín's *The Master: A Novel* (one of the two fictional books about James noted in the review) it seems as if the term *novel* allows the author to have things both ways: the gravitas of biography and the freedom to identify and psychologize that comes with the writing of a certain kind of fiction.

Insincerely Yours

Half a century ago René Wellek and Austin Warren wrote briskly in their *Theory of Literature* about the relationship between literature and biography—a relationship they considered dangerously misleading:

> No biographical evidence can change or influence critical evaluation. The frequently adduced criterion of "sincerity" is thoroughly false if it judges literature in terms of biographical truthfulnesss, correspondence to the author's experience or feelings as they are attested by outside evidence. There is no relationship between "sincerity" and value as art.[78]

As specific counterexamples, they adduce "the volumes of agonizingly felt love poetry perpetrated by adolescents," and "the dreary (however fervently felt) religious verse which fills libraries."

The sincerity issue (Wellek and Warren are clearly speaking back to Lionel Trilling) connects to biography and to the memoir. Their point, firmly stated and reinforced by examples, was that any assumption about a direct or causative relationship between the facts of a life and the work of a writer disregards something fundamental about the nature of literature: "The whole view that art is self-expression pure and simple, the transcript of personal feelings and experiences," they contend, "is demonstrably false." Again, "the biographical approach actually obscures a proper comprehension of the literary process, since it breaks up the order of literary tradition to substitute the life-cycle of an individual." It also "ignores" what they call "quite simple psychological facts": that a work of art may embody the "dream," "mask," or "anti-self" of its author, rather than facets of the actual life.[79] So for Wellek and Warren, much literary biography is not literary.

Perhaps inevitably, their chief example is a selection of biographies of Shakespeare, which from the vantage point of midcentury meant the work of Georg Brandes, Frank Harris, and their nineteenth-century precursors, Hazlitt, Schlegel, and Dowden. Since "we have absolutely nothing in the form of letters, diaries, reminiscences, except a few anecdotes of doubtful authenticity," they point out, there is no real biographical information, only "facts of chronology" and illustrations of Shakespeare's "social status and associations."

> The vast effort which has been expended upon the study of Shakespeare's life has yielded only few results of literary profit . . . One cannot, from fictional statements, especially those made in plays, draw any valid inference as to the biography of a writer.

There is no logic to the idea that emotions and fictional descriptions are linked by anything causal. "One may gravely doubt," write Wellek and Warren, "even the usual view that Shakespeare passes through a period of depression, in which he wrote his tragedies and his bitter comedies, to achieve some serenity of resolution in *The Tempest*. It is not self-evident that a writer needs to be in a tragic mood to write tragedies or that he writes comedies when he is pleased with life. There is simply no proof for the sorrows of Shakespeare."[80]

They insist that there is no more reason to identify the playwright's views with that of a wise protagonist like Prospero, or a disaffected speaker like Timon of Athens, than with those of Doll Tearsheet or Iago: "authors cannot be assigned the ideas, feelings, views, virtues and vices of their heroes."[81] Moreover, the same is true of the first-person *I* of a lyric poem. Whether Wordsworth wandered lonely as a cloud or not has no effect upon the artistic merit or propositional truth of his verse.

So what uses might biography have? Again Wellek and Warren are clear. Biographical information can explain allusions in the work, can accumulate materials for literary history (what the author read, where he or she traveled, etc.). By *literary history* they mean tradition, influences, sources. But where they draw the line, as we have seen, is at evaluation. Biography has no "*critical* importance." A work of literature need have no correlation with events or data related to the author's life, nor do those events explain (or cause) the work.

If biography is not literature—or if only some biographies are literature, and those are considered so for reasons of style and form rather than a supposed fidelity to facts—then why worry about the uses of biography? One response would be that the truth claims—and explanatory claims—made on behalf of biographical, autobiographical, or personal facts have, to a certain extent, preempted or short-circuited the role of criticism and interpretation when it comes to assessing literature, not only for "the common reader" but for many specialists as well.

If it is not only the acknowledged faux or hoax memoirs that are fictions, but also all memoirs, and much biographical writing of the speculative ("if he knew *this*, did it influence him when he did *that*") mode, then their truth claims, which may be compelling (or not), have the status, precisely, of *fictional truth*. Aristotle famously said about plots that he preferred a plausible impossibility to an implausible possibility, and "truth" in this sense, with or without quotation marks, is Coleridge's willing suspension of disbelief. The most effective (and compellingly literary) passage on this matter remains that of Nietzsche, in "On Truth or Lie in an Extra-Moral Sense":

What, then, is truth? A mobile army of metaphors, metonyms, and anthropomorphisms—in short, a sum of human relations, which have been enhanced, transposed, and embellished poetically and rhetorically, and which after long use seem firm, canonical, and obligatory to a people: truths are illusions about which one has forgotten that this is what they are; metaphors which are worn out and without sensuous power; coins which have lost their pictures and now matter only as metal, no longer as coins.[82]

This remarkable paragraph is often assumed by hasty readers—especially those who associate it with deconstruction and thus, by a series of leaps, with nihilism—to be a rejection of the idea of truth rather than a genealogy of truth's maturity. In fact, we could read the passage as "the biography of truth." One of its lineal relations is Francis Bacon's "Truth is the daughter of time, not authority." Nietzsche's essay doesn't say that there is no such thing as truth, but that what is true may change over time, depending upon the intellectual and cultural framework. "Truths are illusions about which one has forgotten that this is what they are." Human beings, Nietzsche claims, "lie unconsciously" in this way, and "precisely *because of this unconsciousness,* precisely because of this forgetting, they arrive at the feeling of truth."[83]

Enough About Me

The art of biography, for all the reasons we've noted, seems to be at an interesting crossroads. We have entered a time when books about the lives of writers sometimes elect to take the form of memoirs, describing the author's experience of reading. Consider two striking cases in point, both about Marcel Proust (and both published in 1997): Alain de Botton, *How Proust Can Change Your Life: Not a Novel,* and Phyllis Rose, *The Year of Reading Proust: A Memoir in Real Time.* Rose is a biographer by profession, the author of well-received books on Victorian marriages and on the black jazz performer Josephine Baker. De Botton is a fiction writer and cultural critic. Like his book's title, his chapter headings read, cleverly, like the titles of self-help books: "How to Suffer Successfully"; "How to Express Your Emotions"; "How to Be Happy in Love." If not Proust Lite, or even Proust Without Tears, this is Proust Without the Eggheads. And, to a certain extent, Proust Without the Proust.

Like the famous Bette Midler line, "But enough about me. What do *you* think of me?," these snapshots of readers watching themselves reading—or living—are engaging on first bounce. In a review of Rose's memoir, Victor Brombert remarks that despite the presence of Proust's name in the title, "he plays a minimal role" in the book, and observes that this decision may have discouraged readers not familiar with Proust's work and frustrated those who were.[84] (Brombert's review begins by recalling André Malraux's comment in *Anti-Memoirs:* "What do I care about what only I care about?")

Michiko Kakutani described de Botton's book as "quirky" but possessed of a "certain genial charm," and she noted that its author had "hit upon a formula for talking about art and highbrow concerns in a deliberately lowbrow way."[85] De Botton went on to "expand upon that formula" with *The Consolations of Philosophy,* finding helpful hints in the works of philosophers like Seneca, Montaigne, Schopenhauer, and Socrates. The book begat a television program in England, where its author was metamorphosed into a philosophical advice-giving figure known as Dr. Love. This is presumably one of the uses of literature, after a fashion. How-to is definitely *use;* whether these adapted sound bites from Montaigne (or Proust) retain their tang as literature or have crossed over into the soothing realm of banality is another question.

Perhaps inevitably, Pierre Bayard's book on how not to read a book (*How to Talk About Books You Haven't Read*)[86] focuses, at the outset, on Proust, an author Bayard is proud not to have read, and who—as he hastens to tell us—Paul Valéry also hadn't read and made much of not reading. Bayard gets lots of mileage in this short book by citing long passages from writers who discuss not reading. Whether he himself has read these books (or skimmed them, or heard of them, to use two of his book's chosen designations) is unclear and, in the long (or short) run, unimportant. What does seem at least fleetingly important is that such a book can not only be published but gain a fandom of sorts. Its most praised section, on the anthropologist Laura Bohannan's retelling of the plot of *Hamlet* to an African tribe, is a familiar story based upon a well-known essay, retold here as if there were no history of discussions of this famous incident.[87] Bayard's book is not a book about reading, and it is not a book about not reading, and it is not even a book about the social pretense (and pretension) of "having read." It is a book about the *theme* of not reading as located in a few idiosyncratically chosen texts.

The back cover of *How to Talk About Books You Haven't Read* asks which of a group of great books the reader has ever talked about without reading: *Moby-Dick, Ulysses, Heart of Darkness, Invisible Man, A Room of One's Own, Being and Nothingness, In Cold Blood, The Scarlet Letter, The Man Without Qualities, Lolita, Jane Eyre, The Sun Also Rises.* But of this list, Bayard discusses only one, Robert Musil's *The Man Without Qualities.* This slim volume is full of long block quotations, separated by passages of plot summary for those who haven't read what Bayard hasn't read, and occasional in-your-face bromides. If he weren't French and telegenic, he would never have gotten away with it.

Taken together, de Botton's book on Proust as a self-help manual and Bayard's book about the theme of not reading may say something about the cachet of French cultural essayists in the American market, or about the defensive self-congratulation of American anti-intellectualism (here validated by a generation of French "intellectuals" who write in a style distinctly different from the "difficult" Derrida, Lacan, or Foucault) or about what it means to be "after the humanities" in the most negative sense. To the extent that the books discuss the use of literature, that use is turned, however wittily, into a social function rather than an intellectual or aesthetic one. As such, books like these are symptomatic. They are the "On Bullshit" of literary life.

A third book we might put on the shelf of books about repurposing the reading of great books is Stuart Kelly's *The Book of Lost Books,* subtitled, in that explanatory way to which we have become accustomed in subtitles of late, *An Incomplete History of All the Great Books You'll Never Read.*[88] Kelly is not French, and his book even has an index, albeit a brief one. In a series of short chapters (typically three to five pages), he identifies, historicizes, and speculates about lost books by famous writers, from Anonymous and Homer to Sylvia Plath and Georges Perec. For some reason, the most recent authors are listed by their full formal names (Dylan Marlais Thomas, William Seward Burroughs, Robert Traill Spence Lowell IV), making them sound vaguely parodic. And not all of the lost works are equally persuasive; Shakespeare's *Love's Labour's Won* is a constant source of speculation, Lowell's notional epic on the crusades less so. Basically, the book is literary gossip. It's probably unfair to quote from the jacket flap—which the author almost surely didn't write—but the cascade of adverbs and adjectives is indicative: "In compulsively readable fashion, Stuart Kelly reveals details about tantalizing vanished works by the famous, the acclaimed, and the influential, from the time of cave drawings to the late twentieth century. Here are the true stories behind stories, poems, and plays that now exist only in imagination."

Why do I classify this book with *How to Talk* and the Proust books? Because all are para-literary, alluding to literature obliquely. None requires that the reader actually have a firsthand encounter with the great works on which they are propped. In the case of Kelly's book, all the works are conveniently unavailable, objects of speculation rather than contemplation. For Bayard, reading is not only unnecessary but sometimes counterproductive; for de Botton, Proust becomes a sophisticated advice giver, a Dr. Marcel to rival television's Dr. Phil. Decades after the culture wars worried about whether college students were being taught the right stuff, these books suggest that you can have a literary experience without having to bother to experience literature, and that it's stylish—even cool—to do so.

EIGHT

Mixed Metaphors

There was a time when Hugh Blair's *Lectures on Rhetoric and Belles Lettres*, written by the first Regius Professor of Rhetoric at the University of Edinburgh and initially published in 1783, was the most popular and widely taught language text in Britain and the United States. Blair's lectures, on topics like Taste, the Sublime in Writing, Metaphor, the History of Eloquence, the Nature of Poetry, Dramatic Poetry, and Versification, contained extended discussions of major works in English literature. The lectures were intended, Blair explained, for those who sought professional employment in composition and public speaking, and also for those who simply wanted to improve their taste so that they could judge works of literature for themselves. But Blair also suggested that his course of study could be of assistance in fashionable society:

> In an age when works of genius and literature are so frequently the subjects of discourse, when every one erects himself into a judge, and when we can hardly mingle in polite society without bearing some share in such discussions; studies of this kind, it is not to be doubted, will appear to derive part of their importance from the use to which they may be applied in furnishing materials for those fashionable topics of discourse, and thereby enabling us to support a proper rank in social life.[1]

Reading "works of genius and literature" was to provide the aspiring socialite with "fashionable topics of discourse." So one use to which literature could be put, for the polite society of the eighteenth and nineteenth centuries, was the achievement, and maintenance, of a proper social place or rank. This was not Blair's preferred application of his precepts and examples—he would have preferred something "of solid and intrinsical use, independent, of appearance and show"—but he readily acknowledged that the eighteenth-century equivalent of "walking to and fro, talking of Michelangelo" could have positive social and intellectual results.

It's worth noting that eloquence in the current political climate is often as much distrusted as it is admired. As we've noted, in the 2008 presidential race, the word *eloquent* went from a term of praise to an epithet in a campaign minute, as rivals to Barack Obama—both in his own party and in the opposition—deployed it against the eventual winner. "I admire so much Senator Obama's eloquence," said his Republican opponent, John McCain, before turning to a perceived difference between words and actions. Twice in the same debate, McCain used "the eloquence of Senator Obama" as a preface to a put-down, a practice that had been earlier used by several conservative broadcasters and columnists, and even by Obama's chief rival for the Democratic nomination, Hillary Clinton. "It's time to get real about how we actually win this election," said Clinton at a campaign rally. "It's time that we move from good words to good works, from sound bites to sound solutions."[2] This formulation, itself an eloquent model of tropes in action (*anaphora,* the beginning of consecutive sentences, clauses, or phrases with the same phrase or word; *prosonomasia,* a punning on words that resemble one another), is a typical and often successful debater's move. In any case, we might wish to contrast such eloquent flights, even those that apparently speak ill of eloquence, with the full-blown collapse of syntax and figure, characteristic of such plain-spoken politicians as Sarah Palin and George W. Bush, that is taken to be unpretentious, honest, and authentic—the opposite of "sophistic," "sophistical," or sophisticated.[3] Although these two politicians are Republicans, I should say at once that resistance to syntax or rhetorical style is an equal-opportunity failing (or success, depending upon your point of view).

The distrust of eloquence echoes the distrust of rhetoric expressed in classical times by those who excoriated the sophists, who were professional rhetoricians, because their eloquence was purchased for a price. We might compare this practice to that of a modern defense attorney or speechwriter or advertising copywriter, all of whom deploy language and rhetoric in the service of a professional task for which they are compensated. No one requires these professionals to believe in their products or their candidates or their client's innocence, although sometimes the persuaders persuade themselves.

Today, however, discussion of the power of figurative language has moved away from literature and toward cognition theory and brain science. Cognitive psychologists and cognitive linguists seek to read *through* metaphor and other rhetorical figures to discover something about the functioning of the mind.

The Metaphor of Metaphor

George Lakoff and Mark Johnson's book *Metaphors We Live By* (1980) focuses on metaphor's "power to define reality." In most cases, they argue, "what is at issue is not the truth or the falsity of a metaphor but the perceptions and inferences that follow from it."[4] Metaphor, according to Lakoff and Johnson, is an aspect of cognitive thinking, "pervasive in everyday life, not just in language but in thought and action."[5] *Metaphors We Live By* offers examples like "Argument Is War," "Time Is Money," "Life Is a Journey," and then, in a chapter called "Some Further Examples," a list of concepts, each an umbrella topic under which actual metaphors could be grouped, such as "Theories Are Buildings" (sample metaphorical terms: *foundation, buttress*), "Ideas Are Food" (*half-baked, fishy, can't swallow*), "Love Is Magic" (*cast a spell, entranced, bewitching*), and so on.[6] Ideas, as Lakoff and Johnson would have it, can be not only food but also people, plants, products, commodities, money, cutting instruments, and fashions, while love can be magic, madness, war, a magnet, or a patient. In other words, language is figure. The notion that metaphor is not "just" language but also influences thought and action means that—as poets, linguists, philosophers, rhetoricians, and politicians have known for quite a while—what people say and how they say it affects, shapes, and directs understanding and response. But the phrase *not just in language* is indicative of a devaluation of the power and nature of words and rhetoric, and it contributes to the remanding of the literary to a secondary or tertiary role. This point is underscored in an afterword, where the supposed primacy of the conceptual is described under the heading "Persistent Fallacies":

> The single biggest obstacle to understanding our findings has been the refusal to recognize the *conceptual* nature of metaphor. The idea that metaphors are nothing but linguistic expressions—a mere matter of words—is such a common fallacy that it has kept many readers from even entertaining the idea that we think metaphorically.[7]

Notice the rhetoric of diminishment: "nothing but linguistic expressions"; "a mere matter of words." Could we call this, following Lakoff and Johnson, the metaphor of "Language Is Negligible"?

"Life is a journey" and "time is money" are cultural clichés of the kind that we associate with the greeting-card industry. Actually most of the metaphors mentioned above or listed in *Metaphors to Live By* are often (and erroneously) called dead metaphors, which is to say, metaphors whose originality of expression has eroded over time so that we no longer encounter them as figurative (for example, the *horsepower* of an engine, or the *foot* of a page). Do readers who encounter the phrase *half-baked ideas* think, consciously or subliminally, of cookie dough? In short, the concept of metaphor becomes a metaphor in Lakoff and Johnson's work. "Happy Is Up" (to use another of their examples, the one they call "the major metaphor in our culture")[8] is *not* a metaphor; it is a concept.

In subsequent books, George Lakoff pushes his claim about metaphor to encompass, for example, the political differences between progressives (who, he claims, cleave to a Nurturant Parent Model) and conservatives (who prefer a Strict Father Model). The index to *Moral Politics: How Liberals and Conservatives Think* includes two columns of metaphors, with keywords capitalized in what had by that time become the author's trademark style. These include the Moral Accounting metaphor, the Moral Action as Financial Transaction metaphor, the Moral Boundaries metaphor, the Moral Essence metaphor, the Moral Growth metaphor, the Morality as Empathy metaphor, and many other capitalized metaphors of the same kind. Thus the section on Moral Health includes the propositions "Morality Is Health" and "Immorality Is Disease." Without question, these are powerful paradigms, but they are even more powerful when the figure precedes the ground or, to use the standard phrase about metaphors, the vehicle precedes the tenor.

The "X is Y" formulation irresistibly suggests the George Orwell of both *1984* and *Animal Farm* but these literary and critical examples, together with the ironies and interpretive dangers they present, are few and far between. Orwell is, however, mentioned as the inventor of Big Brother, the "nightmare head of state" whose title illustrates the pervasiveness of "the Nation as Family metaphor."[9] In fact George Orwell is the *only* literary author mentioned in *Moral Politics,* a book that cites Christine Todd Whitman but not Walt Whitman, William Bennett but not Arnold Bennett, Katherine Harris but not Joel Chandler Harris, Sandra Day O'Connor but not Flannery O'Connor. Lakoff and another collaborator, Mark Turner, did, however, address the question of metaphors in literature in a book called *More Than Cool Reason: A Field Guide to Poetic Metaphor.* With advanced degrees in both mathematics and English literature, Turner was well placed to participate in ongoing conversations about such cognitive topics as "conceptual blending," "conceptual integration," and "the mind as an autocatalytic vortex." He would later write several influential books that combined literary study and neuroscience. What is especially notable may be that his own career has migrated from English studies to cognitive science, where his professorial appointment is located.

In the preface to his book *The Literary Mind* Turner makes a set of claims about the centrality of literary thinking that might be considered compatible with the argument I'm making here. He sets out three "principles of mind," which he calls *story, projection,* and *parable,* and makes a case for considering them fundamental to all thinking, not just the specialized processes and practices that are often called literary.

> *Story* is a basic principle of mind. Most of our experience, our knowledge, and our thinking is organized as stories. The mental scope of

story is magnified by *projection*—one story helps us make sense of another. The projection of one story onto another is *parable,* a basic cognitive principle . . .

"In this book," he continues, "I explore technical details of the brain sciences and the mind sciences that cast light on our use of parable . . . I explore the possibility that language is not the source of parable but instead its complex product."

In itself, this is not a surprising idea. Narratologists from Vladimir Propp to Tzvetan Todorov to Gerard Genette have made claims for the role of story and fable. As early as the 1920s, Propp's *Morphology of the Folktale* distinguished between *fabula* (the content of the story) and *sujet* (the form that the telling of the tale imposes on that content).[10] In the late sixties, when ideas about the scientific (or social scientific) basis of literature provided an impetus for literary theorists, some of this work became important in the anthropological and critical practice known as structuralism. Man as the fiction-making animal was a favorite trope of the mid-twentieth century, in disciplines from literary studies to anthropology. Thus, for example, an innovative course, "Man and His Fictions"—otherwise known as Literature X—was the starting point of the new literature major at Yale in the 1970s. Subsequently, the diverse set of literary critical practices generally described under the rubric of post-structuralism challenged the belief in a stable set of significations, or meanings, across cultures, and in the concept of the universal category of "man."

These are just the kinds of claims that are again being made under the rubric of brain science and cognition rather than the human sciences or social sciences. The wheel has come full circle. Cognitive science's holistic assertions about the brain and basic principles of mind, as appealing as they may be, make the literary mind a repository of narrative fictions, without acknowledging that words and rhetorical forms are themselves unstable, producing alternative and often antithetical narratives of their own. It's precisely the tendency to think in stories or parables that often leads to underreading, by presuming that the outcome is already shaped

by the narrative form—that "one story helps us make sense of another."
(Not to mention the diversity of interpretation that may attend upon
such stories and parables, as any rigorous study of biblical scholarship
will attest.) Linking one cultural metaphor to another, rather than paying
close attention to individual words, tropes, figures of speech, and rhetorical inflections, makes literature into a kind of master code or anthology
of expectable moves. Turner's assertion in the preface, that "the literary
mind is the fundamental mind," may seem like a compliment to literature, rescuing it from what he describes as "the common view—firmly
in place for two and a half millennia—[that] sees the everyday mind as
unliterary and the literary mind as optional." But in fact this sweeping
claim sweeps the literary away.

Translating Metaphor

Let's return for a moment to the idea of metaphor, a word that means
carrying across, or transporting. As several theorists and philosophers
note, this is the same etymological meaning as *translation,* also a carrying *(trans)* across. The conveyances that in American English are called
moving vans (and in British English, removal trucks) are in modern
Greece marked with the word *metaphora,* indicating their function—
much to the delight of observers from the philosopher Paul Ricoeur to
the biologist Stephen Jay Gould.[11] It was the critic I. A. Richards (in his
Philosophy of Rhetoric, 1936) who invented the terms *vehicle* and *tenor*
for the two parts of a metaphor, the "literal subject" and the figurative
connection. I enclose the word "literal" in quotation marks here, at the
risk of irritating the reader, because it is the argument of many literary
theorists that all language is figurative. Perhaps it would be better to call
this the *referent,* although that term, too, has become critically loaded. In
a phrase like *My love is like a red, red rose,* or (to use a less poetic figure)
life is a bitch, the vehicles are *love* and *life,* and the tenors (holding the
referents) *rose* and *bitch.*

"Metaphor is the transference of a term from one thing to another," as Aristotle explained in the *Poetics,* "whether from genus to species, species to genus, species to species, or by analogy."[12] And he expands on this concept in *Rhetoric:*

> Metaphors, like epithets, must be fitting, which means that they must fairly correspond to the thing signified: failing this, their inap-propriateness will be conspicuous: the want of harmony between two things is emphasized by their being placed side by side . . . And if you wish to pay a compliment, you must take your metaphor from something better in the same line; if to disparage, something worse. To illustrate my meaning: . . . somebody calls actors hangers-on of Dionysus, but they call themselves artists: each of these terms is a metaphor, the one intended to throw dirt at the actor, the other to dignify him. And pirates now call themselves purveyors. We can thus call a crime a mistake, or a mistake a crime.[13]

"Metaphor is the dreamwork of language," wrote the philosopher Donald Davidson, "and, like all dreamwork, its interpretation reflects as much on the interpreter as on the originator. The interpretation of dreams requires collaboration between a dreamer and a waker, even if they be the same person; and the act of interpretation is itself a work of the imagination. So too understanding a metaphor is as much a creative endeavour as making a metaphor, and as little guided by rules."[14]

As Aristotle suggested, we can "call a crime a mistake, or a mistake a crime." Understanding a metaphor is as much a creative endeavor as making one, and neither is guided by rules. This is a different notion of metaphor from the conceptual belief that seems to imply a common cul-tural unconscious. It implies that metaphors are made rather than found, and that they are not only modes of translation and transference, but also of transgression: they step across boundaries ("from genus to species, from species to genus"); they can be complimentary or disparaging; they do not articulate or obey rules, except perhaps the rule of compulsory disobedience. Metaphors are a kind of intentional or motivated solecism: a mistake or a crime elevated to a position of rhetorical power.

When the literary critic Paul de Man approached the question of metaphor's constitutive transgressiveness via the route of epistemology, he did so with characteristic rigor, beginning with his opening salvo: "Metaphors, tropes, and figural language in general have been a perennial problem and, at times, a recognized source of embarrassment for philosophical discourse and, by extension, for all discursive uses of language including historiography and literary analysis." Try as one might, it is impossible to free oneself from figural language. Moreover, "we have no way of defining, of policing, the boundaries that separate the name of one entity from another: tropes are not just travelers, they tend to be smugglers and probably smugglers of stolen goods at that. What makes matters even worse is that there is no way of finding out whether they do so with criminal intent or not."[15]

De Man is not talking about Aristotle but, rather, the "use and abuse of words" as this topic is discussed in John Locke's "Essay Concerning Human Understanding." Nonetheless, his language echoes some of the key terms we have just noted in Aristotle's *Rhetoric:* pirates as purveyors, crime as mistake and mistake as crime. And the *use and abuse* phrase will recur several times, not merely as a grace note but as what can gradually be seen as the core of the problem, for Locke in particular but also for metaphor in general:

> Once the reflection on the figurality of language is started, there is no telling where it may lead. Yet there is no way *not* to raise the question if there is to be any understanding. The use and abuse of language cannot be separated from one another.[16]

Moreover, as de Man goes on, "Abuse of language is, of course, itself the name of a trope: catachresis." Locke had chastised those who made what he regarded as a category error, as well as an error in understanding. "He that thinks the name *centaur* stands for some real being, imposes on himself and mistakes words for things."[17] But a word *is* a thing. All words are figures, and a *horse* or a *man* is no less a figure than a centaur. As de Man will argue "the condemnation, by Locke's own argument, now takes all of language for its target, for at no point in the demonstration can the empirical entity be sheltered from tropological defiguration." *Catachresis* (etymologically, misuse or perversion, a term "Englished" in George

Puttenham's sixteenth-century treatise as "the Figure of Abuse") is not a violation of rhetoric, but itself resides *within* rhetoric.

Catachresis became an important topic for certain literary theorists in the late twentieth century precisely because it provided a third way of looking at the idea of figure, one that challenged the binary of use and abuse. "On the one hand," wrote Andrzej Warminski, "catachresis is clearly a transfer from one realm (often the human body) to another and thus is definitely a figurative use of language. To give a 'face' to a mountain or a 'head' to cabbage or lettuce is clearly a figure. On the other hand, since this figurative (ab)use does not take the place of an already existent, established literal use but rather replaces the lack of the literal, the lack of the proper expression, it is not just figurative; it can often become the proper, the only way to say the *x* of a mountain. But it would be a mistake to call it 'literal.'"[18] The classical example here is the "leg" of a table, where "leg" is a figure of speech, but does not replace or substitute for any other word.

This "uncanny doubleness" of catachresis, putting in question "the relation between literal and figurative, proper and transferred," suggests that it may be a "conceptual" mistake to think of metaphors as concepts prior to their occurrence in language. "The leg of a table" is not a concept but a poem naturalized into ordinary language.

Affecting Metaphysics

I will return briefly at the end of this chapter to the "mixed mode" figures (like the centaurs to which John Locke took such exception), since they appear importantly, and indeed as instructive "figures of abuse," in one of Shakespeare's best-loved plays. But rather than pursue this question in Locke or in philosophy, I'd like to bring it home to literature, and to metaphors and figures in poetry, by citing one of the most famous critical attacks on figures of speech (especially metaphors and/ or catachreses) in the annals of English criticism, Dr. Samuel Johnson's critique of those writers who—because of the attack—would come to be known in the history of English studies as "the metaphysical poets."

Here is Johnson's opinion of the style of this school, poets like Abraham Cowley, John Cleveland, and John Donne.

> The most heterogeneous ideas are yoked by violence together; nature and art are ransacked for illustrations, comparisons, and allusions; their learning instructs, and their subtlety surprises; but the reader commonly thinks his improvement dearly bought, and though he sometimes admires, is seldom pleased.

And:

> Their attempts were always analytic; they broke every image into fragments; and could no more represent, by their slender conceits and laboured particularities, the prospects of nature, or the scenes of life, than he who dissects a sunbeam with a prism can exhibit the wide effulgence of a summer noon.[19]

The term *metaphysical,* which refers to the branch of philosophy concerned with questions of being and knowing, was suggested in John Dryden's complaint about Donne, "He affects the metaphysics, not only in his satires, but in his amorous verses, where nature only should reign; and perplexes the minds of the fair sex with nice speculations of philosophy, when he should engage their hearts, and entertain them with the softnesses of love."[20] Whether the comparisons favored by Donne from the new science are really metaphysical, or in fact intensely material and physical (lovers as "stiff twin compasses," tears compared to a globe full of continents, specific and arcane medical knowledge), it is clear that they irritated Dr. Johnson and offended his belief that "great thoughts are always general."[21] "Who but Donne would have thought that a good man is a telescope?" he asks, citing these lines:

> Though God be our true glass through which we see
> All, since the being of all things is he,
> Yet are the trunks, which do to us derive
> Things in proportion fit, by perspective
> Deeds of good men; for by their living here,
> Virtues, indeed remote, seem to be near.

Likewise, he declares that "their fictions were often violent and unnatural," giving as his example a passage from Abraham Cowley's "Bathing in the River":

> The fish around her crowded, as they do
> To the false light that treacherous fishes show,
> And all with as much ease might taken be,
>> As she at first took me:
>> For ne'er did light so clear
>> Among the waves appear
> Though every night the sun himself set there. [22]

Whether or not the reader concurs with Dr. Johnson about the effect and value of these passages, I think it is probable that it would not do them— or Johnson—justice to describe them as conceptual metaphors in the cognitive style: the "Man Is a Telescope" metaphor, or the "Beloved Is a Bioluminescent Fish" metaphor. Johnson's criticisms were not unmixed with praise, as in this judicious, if slightly grudging sentiment: "Yet great labour, directed by great abilities, is never wholly lost: if they frequently threw away their wit upon false conceits, they likewise sometimes struck out unexpected truth; if their conceits were far-fetched, they were often worth the carriage. To write on their plan, it was at least necessary to read and think."[23]

T. S. Eliot endorsed this view, with equal eloquence and considerably more enthusiasm in his essay on "The Metaphysical Poets." Seeking to distinguish between "the intellectual poet" of the seventeenth century and "the reflective poet" of the nineteenth, Eliot had recourse to some cognitive metaphors of his own. Here is his famous account of the difference between Donne and a Victorian writer like Tennyson or Browning:

> Tennyson and Browning are poets, and they think; but they do not feel their thought as immediately as the odour of a rose. A thought to Donne was an experience; it modified his sensibility. When a poet's mind is perfectly equipped for its work, it is constantly amalgamating disparate experience; the ordinary man's experience is chaotic, irregular, fragmentary. The latter falls in love, or reads Spinoza, and

these two experiences have nothing to do with each other, or with the noise of the typewriter or the smell of cooking; in the mind of the poet these experiences are always forming new wholes.[24]

Of the poets called *metaphysical,* he writes, in a sentence from the same essay that seems half-consciously to echo Johnson on the necessity to read and think, "they were, at best, engaged in the task of trying to find the verbal equivalent for states of mind and feeling."[25] He draws some comparisons between French poetry and poetry in English, and returns to the physical body and the senses:

> Those who object to the "artificiality" of Milton or Dryden some-times tell us to "look into our hearts and write." But that is not look-ing deep enough; Racine or Donne looked into a good deal more than the heart. One must look into the cerebral cortex, the nervous system, and the digestive tracts.[26]

Is T. S. Eliot, then, a cognitive theorist *avant la lettre*? Does his invocation of the cerebral cortex and the nervous system suggest that he finds in Donne's work some hardwired connections or some metaphors to live by? I think his argument points in the reverse direction, toward the mind of the poet, not the poetry of the mind. Here is a passage from the essay in which he tries to explain how these poets use rhetorical figures in their work:

> Donne, and often Cowley, employ a device which is sometimes considered characteristically "metaphysical"; the elaboration (con-trasted with condensation) of a figure of speech to the farthest stage to which ingenuity can carry it. Thus Cowley develops the com-monplace comparison of the world to a chess-board through long stanzas *(To Destiny)*, and Donne, with more grace, in *A Valediction [Forbidding Mourning]*, the comparison of two lovers to a pair of compasses. But elsewhere we find, instead of the mere explication of the content of a comparison, a development by rapid association of thought which requires considerable agility on the part of the reader.

> On a round ball
> A workman that hath copies by, can lay
> An Europe, Afrique, and an Asia,
> And quickly make that, which was nothing, All,
> So doth each teare,
> Which thee doth weare,
> A globe, yea, world by that impression grow,
> Till thy tears mixt with mine doe overflow
> This world, by waters sent from thee, my heaven dissolved so.

Here we find at least two connexions which are not implicit in the first figure, but are forced upon it by the poet; from the geographer's glove to the tear, and the tear to the deluge. On the other hand, some of Donne's most successful and characteristic effects are secured by brief words and sudden contrasts:

> A bracelet of bright hair about the bone.

where the most powerful effect is produced by the sudden contrast of associations of "bright hair" and of "bone." This telescoping of images and multiplied associations is characteristic of the phrase of the dramatists of the period which Donne knew; not to mention Shakespeare, it is frequent in Middleton, Webster, and Tourneur, and is one of the sources of the vitality of their language.[27]

Eliot's interest is certainly in cognition, but it is the cognition of the poet and the reader. Notice his attention to a "development by rapid association of thought which requires considerable agility on the part of the reader." In this analysis, the reader does not exhibit the necessary agility because he or she has assimilated a conceptual metaphor like "Tears Are Globes" (or perhaps "The World Is Made of Tears"—needless to say both of these "concepts" are my fabrications, unauthorized and unsanctioned). Moreover, while "a bracelet of bright hair about the bone" could connect to any one of the thirteen metaphors about death listed in Lakoff and Turner's field guide to poetic metaphor ("Death Is a Devourer," "Death Is an Adversary," "Death Is a Reaper," "Death Is Darkness," etc.), its power lies precisely in eluding any such familiar conceptual categorization. It is not banal. It shocks with its unexpectedness, its precision, its physicality, its mise-en-scène, its alliterative B's that lead inexorably from *bracelet* to *bone,* its single adjective *(bright)* that seems at first to offer relief from the starkness of image and syntax but actually makes the verbal bridge between *bracelet* and *bone.* Historical research and cultural context—of a kind that is notable by its absence in Lakoff and Turner—would remind the reader that keepsakes made of woven or braided hair were common love tokens, so this macabre image is also, disturbingly, commonplace. Which is not to say that it is remotely ordinary.

In his poetry as well as his literary criticism T. S. Eliot engages this sense of the body—which is not the same as what cognitive theorists call embodiment or embodied cognition, since what intrigues Eliot is the specific writing of poetry, not the presumed universal response to it:

Webster was much possessed by death
And saw the skull beneath the skin;
And breastless creatures under ground
Leaned backward with a lipless grin.

   Daffodil bulbs instead of balls
Stared from the sockets of the eyes!
He knew that thought clings round dead limbs
Tightening its lusts and luxuries.

   Donne, I suppose, was such another
Who found no substitute for sense,
To seize and clutch and penetrate;
Expert beyond experience,

   He knew the anguish of the marrow
The ague of the skeleton;
No contact possible to flesh
Allayed the fever of the bone.[28]

These stanzas, from a poem called "Whispers of Immortality," might be catalogued under "Death Is an Adversary," "Death Is a Devourer," or,

I suppose, "Death Is Going to a Final Destination," but it is difficult to see how those "conceptual" categories would assist, in any way, to produce a subtle, nuanced reading of this (or indeed any) poem.

Hunting the Wild Metaphor

In their field guide, Lakoff and Turner mention no literary critics or theorists, no ancient or modern rhetoricians, no historical scholars, no periods or schools of poetry or literature, nothing at all to indicate that there is a tradition, thousands of years old, for the consideration of poetry, of rhetorical figures, of literary influence and literary resistance. Something called the "Great Chain Metaphor" is singled out for extensive discussion without any mention of works like Arthur O. Lovejoy's 1936 classic *The Great Chain of Being: A Study in the History of an Idea*, not to mention E. M. W. Tillyard's use of it in *The Elizabethan World Picture* (1940), or any of the several responses to Tillyard and to Lovejoy that have enlivened literary criticism and theory in the intervening years—nor to earlier articulations and discussions of this metaphor in the works of Dante, Boethius, Descartes, Spinoza, Leibniz, Pico della Mirandola, or the theory of the divine right of kings. What is the field to which this is a guide? The book's subtitle alludes not to any intellectual or disciplinary field but to the genre of handbooks or guidebooks used to assist the reader in identifying wildlife or other objects in nature: birds, plants, rocks, trees, insects, and so forth—a practical, browsable, publicly accessible handbook like Roger Tory Peterson's *Field Guide to the Birds of North America*. "Poetic metaphor" in Lakoff and Turner's guide is a "tool" that "allows us to understand ourselves and our world."[29] As for poets, they are "us," with a linked-in database of conceptual metaphors, into which their poems can be neatly docketed:

> Great poets can speak to us because they use the modes of thought we all possess. Using the capacities we all share, poets can illuminate our experience, explore the consequences of our beliefs, challenge the ways we think, and criticize our ideologies.[30]

Words like *we, us,* and *our,* when deployed in "philosophical" utterances, should probably come with a warning label, since they are both universalizing and coercive. Even in apparently open assertions where the specific nature of "our" experiences, ideologies, etc., is left to the reader, the claim is made that "we" all possess modes of thought that "respond" to the works of great poets. This claim is not made more convincing by the book's recurrent citation from a single translated volume of Sanskrit verse—mentioned, with textual examples, six different times in the text, presumably as a nod to the "universal" nature of poetic metaphor—or by a Navaho war god's horse song cited from an anthology of "poetries from Africa, America, Asia, Europe and Oceania."[31] In any case, it is a profoundly uninteresting claim from the point of view of literature.

About the horse song, the reader learns, in commentary on the (translated) line "My horse with a mane made of short rainbows," that "The structure of a rainbow, its band of curved lines, is mapped onto an arc of curved hair, and many rainbows onto many such arcs on the horse's mane. Such image-mapping prompts us to map our evaluation of the source domain onto the target. We know that rainbows are beautiful, special, inspiring, larger than life, almost mystic, and that seeing them makes us happy and awestruck. This knowledge is mapped onto what we know of the horse: it too is awe-inspiring, beautiful, larger than life, almost mystic."[32] Here is that troublesome *we* again—"we know that rainbows are beautiful, special, inspiring, larger than life, almost mystic." Well, maybe. It depends on the literary context and on the culture. A person familiar with the book of Genesis might have a different set of associations with the rainbow, as might an aficionado of leprechauns in Irish folklore, a reader of D. H. Lawrence, or a fan of Judy Garland. None of these associations would, presumably, be germane to the Navaho war god's song. But why should the reader believe that *we*, a transhistorical, transnational, transglobal *we*, "know" that rainbows are beautiful, special, make us happy etc., and that *therefore* this is a pertinent interpretation of a line of verse translated into English from a Navaho poem?

Having given us the line and these truisms about their own assumptions on the universal meaning of rainbows, the authors then quote a larger section of the translated poem (still with no indication of whether it is the entire poem or an excerpt, and with no notations about Navaho culture, the tradition of Navaho verse-making, or even the poem's date). "This line," they say, "comes from a poem containing a series of such image-mappings":

> My horse with a hoof like a striped agate,
> with his fetlock like a fine eagle plume:
> my horse whose legs are like quick lightning
> whose body is an eagle-plumed arrow:
> my horse whose tail is like a trailing black cloud.

Working without any context, a reader can still see some poetic elements here that repay discussion, like the repeated refrain beginning "my horse," the stripes that seem to characterize both rainbow and agate, the repetition of the eagle plume as a point of comparison, the triad of terms associated with storms and signs in the sky (rainbow, lightning, cloud), the progression from head to tail. But for the authors, these are all important because they are image maps, "prompts for us to perform mapping from one conventional image to another at the conceptual level."[33] What interests them is not the poem but what they think it tells them about the workings of the mind.

I say *the* mind because the stress is on "our ordinary comprehension of the world," a common reading of poetry that is not interested in individual poets, particular languages, historical time periods, or specific poems. This use of literature is like the use of a ladder or a yardstick, employed to reach or measure *something else*. Or, to adopt the image the authors propose, it is like the use of a map, but a satellite map from thousands of feet up in the air. From that distance, the maps of, say, Paris, Venice, and Las Vegas will have certain elements in common; indeed Las Vegas has both an Eiffel Tower and a Grand Canal.

When Macbeth's "Out, out, brief candle!" and Othello's "Put out the light, and then put out the light" speeches are offered as versions of the conceptual metaphor "Life Is a Flame," we are about as far from literary study as we can get while still using a word like *metaphor*. Of these great and complex lines it is not false to say that "the flame of the candle is the flame of life" and that "because life is conceived of as brief, the candle is called brief," but these clichés do not afford the reader any entry into the complexity or nuance of the speeches or the plays. "All our yesterdays have lighted fools the way to dusty death," although cited, goes uncommented upon, presumably covered by the "conceptual" phrase "Life Is a Flame." There is no mention of Lady Macbeth's sleepwalking scene, in which "she has light by her continually at her command," nor of Banquo's "there's husbandry in heaven, their candles are all out," nor of the scene after Duncan's death when "by the clock 'tis day / And yet dark night strangles the traveling lamp," nor, in *Othello,* of the role played by darkness, torches, or calls for light from the opening scene to the final one, from which the quoted speech is taken. The authors "use" literature, and from their point of view, presumably this use is not an abuse. What such work seeks to demonstrate, though, is that the language of poetry is assimilable to notions about workings of the ordinary everyday mind—*the* mind, an abstract universal made concretely universal through neuroscience.

Field Work

The title and the last pages of *More Than Cool Reason* refer to a conversation between Theseus and Hippolyta near the close of Shakespeare's *A Midsummer Night's Dream.* Theseus is described by Lakoff and Turner as taking "a position reminiscent of a literal meaning theorist, arguing that poets are like lovers and madmen: they are fanciful and therefore misperceive the truth." We might note that Theseus and Hippolyta have missed out on most of the imaginative action of the play, the world of the fairies, the transformation of Bottom into an ass, Puck's anointing of the lovers' eyes with the magical "love in idleness," and other crucial events; Shakespeare's play allows the audience in the theater, or the reader of the text, to regard this conversation between two highly placed and self-assured characters with some measure of comic irony. That Theseus and Hippolyta engage in an argument about the power of images that has animated literary studies since Plato, or that both participants in this dialogue are simultaneously right and wrong in their responses, does not fit into the declarative and prescriptive nature of *The Field Guide to Poetic Metaphor.* Again, there is no indication that any literary scholarship exists on any of these famous passages—indeed it is indicative of the level of regard with which the book holds literary scholarship that no critics or scholars are mentioned in these pages, and that the short list of further readings at the end of the book does not direct the reader to anything written by a literary critic. There is an index of metaphors and a general index but not an index of poems or poets: in the book's own metaphorical construction, the conceptual metaphor ("Form Is Motion," "Life Is a Fluid," "Time Is a Healer," "Staying Alive Is a Contest") is the tenor and the poetry merely the vehicle.

For whom is such a field guide intended or useful? According to its authors, "the book should . . . prove valuable to students and researchers in literature, linguistics, philosophy, psychology, anthropology, and cognitive science"—although they also note that they have "tried to write the book in a style accessible to undergraduates."[34] Accessible it may be, and since disciplines and uses vary widely, it might be useful to those studying cognition, philosophy, or the neuroscientific branches of psychology. In terms of literature, however, a handbook like this erases the history of literary scholarship and analysis, discounts the role of interpretation and reading, and above all, denies or resists the creative, transgressive, and excitingly unstable power of language. Reducing literature to concepts, even to conceptual metaphors, is a mode of appropriation that makes the literary disappear.

The 2003 afterword to Lakoff and Johnson's *Metaphors We Live By* included a section on "applications of metaphor theory" that attempted to put into context developments that had occurred in various fields since the book initially appeared. Here is how the Lakoff and Turner collaboration summarized the argument of *More Than Cool Reason:* "[M]etaphors in poetry are, for the most part, extensions and special cases of stable, conventional conceptual metaphors used in everyday thought and language. The metaphoric innovations of poets are shown thereby to consist not in the totally new creation of metaphoric thought but in the marshalling of already existing forms of metaphoric thought to form new extensions and combinations of old metaphoric mappings."[35]

This is actually not so different from what literary theorists have argued—except that the power dynamic is reversed, as is the purpose of making the argument. Where Lakoff and Turner locate the "existing forms of metaphoric thought" in "stable, conventional conceptual metaphors used in everyday thought and language," critics concerned with rhetoric and the powerful *instability* of language have asserted the primacy of literariness, the ungovernable mobility of tropes and figures of speech, and the inevitability of productive *misinterpretation* in the creative act of reading.

A First-Order Phenomenon

Literature is a first-order, not a second-order, phenomenon. It is not simply a clever kind of code developed by the mind to ensure that we all possess a mental Rolodex of figures enabling the nimble linking and blending of commonly held thoughts. It does not merely frame concepts or conceptual metaphors in pleasing or memorable phrases.[36] In other words, language *makes* meaning, or rather, meanings in the plural; it does not merely reflect it. Things that do not exist are often brilliantly brought to life through figures of speech, so that it is the figures that are primary, and the referents, the facts, that follow in their train. In large forms like mythology (or religion) and in smaller ones like individual figures or metaphors, concepts are created by the imaginative leaps that we call poetry or fiction or rhetoric. As Keats magnificently expressed it in one of his letters, "What the imagination seizes as Beauty must be truth—whether it existed before or not."[37] But for Lakoff and Turner, since "metaphors allow us to understand one domain of experience in terms of another . . . there must be some grounding, some concepts that are not completely understood via metaphor to serve as source domains." They offer a list of "source domains" that "are at least partly, if not totally, understood on their own terms: plants, departures, fire, sleep, locations, seeing, and so on." What is at stake is a difference in under-standing about the role and nature of language and figure. It is not that rhetorical theorists doubt the empirical existence of fire, sleep, plants, or departures, but that they do not find conceptual metaphors like "Love Is Fire," "Life Is Fire," "People Are Plants," "Human Death Is the Death of a Plant," or "Change of State Is Change of Location" to have anything to do with "the symbolic power of language" or the use of literature.[38]

The point is not that one view of the power and nature of metaphor is right and another one wrong—to the contrary. There are many uses for these analyses, and the emergence of cognitive linguistics and other areas of cognitive science have been productive as well as provocative. What I am suggesting instead is that this kind of analysis is profoundly unuseful for the interpretation of literature. The claim that imaginative creation needs to be "grounded" in something else—a turn of phrase that recalls the figure-ground conundrums of visual perception—is an empirical claim about the dependence of language and figure on the extra-literary existence of things in the world.

It might be helpful then to consider how these visual images strike the eye and the mind. The famous example of the Rubin vase, included by the Danish psychologist Edgar Rubin in his two-volume book *Visual Figures*, shows a vase in the center of a visual field. The eye sees either the vase as figure and the surrounding area as ground, or two symmetri-cal human profiles, one on the left and one on the right, with the area in the center as ground. Each visual interpretation is valid, but even though the viewer knows they are both present, only one can (ordinarily) be seen at a time. This kind of image (sometimes called an optical illu-sion) was widely influential for Gestalt psychology and also for visual artists of the period. If we take this image as a figure for *figure*, what we can learn from it is that the idea of a ground, in the empirical sense asserted by Lakoff and Turner ("there must be some grounding, some concepts that are not completely understood via metaphor to serve as source domains") depends upon the pre-determination of these undecidable entities: faces or vase? All language is figure, and figuration: it is the idea that we can see through language to encounter the real that is ultimately what might be called the conceptual illusion. Again, this is not to say that nothing is real, an empty claim as well as a foolish one, but that the real is perceived through language. Every act of language is a creative act of figuration, whether the figure is fresh and new or so familiar as to be undetectable (the so-called dead metaphor). Even dead metaphors are not dead, but sleeping, waiting to be awakened by a new poet, a naive speaker, or an inquisitive child. This is one of the sources of wit as well as wisdom that is "bodied forth" in *A Midsummer Night's Dream,* the play from which Lakoff and Turner take their title and to which we will now briefly return.

Misreading Theseus Misreading

The debate between Theseus and Hippolyta offers the literary critic an opportunity for a double reading of Theseus's lines:

> Such tricks hath strong imagination,
> That, if it would but apprehend some joy,
> It comprehends some bringer of that joy;
> Or in the night, imagining some fear,
> How easy is a bush suppos'd a bear! (5.1.18–22)

To suppose the bush a bear, to see or read it as a bear (in the night, in the darkness, in the dream world), is not, or not only, a mistake; it is also a true reading, for the moment, at least. This is the power of strong imagination, and if Theseus's tone is dismissive (like that of Lakoff and Turner's "literal meaning theorist"), his words are truer than he understands them to be: the frightening bush/bear is not a mistake, but a creative act.

The literary critic Rosalie Colie describes what she calls "unmetaphoring" in the work of Shakespeare and other writers, whose practice of "unmetaphoring and remetaphoring familiar literary clichés" creates "new forms and patterns to bequeath to successors."

> An author who treats a conventionalized figure of speech as if it were a description of actuality is unmetaphoring that figure. Shakespeare's quietly making the garden enclosed of virginal love the locus of Romeo's second exchange with Juliet or his transforming a standard prop in the tableaux of noble melancholy into the specific skull of a dead friend [in *Hamlet*] are examples of the sort I mean.[39]

Remetaphoring is, for Colie, in part a reminder by the poet that culture and literary tradition think through figures—not the "conceptual" figures of Lakoff and Turner but *literary* figures, the language "bequeathed" from poet to poet.[40]

"The best in this kind are but shadows," Theseus says to Hippolyta before they sit down to watch the play, explaining his forbearance with imperfect or unschooled performers, and in the play's epilogue, Puck will remind the audience that the actors they have been watching, as well as the denizens of fairyland, are "shadows," too. The fact that Theseus is a fiction—that these speculations on the power and limits of the imagination are spoken by a literary character imagined by a poet/playwright about whom much has been written and imagined—may gesture further toward the work of art as a *mise en abyme:* the frame within a frame, the dream within a dream, the play within a play, the door that opens only onto another door. Which is the figure and which is the ground? Which is the metaphor and which is the concept? Theseus may smile at the idea of a bush (mis)taken for a bear, but then he has not seen what the audience has seen: the "translated" Bottom, whose metaphorical status ("man is but an ass if he go about to expound this dream") is as powerful as his disconcertingly hybrid presence, half man, half beast ("methought I was—and methought I had"). Onstage Bottom is a walking and dreaming catachresis, a man with an ass's head. Would we call such an onstage representation "literal"? It is certainly an example of creative "unmetaphoring." The effect is to make the audience see something of the transformative—and dangerous—effect of figurative language.

Neither Theseus nor Hippolyta grasp the dimensions of this power, which is wielded in their play by the *other* royal pair, Oberon and Titania, the king and queen of fairies. Bottom's metaphorical identity as an ass is violently unmetaphored by Oberon so that his estranged queen will awaken to find herself in love with a monster. Titania seems perfectly content in this erotic space of fantasy—it is her husband who decides to "pity" her "dotage" and to restore her to ordinary sight ("My Oberon, what visions I have seen," she later reports. "Methought I was enamoured of an ass"). The wish and the unwish are both accomplished by the string-pulling Oberon, leaving Bottom unmoved and unscathed, ready to perform his part in yet another play, where yet another hybrid monster (a timorous amateur actor in a lion suit) menaces a young woman. As her histrionic lover, Bottom draws his sword and kills himself, to the amusement, rather than the horror, of the onstage audience watching the play:

BOTTOM [as Pyramus]: Now die, die, die, die, die.

DEMETRIUS: No die, but an ace for him; for he is but one.

LYSANDER: Less than an ace, man; for he is dead, he is nothing.

THESEUS: With the help of a surgeon he might yet recover, and prove an ass.

A Midsummer Night's Dream, 5.1.295–299

Ace and *ass* were pronounced the same in Shakespeare's time. Each was a "low" entity—the ass in the animal kingdom, the ace, the smallest number, so that Demetrius's pun on "die" (the singular of "dice" as well as a familiar Renaissance pun on sexual climax) trivializes both Bottom's language and the "death of Pyramus." These joking spectators have not encountered the transformed figure of Bottom as an ass, but—uncannily—they rename him as one. In other words, their joke unwittingly re-creates the metaphor, the "vision" of Bottom-is-an-ass. They don't know what they know. Their language speaks through them to us. But Lysander and Demetrius are themselves dramatic characters, literary creations. The profoundly trivial and yet astonishingly apt little conversation that we in the audience overhear offers us another insight into the many layers of this world of *Dream*. It is not because they are real that their words function in this dizzying way, but because they are figures: literary or dramatic figures speaking in figures of speech.

Language does change our world. It does make possible what we think and how we think it. This is one vital reason to read and study literature, rather than merely to apply its strategies. As for the conceptual metaphors, from "Life Is Fire" to "Death Is a Reaper"—perhaps we should look to the words of a former politician and rhetorical expert and ask what the meaning of *is* is.

Consider a wisely riddling observation by Harold Bloom from his powerful work of literary theory, *The Anxiety of Influence,* published in 1973 and subtitled *A Theory of Poetry*. "The meaning of a poem can only be another poem."[41] The argument is first set out in the context of a paragraph describing what Bloom calls "antithetical criticism," a term he develops from his reading of—and productive resistance to—his two great critical "precursors," Nietzsche and Freud.

> Antithetical criticism must begin by denying both tautology and reduction: a denial best delivered by the assertion that the meaning of a poem can only be a poem, but *another poem—a poem not itself.*[42]

"Tautology" is a version of what Cleanth Brooks called "paraphrase"; "reduction" is the idea that poetry conveys a message, a moral, or a theme. What Bloom proposes is what he observes in the literary tradition—that poems beget poems, that imaginative thinking produces imaginative thinking, that literature is what I have called a first-order phenomenon, not a conveyor belt for ideas that find their "impact," their "reality," or their "application" elsewhere.

Literature is figure.

NINE

The Impossibility of Closure

Because no interpretation of literature is "final" or "definitive," literary study, like literature, is a process rather than a product. If it progresses, it does so in a way that often involves doubling back upon a track or meandering by the wayside rather than forging ahead, relentlessly and single-mindedly, toward some imagined goal or solution. As we have noticed, one of the defining characteristics of literature and literary study is to open questions, not to close them. This has sometimes been regarded as a trait—as something that makes literature and literary study both unique and also "useless," in contrast with problem-solving disciplines like economics, political theory, or even certain branches of philosophy. And in an era when persistent questions about outcomes and impact have gained ascendancy for legislatures, educational researchers, and the public press, the absence of answers may look like a manifest failure either on the part of imaginative writers, or of critics and scholars, or of both. Hence some of the desire to convert passages of poetry or taglines from novels into social and ethical *doxa*: "Good fences make good neighbors"; "Only connect." Quotations like this, taken out of context, seem like useful advice, or wisdom.

Let me illustrate the difficulty about closure with a brief anecdote. Once, when I was lecturing to my Shakespeare class at Harvard, I decided to give them an object lesson in literary interpretation. I chose a famous crux from one of the plays and offered an extended "answer" to it. Students all over the lecture hall wrote busily in their notebooks. I then observed that although this answer once had been deemed satisfactory, it was no longer highly regarded by critics. All over the hall, students crossed out what they had written. I next offered a newer solution to the crux with the same set of results; students took down every word I said, then reacted with consternation when I remarked that this solution, too, had been questioned by subsequent critics. It took a third "solution" and a third qualification of that solution to begin to make the point, which was that literary interpretation is a conversation taking place over time and space, and that the really interesting questions do not have final answers.

Still, many students in the large introductory course left the lecture hall unsatisfied, frustrated, or worse. I had failed to convince them that such a method, if it could—in their eyes—be called a method, had value in and of itself. Why couldn't I just tell them what the real meaning of the play was, then move on to the meaning of the next? I was the professor; they were there to write down what was true. Since Shakespeare wrote so many years ago, scholars had had all this time to get it right, hadn't they? What was the problem, and why couldn't the professor give them the right answer right away, instead of beating around the bush?

The absence of answers or determinate meanings—that is to say, the *presence* of the qualities that make a passage or a work literary—has given rise to persistent misunderstandings, including many of the rather desperate attempts we have already noted to try to make the literary work useful by "applying" it to something else. Requests on the part of institutions, officials, and government agencies for information on impact and assessment are attempts to figure out what literary study does, or accomplishes, or proves, or solves. But such requests pose the question maladroitly from the perspective of literature, where in formal terms, the beginning and ending are part of the structure, and thus part of the internal process of self-questioning and revision that is at the heart of creative work. To put it another way, a key feature of what might be called the literary unconscious is a tendency on the part of the text to outwit or to confound the activity of closing or ending.

One of the most famous and most praised themes in literature— the idea that the work lives on beyond the life of the author and serves as both a memorial and a revivification—delights in subverting closure through the agency of the living word or the living voice.

So long as men can breathe or eyes can see,
So long lives this, and this gives life to thee.

Shakespeare, Sonnet 18

While there is not a perfect symmetry between the activity of criticism and the activity of writing, the bridge between the two is the reader. Reading and criticism are themselves creative acts, remaking the work: making it new, making it contemporary, making it personal, making it productively strange, and therefore endowing it with fresh and startling power.

Against Closure

Closure as a term has suffered some indignities over the last several years, as it has become a staple of pop psychology. Closure as a synonym for "a sense of personal resolution; a feeling that an emotionally difficult experience has been conclusively settled or accepted"[1] is a fairly recent addition to the lexicon, but it is all over the general media, whether the closure sought (or denied) is that of a surviving spouse, a bereft lover, a witness to a national calamity, or a soldier returned from war. Individuals who have never experienced psychotherapy or serious trauma now talk freely about needing, wanting, or getting closure, whether the closure they have in mind is their own or someone else's.

As we'll see, there is some connection between this wish to resolve or avoid trauma and the process that Freud called, in connection with his clinical practice, "analysis terminable and interminable." But getting to closure in the popular sense is really the antithesis of the experience of literary reading.

"My life closed twice before its close" is how Emily Dickinson began one of her poems. Contrary to what might at first seem to be the case, the poem is about non-closure, not closure, if it can be said to be "about" anything. The non-"about"-ness of literature, its refusal to be grounded or compromised by referentiality, is one of its distinguishing traits, perhaps the one most readily underestimated or disbelieved.

Perhaps my favorite non-ending ending is the last line of Wallace Stevens's poem "The Man on the Dump." Early in the poem, the speaker observes that "The dump is full / Of images," including "the janitor's poems / Of every day, the wrapper on the can of pears, / The cat in the paper-bag, the corset, the box / From Esthonia: the tiger chest, for tea." Here are the final lines, which begin by invoking the traditional bird of poetry, celebrated from Ovid to Keats to (with a twist) T. S. Eliot:

> Did the nightingale torture the ear,
> Pack the heart and scratch the mind? And does the ear
> Solace itself in peevish birds? Is it peace,
> Is it a philosopher's honeymoon, one finds
> On the dump? Is it to sit among mattresses of the dead,
> Bottles, pots, shoes and grass and murmur *aptest eve:*
> Is it to hear the blatter of grackles and say
> *Invisible priest;* is it to eject, to pull
> The day to pieces and cry *stanza my stone?*
> Where was it one first heard of the truth? The the.

The may be part of the philosopher's quest for truth, but it is also the beginning of a poem as well as an ending for one. The inevitable recursiveness of poetry, beginning at its end, ending at its beginning, is here gorgeously and economically evoked.

It was a commonplace of formalist literary criticism that poems were inescapably self-referential, that whatever their ostensible topic in the world, they also gestured, in an unmistakable and important way, toward their own shape and structure. The idea was that beginnings and endings mattered, that the poem or work would re-begin itself at the supposed "end." The poem might be imagined as taking the form of the ouroboros, the snake (or dragon) with its tail in its mouth, the ancient symbol of psychic continuity, or of eternal process, or of redemption, or of self-sufficiency, or of infinity. Its perfection (literally, its "finishedness") lay precisely in its capacity to indicate that in its beginning was its end, but also that in its end was its beginning.

We might look at some specific cases, to see how each folds in the material components of writing (or printing). Here are three examples of this poetic capacity, one having to do with rhyme, another with stanza form, and the third with punctuation. The first is from a magnificent short poem by George Herbert that takes poetic invention as its topic:

JORDAN (I)

Who says that fictions only and false hair
Become a verse? Is there in truth no beauty?
Is all good structure in a winding stair?
May no lines pass, except they do their duty
      Not to a true, but painted chair?

Is it no verse, except enchanted groves
And sudden arbours shadow coarse-spun lines?
Must purling streams refresh a lover's loves?
Must all be veiled while he that reads, divines,
      Catching the sense at two removes?

Shepherds are honest people; let them sing:
Riddle who list, for me, and pull for Prime:
I envy no man's nightingale or spring;
Nor let them punish me with loss of rhyme,
      Who plainly say, *My God, My King.*

Here we have a poem that purports to rail against poetry as a fiction, against "catching the sense at two removes," and against poets poetizing (and falsifying) themselves by calling themselves shepherds. The nightingale is a classical source of poetic inspiration, as is the Pierian spring of the Muses. But the witty (and ardent) denouement comes in the apparent abdication of earthly rhyme ("God" and "King" rhyme only in the sense that they are a perfect fit) while at the same time the final line *does* rhyme with "sing" and "spring," just as in the previous stanzas, the last line rhymes with lines 1 and 3 *(hair / stair / chair; groves/ loves/removes)*. Arguably, the imperfect aural chiming of these last three words sets up the question of rhyme-that-is-not-rhyme, and thus of its obverse, not-rhyme-that-is-rhyme.

It's characteristic of Herbert to use pairs of last lines as a way of turning the poem upside down and compelling a rereading, as he does, equally famously, in poems like "Love (III)" and "The Collar." In all these cases, ending, or closure, is a signal to the reader about self-reference, authorship, authority, continuity, and the place of poetry in the world, the mind, the church, and the heart. Closure is both necessary and impossible.

My second example is a sonnet by William Butler Yeats, an early poem that bears the indicative title "The Fascination of What's Difficult."

> The fascination of what's difficult
> Has dried the sap out of my veins, and rent
> Spontaneous joy and natural content
> Out of my heart. There's something ails our colt
> That must, as if it had not holy blood
> Nor on Olympus leaped from cloud to cloud,
> Shiver under the lash, strain, sweat and jolt
> As though it dragged road-metal. My curse on plays
> That have to be set up in fifty ways,
> On the day's war with every knave and dolt,
> Theatre business, management of men.
> I swear before the dawn comes round again
> I'll find the stable and pull out the bolt.

I said that the poem was a sonnet, but a count of the lines will come up one short for the traditional, canonical fourteen-line form. The rhyme scheme is unusual, too: *abba cc adda ee a,* which means that the poet has inserted two couplets (the verse form that, in the Shakespearean or English sonnet, is the emblem of closure) in the midst of the poem, producing a formal impossibility, a thirteen-line inside-out sonnet. The challenge of the first line, the fascination of what's difficult, is triumphantly displayed and achieved. At the same time the argument of the poem seems to rue the dailiness of work ("the day's war with every knave and dolt, / Theatre business, management of men") in a way that might even be glancing, sidelong, at the quotidian life of that earlier poet-playwright after whom the English sonnet form is named.

The third example is also from a modern poet, Robert Graves, in a poem that speaks directly to the question of closure. The poem's title is "Leaving the Rest Unsaid":

Finis, apparent on an earlier page,
With fallen obelisk for colophon,
Must this be here repeated?

Death has been ruefully announced
And to die once is death enough,
Be sure, for any life-time.

Must the book end, as you would end it,
With testamentary appendices
And graveyard indices?

But, no, I will not lay me down
To let your tearful music mar
The decent mystery of my progress.

So now, my solemn ones, leaving the rest unsaid,
Rising in air as on a gander's wing
At a careless comma,

Here the "life-time" and the book speak at once, or as one. The colophon, a typographical element placed at the end of a book or manuscript—sometimes in the form of a picture, sometimes an emblem—gives the title, the printer's name, and the dates and places of printing. An obelisk is a four-sided pillar or column, a common image for a colophon. But an obelisk is also, in the history of printing, a diacritical mark sometimes known as a dagger († or ‡), used for marginal references, footnotes, and so on. *The Indexer,* the journal of the Society of Indexers, noted at one point that "Suffixing a name by an obelisk . . . indicates that the person is dead."[2] The word *finis* (Latin *end*) was also formerly placed at the end of a book and from the literary or printers' use came to mean *end of life, death.*

First the book, then the life; first the finis, then the death. Graves, perfectly aware of his own resonant name, opts to end in the middle, with a "careless comma,": how "careless" the comma is may be debatable, but in this poem about closure, literary, typographical, and mortal, we encounter what amounts to a diacritical revolt. By closing the poem with a comma as well as with the word *comma* the poet fulfills the promise of his title by refusing to complete the verse line. Which is the figure? Literature, or life? As posed here, the question is undecidable, and in fact the question of decision, conclusion, or judgment (from *decider*, to cut or cut off) is suspended, as it were, in midair.

"Death is a displaced name for a linguistic predicament," wrote Paul de Man in an essay on autobiography, romanticism, epitaphs, and the poetry of Wordsworth. The phrase could be a somewhat fanciful but not entirely inaccurate replacement for the engraved motto *Et in Arcadia ego* on the shepherd's tomb in a celebrated painting by Poussin. The inscription has a famous double reading: "I [Death] am also in Arcady" is one possibility. But the other—as Erwin Panofsky marvelously demonstrated[3]—pulls in an opposite direction: "I [the dead shepherd buried in the tomb] once also lived in Arcady." Either "in the midst of life we are in death" or "death cannot erase the joys and accomplishments of living." Or, indeed, the pleasures of writing and reading, since the speaking tomb here is gestured toward, and deciphered, by shepherds who trace the letters, carefully, with their fingers. "Death is a displaced name for a linguistic predicament." There is something shocking, as well as something puzzling, about this apparently dispassionate statement. We might think that only an artist like Mark Tansey would inscribe such a thing on a tomb. The absence of a qualifying word like *only* or *just* heightens the shock value: the sentiment seems devoid of pathos. We are used to regarding death as "the thing itself," rather than as a figure for, much less a displacement of, something else. But in terms of that ambivalent thing called "closure," too readily applied to an emotional state and a literary and interpretive act, death is a displaced name for a *formal* predicament. Ending does not end.

Productive Tensions

In her book *Poetic Closure,* the literary critic and theorist Barbara Herrn-stein Smith wrote convincingly about the "tensions created by local deferments of resolution and evasions of expectation" that are derived from the experience of art. Writing in 1968, Smith was prescient about developments that were later to take place in the field of cognitive theory, suggesting that terms such as "tension" and "states of expectation" are "likely to appear naïve and become obsolete when the psychology and presumably the physiology of perception are better understood."[4] Such tensions and expectations formed the central argument of Freud's *Beyond the Pleasure Principle* (1920), which in turn provided a narrative arc for Peter Brooks's argument about narrative in his 1984 *Reading for the Plot.* Here is Brooks, reading Freud, and envisaging the writing and reading processes as patterns of vital and sexualized tension:

> Textual energy, all that is aroused into expectancy and possibility in a text, can become usable by plot only when it has been bound or formalized. It cannot otherwise be plotted in a course to significant discharge, which is what the pleasure principle is charged with doing . . . these formalizations and the recognitions they provoke may in some sense be painful: they create a delay, a postponement in the discharge of energy, a turning back from immediate pleasure, to ensure that the ultimate pleasurable discharge will be more complete. The most effective or, at the least, the most challenging texts may be those that are most delayed, most highly bound, most painful.[5]

When it first appeared, Brooks's influential argument about the structure of plot and the deferral of discharge attracted some attention from feminist scholars who saw the pattern he adumbrated as that of (singular) male orgasm rather than (multiple) female pleasure.[6] With or without this physiological substrate, the claim—made by Freud, Brooks, and a number of other theorists of narrative—was that the ending was both desired and withheld, and that the pleasure of waiting, of anticipation and of delay, was part of the pleasure of stories, storytelling, fiction, and plot. Freud's discussion, which focused in part on what he called the death drive or the death instinct in human behavior, drew the same kind of analogy between the "little death" of sexual orgasm and the Big One.

Roland Barthes makes a discussion of "la petite mort" and the experience of reading literature central to his own literary theory—and his theory of pleasure in and of the text. Here is an extended description by Barthes of what he nicely calls "these dilatory maneuvers, these endlessly receding projects," which, in his analysis, "may be writing itself."

> First of all, the work is never anything but the metabook (the temporary commentary) of a work to come which, *not being written*, becomes the work itself: Proust, Fourier never wrote anything but such a "Prospectus." Afterward, the work is never monumental: it is a *proposition* which each will come to saturate as he likes, as he can . . .

> Finally, the work is a (theatrical) *rehearsal*, and this rehearsal . . . is verbose, infinite, interlaced with commentaries, excursuses, shot through with other matters. In a word, the work is a tangle; its being is the *degree*, the step: a staircase that never stops.[7]

This "staircase that never stops" might remind us of Piranesi's prisons and dreamscapes, so evocatively described by Thomas de Quincey in his *Confessions of an Opium-Eater* (1820). De Quincey is reporting what he heard from his friend Coleridge, so this vivid description is actually secondhand.

> Creeping along the sides of the walls, you perceived a staircase; and upon it, groping his way upwards, was Piranesi himself: follow the stairs a little further, and you perceive it come to a sudden abrupt termination, without any balustrade, and allowing no step onwards to him who had reached the extremity, except into the depths below . . . But raise your eyes, and behold a second flight of stairs still higher: on which again Piranesi is perceived, but this time standing on the

very brink of the abyss. Again elevate your eye, and a still more aerial flight of stairs is beheld: and again is poor Piranesi busy on his aspiring labors: and so on, until the unfinished stairs and Piranesi both are lost in the upper gloom of the hall.[8]

We might compare this concretely imagined vision to the "unfinished" endlessness of literature and its interpretations. But before we turn directly to the experience of interpretation, it may be of interest to consider some other material evidence of the impossibility of closure *within* literary texts.

One consistent example is provided by Shakespeare, whose plays all close with gestures toward the future. Not merely the *idea* of the future but of *events*—like marriages and coronations and state funerals—that, while aimed at throughout the five acts of the play, will actually take place (if they do) in some future time beyond the boundaries of the performed (or scripted) play. Examples abound and are in fact found in every one of the plays. I'll list a few of the most obvious ones.

At the end of *Much Ado About Nothing,* Benedick suggests that the lovers "have a dance ere we are married," and although the old father Leonato urges, "We'll have dancing afterward" (5.4.118–119; 120) the marriages are not performed before the play ends.

At the end of *Twelfth Night,* Orsino says that he will marry Viola once he sees her in women's clothing (rather than in the boy's clothes she has adopted as a disguise). But the "other habits" in which he asks to see her before proclaiming her as his "mistress and his fancy's queen" (5.1.380) are not returned within the playing space of the drama, and the transformation and consequent marriage are deferred until after the fifth (and final) act.

At the end of *Macbeth,* Malcolm invites the Scottish nobles, now called earls rather than thanes, to see him crowned at Scone (5.9.41). But the scene does not shift to Scone or to the coronation: that event is predicted and expected but not acted, performed, or shown.

At the end of *Henry V,* when it seems every major kind of closure has been achieved—a war successfully waged, a bride successfully wooed—the chorus enters to remind the audience how brief was the victory and how profound the subsequent reversal. After a brief reign Henry V died, his infant son, badly counseled and ill equipped to govern, lost all the French territory that had been gained, and the nation was divided by civil war, "Which oft our stage hath shown" (Epilogue, 12). So instead of offering closure (either structural or cathartic), this play points backward to Shakespeare's earlier tetralogy, which told the story of Henry VI and the Wars of the Roses. Just when the story seems to be coming to a triumphant end, there is a vertiginous sense of loss and a metatheatrical injunction to go back to the beginning of the playwright's career. Closure in dramatic terms—as well as in history—is always a caesura rather than a period or full stop.

Renaissance playwrights, like modern ones, regularly rewrote speeches, scenes, and characters in response to audiences and critics, whether the audience was a single powerful monarch or a playhouse full of commoners. It's not only Shakespeare plays that help to make this point. The third act of Tennessee Williams's *Cat on a Hot Tin Roof* was extensively rewritten by the playwright, at the suggestion of director Elia Kazan. Both versions are printed in current editions, together with Williams's explanation for why he preferred the original script. The concept of the pre-Broadway tryout was developed to allow experimentation and change while a show was on the road. Film adaptations of novels, plays, or other films always make alterations, often significant ones, to the "original" text or script.

Nor have we yet mentioned what was perhaps the most striking nineteenth-century phenomenon of literary open-endedness: the serial writing and publication of novels, chapter by chapter, ongoing and in real time, rather than retrospectively after the novel was completed. As employed, and deployed, by creative masters of the form like Charles Dickens and Edith Wharton, this process generated remarkable acts of authorial invention, authorial forgetfulness, changes of mind, design, plot, and character personality, as well as responses to the reading public in medias res. Novels like Wharton's *The Age of Innocence* and *The House of Mirth* appeared in installments in periodicals prior to their publication in book form. Dickens's novels, from *The Pickwick Papers* to *Our Mutual Friend,* were all published serially—some in monthly installments, some weekly. The journals he founded, *Master Humphrey's Clock, Household Words,* and *All the Year Round,* were principal vehicles and venues for the publication of the novels, and they appeared punctually, in each case the author writing to a strict deadline. Dickens's last novel, *The Mystery of Edwin Drood,* was to be published in twelve— rather than the usual twenty—monthly installments, but he died after only six parts were written and released.[9] In this case, one kind of closure precluded another, leaving readers confronted with a genuine mystery, a story without an ending.

End Games

Closure is not quite synonymous with *ending:* it seems to imply a wrapping up, a completing of the circuit, a satisfaction (or relief) that puts the previous events, or text, or emotional experience, firmly if not always completely, comfortably in the past. Nonetheless, it is of some interest, historically and symptomatically, to see that the literary study of endings took on renewed energy and point in the 1960s, a time when the United States and its allies were preoccupied with the Vietnam War, when countercultures began to assert themselves, from issues of race and gender equality to sex, drugs, and rock and roll, and when literary criticism was on the verge of a theory revolution. In addition to Barbara Herrnstein Smith's *Poetic Closure* (1968), we might mention Frank Kermode's *The Sense of an Ending* (1966), subtitled *Studies in the Theory of Fiction,* which begins, deftly, with a chapter called "The End." Kermode is interested in ideas of the apocalypse, biblically and fictionally, even in the modern world:

> Men, like poets, rush "into the middest," *in medias res,* when they are born; they also die *in mediis rebus,* and to make sense of their space they need fictive concords with origins and ends, such as give meaning to lives and to poems.[10]

In literature, as Kermode goes on to suggest, variation and innovation are what make for interest: "We cannot, of course, be denied an end; it is one of the great charms of books that they have to end. But unless we are extremely naïve, as some apocalyptic sects are, we do not ask that the progress toward that end precisely as we have been given to believe. In fact we should expect only the most trivial work to conform to pre-existent types." Alluding to Wallace Stevens's great poem "Notes Toward a Supreme Fiction," Kermode adds, "the fictions must change, or if they are fixed, the interpretations must change."[11]

Another important book of this period, by the literary critic Edward Said, might seem at first to be the obverse of "the sense of an ending" or "how poems end," since its title is *Beginnings*. But Said's list of words and ideas that "hover about the concept of 'beginnings' " is also a list that has everything to do with the impossibility of closure: *innovation, novelty, originality, revolution, change, convention, tradition, period, authority*, and *influence*.[12] Said's study, as he explains in a preface to an edition released ten years after the first, was at least in part intended to "describe the immense effort that goes into historical retrospection as it set out to describe things from the beginning, *in history*."[13] So "beginning" itself is a concept viewed—and possibly constructed—retrospectively from some later position. In the end is the beginning.

Said ends his book about beginnings with some remarks about its relevance to literary scholarship. "A beginning," he says, "is what I think scholarship ought to see itself as, for in that light scholarship or criticism revitalizes itself." And "a beginning methodologically unites a practical need with a theory, an intention with a method." And again, "beginnings for the critic restructure and animate knowledge."[14] If we link this idea to Kermode's apt paraphrase of Wallace Stevens, "the fictions must change, or if they are fixed, the interpretations must change," we can ourselves begin to see that the activity of rebeginning, of making new, of revitalization is the work not only of the poet or the novelist but also of the literary critic, the literary theorist, and the literary reader.

That such new beginnings have social and cultural effects and motives is part of Said's argument. *Beginning*, he insists, is a very different concept from *origin:* "the latter divine, mythical, and privileged, the former secular, humanly produced, and ceaselessly re-examined." The work of critics writing in the years following the appearance of his book, he notes approvingly, engaged such topics as "the critique of domination, the re-examination of suppressed history (feminine, non-white, non-European, etc.), the cross-disciplinary interest in textuality, the notion of counter-memory and archive, the analysis of traditions . . . professions, disciplines and corporations," and the "social history of intellectual practices, from the manipulation and control of discourse to the representation of truth and 'the Other.'"[15] Citing some by name and others by the catchwords and phrases that had become associated with their work, Said thus argues that new beginnings were undertaken by theorists from Michel Foucault to Eric Hobsbawm to Jacques Lacan and Emmanuel Levinas. That some of the seminal work of these theorists appeared prior to the publication of *Beginnings* and was being newly read and put to new critical uses, presumably would have supported, rather than undercut, the central point.

"There are," suggests Jacques Derrida, "two interpretations of interpretation." The first "seeks to decipher, dreams of deciphering a truth and an origin." The other, "which is no longer turned toward the origin, affirms play," what he calls "the joyous affirmation of the play of the world," "the affirmation of a world of signs without fault, without truth, and without origin." The two kinds of interpretation, he says, were "absolutely irreconcilable even if we live them simultaneously."[16] Both are part of the history of the interpretation of literature and also of its practice. Arguably, they are not only co-extensive but also complementary. But it is the second that accords more directly with what I have called the literary.

We have already seen, in the chapter called "Why Literature Is Always Contemporary," that however deeply rooted in a particular time period a work may be, it is always being read in "the present," a shifting concept that is itself always open, never closed. The progressive tense of *being read* is a further tip-off, should we need one, since many readers may re-read, or re-consider, or re-discuss the novel, poem, or play in a class, in a reading group, upon revisiting the volume on a bookshelf, when a child or friend first encounters the same text, etc. If every production of a play is an interpretation, then so is every reading of that play. This is equally true for lyric poetry, for fiction, for sermons, for treatises, for political speeches, for any work in language that makes a claim upon our literary attention.

By *attention*, I mean to suggest not only a close analysis of language, rhetoric, grammar, figure, and argument but also the complex psychic process that has engaged the interest of modern-day observers from William James, Sigmund Freud, and Walter Benjamin to contemporary cognitive theorists. James defined attention as "taking possession by the mind, in clear and vivid form," and he opposed it to "the confused, dazed, scatterbrained state which in French is called *distraction*, and *Zerstreutheit* in German."[17]

Walter Benjamin addressed the question of *distraction*, which for James was the opposite of attention, and found in it an alternative modern mode of cognition: art and architecture, he thought, were apprehended "much less through rapt attention than by noticing the object in incidental fashion." Indeed, "reception in a state of distraction" was "increasing noticeably in all fields of art" and was "symptomatic of profound changes in apperception." But the preeminent modern genre for reception in a state of distraction was the film. At the movies, the public is put "in the position of the critic." But at the movies, "this position requires no attention."[18]

And yet "no attention" can also be a different *kind* of paying attention.

Freud, analyzing the dream state and the "preconscious," distinguished between the application of attention to issues of conscious thought and the ongoing processes by which "the train of thought which has . . . been initiated and dropped can continue to spin itself out without attention being drawn to it again, unless at some point or other it reaches a specially high degree of intensity which forces attention to it."[19] Such preconscious or unconscious rumination, the train of thought running, so to speak, on a side track until it is ready to rejoin the main line—is how much intellectual work takes place: distraction, or sleep, or dream, or any other apparent act of inattention often accomplishes what conscious attention cannot, in reframing or rephrasing the issue or problem in order to present a different kind of attack upon it. This is another instance of "the impossibility of closure." The way Freud describes a dream is closely analogous to how we might describe a work of literature, and the activity animating and energizing these mental artifacts or rebuses is what we have come to call, as in the English-language title of Freud's own great book on the topic, *interpretation.*

Interpreting Interpretation

In early use, *interpretation* was a term applied to religious scripture, to writing of all kinds, and to law, but over time it also came to apply to the decipherment of human character, the assessment of military information, the translation from one language to another, and the rendering of a musical, dramatic, or artistic composition (a song, a play, a landscape). It seems important to distinguish interpretation from definition or any other "conclusive" practice; as the examples of artwork, law, spy photographs, and linguistic translation all suggest in their different ways, interpretations can be motivated, personal, fallible, opinionated, compelling, insightful, and/or brilliant. They may also be time-bound or time-linked. Biblical or scriptural interpretation (and the secular editorial practices that followed from it) was frequently cumulative: an interpreter's views became part of the textual apparatus, to be read and interpreted, in turn, by those who came afterward. Biblical exegesis is one prevalent model for this practice, and it was, together with classical philology, the framework on which modern literary studies was based— and from which it has evolved. The expounding of an interpretation, once part of homiletics or preaching, is a matter of (learned) opinion, whether put forward by a cleric, a literary critic, or, as in the case of Freud and dream interpretation, a psychoanalyst. In any case, interpretation remains, as a practice, open-ended, always subject to revision, challenge, augmentation, change.

In 1937, long after the publication of his landmark *Interpretation of Dreams,* Freud wrote an essay that speaks even more directly to the question of closure. The essay's title, translated into English, was "Analysis Terminable and Interminable," and it is one of the few papers on technique that Freud published this late in his career (he died two years later, putting closure of a different kind on a remarkable lifetime of work). Freud was seeing few clinical patients then; almost all the analytic sessions he conducted were training analyses—that is, the analysis of other analysts.

What would be meant by the end of an analysis? Freud asked rhetorically, and he then proceeded to offer a range of possible answers. An analysis could be ended because the patient felt he was no longer experiencing symptoms, or because the analyst felt that "so much repressed material has been made conscious, so much that was unintelligible has been explained, that there is no need to fear a repetition of the pathological processes concerned."[20] But there was also what Freud called a more "ambitious" meaning to the end of the "end" of an analysis. "In this sense of it, what we are asking is whether the analyst has had such a far-reaching influence on the patient that no further change could be expected to take place in him if his analysis were continued. It is as though it were possible by means of analysis to attain to a level of absolute psychical normality—a level, moreover, which we could feel confident would be able to remain stable, as though, perhaps, we had succeeded in resolving every one of the patient's repressions and in filling all the gaps in his memory."[21]

There are so many differences between the psychoanalyst-patient relationship and the literary analyst–literary work relationship that it is easy to jettison the analogy completely. For one thing, why not imagine that the literary work is the analyst, rather than the patient? Surely it reads us as much as we read it. And even if we were to agree with the suggestion that there is something called "normality" attached to the psychic health of human beings, there seems no possible equivalent in the realm of literature, where works are, like Tolstoy's famous families, each, happily, unhappy in its own way. But the idea of repressed material and things that seem unintelligible does seem related to the kind of questions we ask of literary works.

Freud may help us out a little by proceeding, in his argument, to draw a textual analogy of his own as a way of describing what he means by repression. The analogy he offers ("though I know that in these matters analogies never carry us very far")[22] is one that may strike a modern readership with an uncanny familiarity, since it is the image of a book, a historical record, that has been defaced and blotted out like a security file. I will quote his long passage, which reads rather like a dream narrative:

> Let us imagine what might have happened to a book, at a time when books were not printed in editions but were written out individually. We will suppose that a book of this kind contained statements which in later times we regarded as undesirable—as, for instance, according to Robert Eisler (1929), the writings of Flavius Josephus must have contained passages about Jesus Christ which were offensive to later Christendom. At the present day, the only defensive mechanism to which the official censorship could resort would be to confiscate and destroy every copy of the whole edition. At that time, however, various methods were used for making the book innocuous. One way would be for the offending passages to be thickly crossed through so that they were illegible. In that case the book could not be transcribed, and the next copyist of the book would produce a text which was unexceptionable but which had gaps in certain passages, and so might be unintelligible in them. Another way, however, if the authorities were not satisfied with this, but wanted also to conceal any indication that the text had been mutilated, would be for them to proceed to distort the text. Single words would be left out or replaced by others, and new sentences interpolated. Best of all, the whole passage would be erased and a new one which said exactly the opposite put in place. The next transcriber could then produce a text that aroused no suspicion but which was falsified. It no longer contained what the author wanted to say; and it is highly probable that the corrections had not been made in the direction of truth.[23]

With this dispassionate and chilling, proto-Orwellian vision (*1984* would be written ten years later), Freud presents his analogy, one he wants to insist should not be pursued too strictly, between the operations of repression and the operations of literary censorship, forgery, and bowdlerized editing. The text conceals a secret, or a series of secrets, that have occurred as a result of a process of concealment. The censor is the pleasure principle, which does not want unpleasure to be experienced, and so overwrites, deletes, or defaces the text.

Can we use Freud's analogy to understand the way in which closure is both sought and deferred, claimed and mistaken, in literature and literary interpretation?

The objection that psychoanalysis is not like reading and writing is answered in a way by Freud's own text, which takes as its image for psychic repression or withholding the idea of a defaced or edited book. Although for Freud, the main topic is repression, and the image of the book occurs only as a comparison, a metaphor, or an illustration, the process he is describing can be turned on its head, since the image of unconscious rewriting is at once the story of literary history and the story of reading and interpretation. But where Freud is trying to account for a psychic economy of pleasure for the individual, an allegorical understanding of his analogy might point toward the inevitability of a reading and a writing that not only overwrites and defaces but also continues the editing process until it is newly "legible."

Writing on the Wall

When texts and authors bring this practice to consciousness, the activity of rewriting and defacement is not always or reliably in the direction of pleasure. The most striking example from George Orwell might not be *1984* but, rather, *Animal Farm,* in which the apparent victory of the animals over their human oppressors leads to the painting on a wall "in great white letters that could be read thirty yards away," the Seven Commandments that "would form an unalterable law by which all the animals on Animal Farm must live forever after." These were the commandments:

1. Whatever goes upon two legs is an enemy.
2. Whatever goes upon four legs, or has wings, is a friend.
3. No animal shall wear clothes.
4. No animal shall sleep in a bed.
5. No animal shall drink alcohol.
6. No animal shall kill any other animal.
7. All animals are equal.[24]

One by one, as these commandments are breached or broken by the animal leadership now in power, the commandments are mysteriously rewritten. Pigs begin to sleep in the beds left vacant by the previous human occupants, and the Fourth Commandment is found to say, "No animal shall sleep in a bed *with sheets*."[25] After false confessions of treason are forced from some of the animals and they are summarily executed, the Sixth Commandment is discovered to read, "No animal shall kill any other animal *without cause*."[26] When Napoleon, the tyrant pig, develops a taste for whiskey, the animals come to realize that they must have misremembered the Fifth Commandment: "there were two words that they had forgotten. Actually, the Commandment read, 'No animal shall drink alcohol *to excess*."[27] At the end of this truly disturbing "fairy story" (Orwell's subtitle for the book), when every ideal has been lost, the animals find that instead of the Seven Commandments, only one now appears on the wall, the commandment that most readers remember (though often not in context): "All animals are equal, but some animals are more equal than others."[28] The animals on the farm are bewildered: some, at least, believe that their own memories are faulty and that they have misread, or misremembered, or misunderstood the commandments.

Orwell's novel does supply some ironic closure, in the return of Animal Farm to its previous name, the Manor Farm, and the effective erasure of the entire rebellion and the brief-lived animal utopia. For an adult reader returning to this short novel so frequently taught to children, the untrustworthiness of writing is as disconcerting and as convincing as the untrustworthiness of man. (And since the novel is itself *written* and *read*—or *misread*—as a children's story, it provides an instance of the very process that it holds up to critique.)

Animal Farm was published in 1946. Six years later, there appeared another book about writing and unwriting on an animal farm, this time with a distinctly uplifting tone: E. B. White's *Charlotte's Web*. Written by a major contributor to *The New Yorker,* this "children's book" offered the story of a spider who labored to write messages in her web in order to save her friend Wilbur the pig from slaughter. From "Some Pig" to "Terrific" to "Radiant" and "Humble," the words that "magically" appeared in the web caught the attention of farmers, fairgoers, and the national media. "Right spang in the middle of the web there were the words 'Some Pig,' " Farmer Zuckerman tells his wife.

> "A miracle has happened and a sign has occurred here on earth, right on our farm, and we have no ordinary pig."
> "Well," said Mrs. Zuckerman, "it seems to me you're a little off. It seems to me we have no ordinary *spider.*"
> "Oh, no," said Zuckerman. "It's the pig that's unusual. It says so, right there in the middle of the web."[29]

It's not necessary to see *Charlotte's Web* as a deliberate response to *Animal Farm* in order to note the several connections between them: mysterious writing, a clueless pig hero rather than a manipulative pig tyrant and villain, a team of animals of various kinds working together, a frame story involving thoughtful rather than scheming humans. Both texts, to be sure, have formal closure: in Orwell's powerful satire, the pigs and men become visually indistinguishable ("The creatures outside looked from pig to man, and from man to pig, and from pig to man again, but already it was impossible to say which was which"),[30] while in White's book, despite the heroic death of Charlotte, her spider offspring live on, and so does Wilbur. "Mr. Zuckerman took fine care of Wilbur all the rest of his days, and the pig was often visited by friends and admirers, for nobody ever forgot the year of his triumph and the miracle of the web."[31] In Orwell, animals become more like men, to their detriment; in White, men become more like animals, to their benefit. What remains "open" rather than "closed" however, is not only the ambivalent power of writing but also the question of interpretation. Political satire? Children's story? Moral fable? Through the presence in both novels of the manifest theme of writing, reading, and interpretation, each becomes itself an allegory of the dangerous activity it describes and enacts.

This Möbius-strip structure—the shape of a surface with only one side that can be formed into a continuous loop—is a familiar image from modernist art and sculpture. It was a favorite, for example, of M. C. Escher, as well as a recurring presence in science fiction and time-travel narratives. This image goes back to ancient times, when it was associated, as we've seen, with the ouroboros, the serpent or dragon swallowing its own tail. Is this a figure of closure, or of its impossibility? The riddling form suggests that the answer to both is yes.

For a literary practice that turns this set of ideas and concepts to brilliant account, we might look to the works of Jorge Luis Borges. His short stories, essays, and parables render the sense of history, and literary history, a *mise en abyme* (or, as the title of his collection puts it, a labyrinth) in which ends and beginnings, befores and afters, are put in serious, witty, and profound question. The opening paragraph of "The Library of Babel" sounds strikingly similar to the Piranesi vision of staircases leading ever onward: "The universe (which others call the Library) is composed of an indefinite and perhaps infinite number of hexagonal galleries, with vast air shafts between, surrounded by very low railings. From any of the hexagons one can see, interminably, the upper and lower floors." Borges's compelling story, which has been seen to predict the vastness of the information network and has been subjected to a philosophical analysis by W. V. Quine, concludes with a meditation by the narrator:

> I say that it is not illogical to think that the world is infinite. Those who judge it to be limited postulate that in remote places the corridors and stairways and hexagons can conceivably come to an end—which is absurd. Those who imagine it to be without limit forget that

the possible number of books does have such a limit. I venture to suggest this solution to the ancient problem: *The Library is unlimited and cyclical.* If an eternal traveler were to cross it in any direction after centuries he would see that the same volumes were repeated in the same disorder (which, thus repeated, would be an order: the Order).[32]

As André Maurois comments, "in Borges' narratives the usual distinction between form and content virtually disappears, as does that between the world of literature and the world of the reader."[33] This does not necessarily mean that there *is* no distinction between them but, rather, that Borges plays with consummate skill upon the apparent differences. His stories end where they "ought" to begin; his narrators and heroes find themselves not only quoting other authors but, in the process, becoming them. In his works, characters discover that history copies literature and not the other way around. Here is a discourse—or, if you prefer, a fiction—of literature as a first-order phenomenon, offering readers a chance to rethink priorities, whether we understand "priority" to refer to chronology or to importance. Thus the short parable entitled "Everything and Nothing" closes with the voice of the Lord speaking from a whirlwind to a figure heretofore unidentified in the text: "I have dreamt the world as you dreamt your work, my Shakespeare, and among the forms in my dream are you, who like myself are many and no one."[34]

In Which Nothing Is Concluded

Samuel Johnson's *Rasselas* (1759), a philosophical romance about the pursuit of happiness, ends with a chapter titled "The Conclusion, in Which Nothing Is Concluded." The phrase seems apposite for Dr. Johnson's rather stoical account (the prince, his sister, and their philosopher friend decide that none of their wishes can be obtained, and resolve to return home). But it also strikes me as a fitting way to conclude my much more optimistic narrative.

We sometimes talk about literature and language in a figural way: for example, as an enfilade—doors opening onto other doors that open onto other doors; a vista that stretches out between rows of trees into the infinite distance—or a *mise en abyme*, a term from heraldry describing a shield that bears at its heart the image of another shield. Like the enfilade, the *mise en abyme* is an image not only for self-reflection within a literary work, but also, equally powerfully, for the process of reading, which is never-ending, always opening outward into another scene. The device itself tempts the eye and the mind to move beyond what it can see, to an imagined and imaginable space that is both a plurality of meanings and a future of thought.

Literary interpretation, like literature, does not seek answers or closure. A multiplicity of persuasive and well-argued "meanings" does not mean the death or loss of meaning, but rather the living presence of the literary work in culture, society, and the individual creative imagination. To say that closure is impossible is to acknowledge the richness and fecundity of both the reading and the writing process.

The use of literature begins here.

Notes

INTRODUCTION

1. National Endowment for the Arts, *Reading at Risk: A Study of Literary Reading in America* (Washington, D.C.: National Endowment for the Arts, June 2004), www .arts.gov; "Literary Reading in Dramatic Decline, According to National Endowment of the Arts Survey," National Endowment for the Arts, July 8, 2004, www .arts.gov.
2. *Reading at Risk*, ix–xii.
3. Ibid., 18.
4. Ibid., 2.
5. Ibid., vii.
6. Samuel Johnson, *Life of Milton*, in *Lives of the Poets* (New York: Henry Holt and Co., 1880), 38.
7. Maria Edgeworth, *Moral Tales for Young People* (London: Routledge, 1863), 179.
8. Sir Walter Scott, *The Lay of the Last Minstrel* (New York: C. S. Francis & Co., 1845), 16–17.
9. Oliver Goldsmith, *An Enquiry into the Present State of Polite Learning in Europe* (London: Dodsley, 1759).
10. Thomas A. Trollope, *What I Remember* (New York: Harper and Brothers, 1889), 3:131.
11. Harris Interactive Poll #37, conducted online within the United States between March 11 and March 18, 2008. 2,513 adults, aged eighteen and over, responded. Results released April 7, 2008.
12. "*A letter, a litter.* Une lettre, une ordure. On a équivoqué dans le cénacle de Joyce sur l'homophonie de ces mots en anglais." Jaques Lacan, "Le Seminaire sur 'La lettre volée,' " *Ecrits* (Paris: Seuil, 1966), 25. The actual reference in Joyce is slightly different from Lacan's recollection: "The letter! The litter!" (*Finnegans Wake* 93, l.23) and "type by tope, letter from litter, word at ward" (*FW* 615).
13. Emily Dickinson, letter to Colonel T. W. Higgonson, August 1870, in Martha Bianchi, *The Life and Letters of Emily Dickinson* (Boston and New York: Houghton Mifflin Co., 1924), 276.
14. A. E. Housman, "The Name and Nature of Poetry" (1933), in *The Name and Nature of Poetry and Other Selected Prose* (New York: New Amsterdam Books, 1961), 193.
15. John Keats, letter to J. H. Reynolds, February 3, 1818, in *Selected Letters of John Keats,* ed. Grant F. Scott (Cambridge, MA: Harvard University Press, 2002), 86–87.

16. Henry James, "The Art of Fiction," published in *Longman's Magazine 4* (September 1884) and reprinted in *Partial Portraits* (1888).

17. Matthew Arnold and Thomas Arnold, *Their Influence on English Education* (New York: Scribner, 1898), 104.

18. Adam Phillips, preface to *Promises, Promises: Essays on Psychoanalysis and Literature* (New York: Basic Books, 2001), xvii.

19. Ibid., 366.

20. Sir Philip Sidney, *Defence of Poesie*, ed. Dorothy M. Macardle (London and New York: Macmillan, 1962), 33.

21. Sidney, *Defence*, 15–16.

22. Roland Barthes, "Literature Today," in Barthes, *Critical Essays*, trans. Richard Howard (Evanston, IL: Northwestern University Press, 1972, 1985), 155–56.

23. Immanuel Kant, *Critique of Judgment*, trans. Werner S. Pluhar. *The Norton Anthology of Theory and Criticism*, ed. Vincent Leitch et al. (New York: Norton, 2001), 513, 514, 517, 519, and passim.

24. Barbara Herrnstein Smith, *Contingencies of Value: Alternative Perspectives for Critical Theory* (Cambridge, MA: Harvard University Press, 1988), 33.

25. Matthew Arnold, "The Function of Criticism at the Present Time." First delivered as a lecture at Oxford in 1864, revised and reprinted in 1865 and again in 1875. *The Norton Anthology of Theory and Criticism*, ed. Vincent Leitch et al. (New York: Norton, 2001), 824.

26. Matthew Arnold, "The Study of Poetry," in *Essays English and American*, vol. 28, ed. Charles W. Eliot (1880; New York: P. F. Collier and Son, 1910).

27. Ibid., 65.

28. Ibid., 90.

29. Ibid., 65.

30. James Abbott McNeill Whistler, *The Gentle Art of Making Enemies* (1890). This is not only Whistler's reply to Ruskin's calling his work "a pot of paint flung in the public's face" but also his explanation of why he titled the portrait of his mother *Arrangement in Grey and Black*. "What can or ought the public care about the identity of the portrait?"

31. Théophile Gautier, preface to *Mademoiselle de Maupin*, trans. Joanna Richardson (Harmondsworth, UK: Penguin, 1981), 35–36.

32. Ibid., 37.

33. Ibid., 39.

34. Oscar Wilde, preface to *The Picture of Dorian Gray* in *The Complete Works of Oscar Wilde* (New York: Harper and Row, 1989), 17.

35. Wilde, Letters to Vincent O'Sullivan and Chris Healy. Quoted in Richard Ellmann, *Oscar Wilde* (New York: Knopf, 1984, 1987), 532–33.

36. Ibid., 532.

37. Ibid., 51–52.

38. Theodor W. Adorno, *Aesthetic Theory*, trans. Robert Hullot-Kentor (Minneapolis: University of Minnesota Press, 1997), 236.

39. Adorno, *Aesthetic Theory*, 236–37.

40. Max Horkheimer and Theodor W. Adorno, *Dialectic of Enlightenment*, trans. John Cumming, in *The Norton Anthology of Theory and Criticism*, ed. Vincent B. Leitch, et al. (New York, Norton, 2001), 1239.

41. Raymond Williams, *Marxism and Literature* (Oxford: Oxford University Press, 1977, 1985), 47.

42. Ibid., 49.
43. Williams, *Marxism and Literature*, 51–53.
44. Articles on this topic appeared in every news venue. See, for example, Jack Slater, "How Obama Does the Things He Does: A Professor of Rhetoric Cracks the Candidate's Code." *Slate*, February 14, 2008. Stephanie Holmes, "Obama: Oratory and Originality," BBC News, November 19, 2008. "Era of Obama Rhetoric Is Over," editorial, *Washington Examiner*, June 17, 2010 (online).
45. Chávez's plan for book distribution echoes that of many U.S. cities, like "If All of Seattle Read the Same Book" or "One Book, One Chicago" programs that became popular in the 1990s and continue today.

ONE   *Use and Abuse*

1. Sir Philip Sidney, *Defence of Poesie*, ed. Dorothy M. Macardle (London and New York: Macmillan, 1962), 39.
2. Ibid.
3. Anthony Grafton, *Leon Battista Alberti: Master Builder of the Italian Renaissance* (Cambridge, MA: Harvard University Press, 2000), 31.
4. Alberti, Leon Battista, *The Use and Abuse of Books*, trans. Renée Neu Watkins (Prospect Heights, IL: Waveland Press, 1999), 17.
5. Ibid., 17–18.
6. Ibid., 18.
7. Ibid., 21.
8. The Malone Society is an extremely earnest and learned scholarly enterprise, named after the eighteenth-century editor of the first variorum edition of Shakespeare. Founded in 1906, the society publishes facsimiles of such little-known Renaissance plays as *Hengist, King of Kent*, and *The Wisest Have Their Fools About Them*. When the dance that now ends the annual academic conference was first devised, its originators saw the title as comical, an oxymoron or carnivalization, the equivalent of Shakeapeare's "hot ice and wondrous strange snow." The name has naturalized so much that my current graduate students see nothing unusual about it.
9. Alberti, *The Use and Abuse of Books*, 22.
10. Ibid.
11. Ibid., 23.
12. Ibid., 24.
13. Ibid., 28–29.
14. Ibid., 31.
15. Ibid., 33.
16. Ibid.
17. Ibid., 41.
18. Ibid., 42.
19. Ibid.
20. Ibid., 44.
21. Ibid., 50.
22. Ibid., 51.
23. Karl Marx, *Capital*, vol. 1, *The Process of Capitalist Production*, trans. Samuel Moore and Edward Aveling (New York: International Publishers, 1967), 87.

24. Alberti, *The Use and Abuse of Books*, 53.
25. Ibid., 52.
26. Friedrich Nietzsche, "The Utility and Liability of History," in *Unfashionable Observations*, trans. Richard T. Gray (Stanford: Stanford University Press, 1995), 87.
27. Ibid., 136–37.
28. Ibid., 100.
29. Ibid., 102.
30. Ibid., 167.
31. e. e. cummings, "Poem, or Beauty Hurts, Mr. Vinal," *Collected Poems* (New York: Harcourt, Brace). Cited in Norman Birkett, *The Use and Abuse of Reading* (Cambridge, UK: Cambridge University Press, 1951), 29.
32. Birkett, *The Use and Abuse of Reading*, 30–31.
33. Bacon, "Of Studies," in *The Essays of Francis Bacon*, ed. Clark Sutherland Northup (New York: Houghton Mifflin, 1908), 155.
34. Harold F. Brooks, *The Use and Abuse of Literary Criticism: An Inaugural Lecture Delivered at Birkbeck College 26th June 1974* (London: Ruddock, 1974), 3.
35. Ibid., 4.
36. Ibid., 5.
37. Ibid., 7.
38. Ibid., 8.
39. Ibid.
40. Ibid., 9.
41. Ibid.
42. Ibid., 10.
43. Ibid., 11.
44. Ibid., 16.
45. Ibid.
46. Ibid., 18.
47. Ibid., 20.
48. Ibid., 21.
49. Ibid., 25.
50. Ibid., 24.
51. Ibid., 25.
52. Ibid.
53. Hayden White, *Metahistory: The Historical Imagination in Nineteenth-Century Europe* (Baltimore and London: Johns Hopkins University Press, 1973), ix.
54. Clifford Geertz, *The Interpretation of Cultures* (New York: Basic Books, 1973), 452, 448–49.
55. Clifford Geertz, "Blurred Genres: The Reconfiguration of Social Thought," in *Local Knowledge: Further Essays in Interpretive Anthropology* (New York: 1983), 30.
56. Steven Mullaney, *The Place of the Stage: License, Play, and Power in Renaissance England* (Chicago and London: University of Chicago Press, 1988), x.
57. Stephen Greenblatt, "Invisible Bullets," in *Shakespearean Negotiations: The Circulation of Social Energy in Renaissance England* (Berkeley: University of California Press, 1988), 65.
58. J. Hillis Miller, "Narrative," in Frank Lentricchia and Thomas McLaughlin, eds., *Critical Terms for Literary Study*, 2nd ed. (Chicago and London: University of Chicago Press, 1995), 69.

59. Joyce Appleby, Lynn Hunt, and Margaret Jacob, *Telling the Truth About History* (New York and London: W. W. Norton, 1994), 231.
60. Ibid., 231–36.
61. Ibid., 232–33, quoting Elizabeth Deeds Ermarth, *Sequel to History: Postmodernism and the Crisis of Representational Time* (Princeton, N.J.: Princeton University Press, 1992), 212.
62. Literary critic Steven Mullaney offered in his contribution to this volume a view of the place of literary study that conveyed a sharp difference from where it might have been presumed to be in the 1970s and 1980s: "The literary is thus conceived neither as a separate and separable aesthetic realm nor as a mere product of culture—a reflection of ideas and ideologies produced elsewhere—but as one realm among many for the negotiation and production of social meaning, of historical subjects, and of the systems of power that at once enable and constrain those subjects." Steven Mullaney, "Discursive Forums, Cultural Practices: History and Anthropology in Literary Study," in *The Historic Turn in the Human Sciences*, ed. Terence J. McDonald (Ann Arbor: University of Michigan Press, 1996), 163.
63. McDonald, *The Historic Turn in the Human Sciences*, 1.
64. Roger Kimball, *Tenured Radicals: How Politics Has Corrupted Our Higher Education* (New York: Harper and Row, 1990), xi.

TWO *The Pleasures of the Canon*

1. *The Great Ideas: The University of Chicago and the Ideal of Liberal Education* 5, "Spreading the Gospel," University of Chicago Library Exhibition Catalogue.
2. For this example and much more in this vein, see Dwight Macdonald, "The Book-of-the-Millennium Club," *The New Yorker*, November 29, 1952. *The Complete Greek Tragedies* (University of Chicago Press) were edited by David Grene and Richmond Lattimore and included translations by Grene and Lattimore, as well as Robert Fitzgerald, William Arrowsmith, John Frederick Nims, and others.
3. Macdonald, "The Book-of-the-Millennium Club."
4. Robert M. Hutchins, preface to *The Great Conversation: The Substance of a Liberal Education* (Chicago: Encyclopaedia Britannica, 1952), xxv.
5. Macdonald, "The Book-of-the-Millennium Club."
6. Ibid.
7. Berlin took a saying from the Greek poet Archilochus ("The fox knows many things, but the hedgehog knows one big thing") and applied it to intellectual and cultural life, dividing writers and thinkers into hedgehogs, who view the world through a single defining idea (Plato, Lucretius, Dane, Pascal, Hegel, Dostoyevsky, Nietzsche, Ibsen, Proust), and foxes, who draw on a wide variety of experiences (Herodotus, Aristotle, Erasmus, Shakespeare, Montaigne, Molière, Goethe, Pushkin, Balzac, Joyce). Iaisah Berlin, *The Hedgehog and the Fox: An Essay on Tolstoy's View of History* (London: Weidenfeld & Nicolson, 1953).
8. Edward Albee, in William Flanagan, "The Art of Theater No. 4: Edward Albee," *The Paris Review* 39 (Fall 1966).
9. Kenji Oshino, "Fresh Woods and Pastures New," in "Convictions," *Slate*, March 16, 2008.
10. As one critic wrote about *Tristram Shandy*, "themes, ideas, or systems from all

sorts of places are bodily taken over and absorbed into the Sternean purposes of the work. It happens to *Hamlet* and *Don Quixote,* suggestively at first and then over-whelmingly: it happens to Rabelais, Swift, and Fielding; to the Church Fathers; and to learning so arcane that the standard edition of *Tristram Shandy* is over-whelmed by footnote descriptions of 'sources.' Such allusiveness makes fun of itself, and we are continually made aware of becoming the pedant who sees all, recognizes all, systematizes all." J. Paul Hunter, "Response as Reformation: *Tristram Shandy* and the Art of Interruption," *Novel* 4 (1971), 132–46.

11. T. S. Eliot, *The Complete Poems and Plays* (New York: Harcourt, 1934), 50.
12. William Prynne, *Histriomastix* (1633), f. 566; John Aubrey, *Natural History and Antiquities of Surrey* (1718–19), 1:190. E. K. Chambers, *The Elizabethan Stage* (Oxford: Clarendon Press, 1923), 3:423–24.
13. Cf. W. Jackson Bate, *The Burden of the Past and the English Poet* (Cambridge, MA: Belknap Press, 1970); Harold Bloom, *The Anxiety of Influence: A Theory of Poetry* (New York: Oxford University Press, 1973); Sandra M. Gilbert and Susan Gubar, *The Madwoman in the Attic: The Woman Writer and the Nineteenth Century Literary Imagination* (New Haven: Yale University Press, 1979); Harold Bloom, *The Western Canon: The Books and School of the Ages* (New York: Harcourt Brace, 1994), etc.
14. *Oxford English Dictionary:* canon 2.3, "A standard of judgment or authority; a test, criterion, means of discrimination."

THREE   *What Isn't Literature*

1. Fredric Wertham, *Seduction of the Innocent* (New York and Toronto: Rinehart and Company, 1954), 15.
2. Ibid., 22.
3. Charles and Mary Lamb, *Tales from Shakespeare* (1807; London: Dent, 1961), 141.
4. Wertham, *Seduction,* 143.
5. Jan Baetens, ed., *The Graphic Novel* (Leuven: Leuven University Press, 2001), 8.
6. Charles McGrath, "Not Funnies," *The New York Times,* July 11, 2004.
7. "All-TIME 100 Novels," selected by Lev Grossman and Richard Lacayo, www.time.com/2005/100books/the_complete_list.html.
8. George Gene Gustines, "A Superhero in a Prism, Antiheroes in Deep Focus," *The New York Times,* July 31, 2009.
9. Wertham, *Seduction of the Innocent,* 121.
10. See, for example, Mark Rose, *Authors and Owners* (Cambridge, MA: Harvard University Press, 1993); John Guillory, *Cultural Capital* (Chicago: University of Chicago Press, 1993); Thomas Docherty, *Criticism and Modernity* (Oxford: Oxford University Press, 1999); Lee Morrissey, *The Constitution of Literature: Literacy, Democracy, and Early English Literary Criticism* (Stanford: Stanford University Press, 2008).
11. *Letters of Thomas Bodley to Thomas James, First Keeper of the Bodleian Library,* ed. G. W. Wheeler (Oxford: Oxford University Press, 1926), 219.
12. *The Ephemera Journal* 12 (April 2008).
13. "[The] notion that writing endows the oral with materiality is another facet of the collector's interest in establishing the ephemerality of the oral, and interest that puts

the oral in urgent need of rescue. In other words, the writing of oral genres always results in a residue of lost context and lost presence that literary culture . . . imbues with a sense of nostalgia and even regret." Susan Stewart, "Scandals of the Ballad," in *Crimes of Writing: Problems in the Containment of Representation* (Oxford: Oxford University Press, 1991), 104.

14. "Sibyl with Guitar," *Time*, November 23, 1962. Cited in John Burgess, "Francis James Child," *Harvard* magazine, May–June 2006, 52.
15. Stewart, "Scandals of the Ballad," in *Crimes of Writing*, 102–3.
16. Ernst, in *United States* v. *One Book called "Ulysses,"* 5 F. Supp. 182 (Southern District of New York, 1933). In James Joyce, *Ulysses* (New York: Random House, 1946), xi.
17. Ibid., xii.
18. Ibid., xiii–xix.
19. Gerald Gunther, *Learned Hand: The Man and the Judge* (New York: Knopf, 1994), 338.
20. *United States* v. *One Book called "Ulysses,"* xi–xii.
21. Ibid., xii.
22. Ibid., xiv.
23. Marjorie Heins, *Not in Front of the Children: "Indecency," Censorship, and the Innocence of Youth* (New York: Hill and Wang, 2001), 40–41; Paul Vanderham, *James Joyce and Censorship: The Trials of* Ulysses (New York: NYU Press, 1998), 32–34; Margaret Anderson, *My Thirty Years' War* (New York: Horizon, 1969), 174–75.
24. Mervyn Griffith-Jones, lead prosecutor, opening address to the jury, October 20, 1961. C. H. Rolph, ed., *The Trial of Lady Chatterley* (London: Penguin, 1961), 17.
25. Ernst, in *Ulysses*, viii.
26. James Douglas, "A Book That Must Be Suppressed," *Sunday Express*, August 19, 1928.
27. Sally Cline, *Radclyffe-Hall: A Woman Called John* (Woodstock: Overlook Press, 1998), 248–49.
28. Virginia Woolf, *The Diary of Virginia Woolf,* ed. Anne Olivier Bell (New York: Harcourt Brace, 1980), 3:193, entry August 31, 1928.
29. Woolf, *Diary* 3:206–7 and n., entry November 10, 1928.
30. Quoted in Leslie A. Taylor, " 'I Made Up My Mind to Get It': The American Trial of *The Well of Loneliness*, New York City, 1928–1929," *Journal of the History of Sexuality* 10 (2): 250–86.
31. See Charles Rembar, *The End of Obscenity* (New York: Harper and Row, 1986), 476.
32. Justice Tom Clark, Dissenting Opinion in "A Book Named 'John Cleland's Memoirs of a Woman of Pleasure' v. Attorney General of Massachusetts," 383. U.S. 416, March 21, 1966.
33. Rembar, *The End of Obscenity*, 481.
34. "Decency Squabble," *Time*, March 31, 1930.
35. See, for example, Perry L. Glantzer, "In Defense of Harry . . . But Not His Defenders: Beyond Censorship to Justice," *The English Journal* 93, no. 4 (March 2004), 58–63; Jennifer Russuck, "Banned Books: A Study of Censorship," *The English Journal* 86, no. 2 (February 1997), 67–70; and Nicholas J. Karolides, Margaret Blas, and Dawn B. Sova, *100 Banned Books: Censorship Histories of World Literature* (New York: Checkmark Books, 1999), 274, 365.
36. Robert Louis Stevenson, "Samuel Pepys," in *Essays: English and American*, The Harvard Classics (1909–14). (New York: Collier, 1910), vol. 28.

37. Virginia Woolf, "Montaigne," in *The Common Reader: First Series*, 1925 (New York: Harcourt Brace, 1984), 58.

38. Meyer Levin, "Life in the Secret Annex," *The New York Times Book Review*, June 15, 1952.

39. Theodor W. Adorno, "The Meaning of Working Through the Past," in *Critical Models* (New York: Columbia University Press, 1998), 101.

40. Cynthia Ozick, "Who Owns Anne Frank?," *The New Yorker*, October 6, 1997, 76, reprinted in Ozick, *Quarrel & Quandary* (New York: Vintage, 2000), 77. See also Frank Rich, "Betrayed by Broadway," *The New York Times*, September 17, 1995; Lawrence Graver, *An Obsession with Anne Frank: Meyer Levin and the Diary* (Berkeley: University of California Press, 1995); Ralph Melnick, *The Stolen Legacy of Anne Frank* (New Haven: Yale University Press, 1997); Lawrence Langer, "Anne Frank Revisited," in *Using and Abusing the Holocaust* (Bloomington: Indiana University Press, 2006); Bruno Bettelheim, "The Ignored Lesson of Anne Frank," *Harper's* (November 1960), 45–50.

41. Karen Spector and Stephanie Jones, "Constructing Anne Frank: Critical Literacy and the Holocaust in Eighth-Grade English," *Journal of Adolescent & Adult Literacy* 51, no. 1 (September 2007), 36–48.

42. See, for example, Roger Rosenblatt, "Anne Frank," in *The Time 100*, June 14, 1999. "The reason for her immortality was basically literary. She was an extraordinarily good writer, for any age. . . ." And "It is the cry of the Jew in the attic, but it is also the cry of the 20th century mind."

43. Thomas Bowdler, the English physician who produced *The Family Shakespeare* (from 1807 to 1810), though often caricatured as a repressed Victorian who dared to alter a classic, was praised by some later readers, including the poet Swinburne, as someone who had performed a service to Shakespeare by making it possible for children to read his plays.

44. Francine Prose raises the question of whether the diary has even "been taken seriously as literature," speculating that the failure to give Anne Frank her due as a writer may derive from the fact that the book is a diary, "or, more likely, because its author was a girl." Prose, *Anne Frank: The Book, the Life, the Afterlife* (New York: HarperCollins, 2009), 7.

45. T. S. Eliot, "The Metaphysical Poets," in *Selected Essays* (New York: Harcourt, Brace, and World, 1932, 1960), 248.

46. *The Cambridge History of English and American Literature*, eds. A. W. Ward, A. R. Waller, W. P. Trent, J. Erskine, S. P. Sherman, and C. Van Doren (New York: G.P. Putnam's Sons, 1907–21), vol. 2, section 7, part 4, 165.

47. John Dryden, preface to *Fables Ancient and Modern* (1700), in *Selected Works of John Dryden*, ed. William Frost (New York: Holt, Rinehart and Winston, 1962), 398.

48. Ibid., 404–5.

49. Ibid., 405–6.

50. Washington Irving, *The Life of Oliver Goldsmith* (New York: John W. Lovell, 1849), 182.

51. Ibid.

52. James Boswell, *Life of Johnson* (London and New York: Oxford University Press, 1965), 751–52.

53. Henry James, "The Birthplace," in *Selected Short Stories* (New York: Rinehart, 1955), 246.

54. "Chatterton, the marvellous Boy / The sleepless Soul that perished in its pride." William Wordsworth, "Resolution and Independence" (43–44), in *William Wordsworth: Selected Poems,* ed. Stephen Gill (London: Penguin Books, 2004), 139.

55. Benjamin Bailey, quoted in Walter Jackson Bate, *John Keats* (Cambridge, MA: Harvard University Press, 1963), 216.

56. W. W. Skeat, *The Poetical Works of Thomas Chatterton* (London: Bell and Daldy, 1871), 1: Preface, xi.

57. Boswell, *Life of Johnson,* 579.

58. Blair, an important figure in the Scottish Enlightenment, had a big influence on education in the United States. He maintained that the chief use of literature was to enable upward mobility in society and to promote morality and virtue, and his lectures on rhetoric and belles lettres were often reprinted and used by universities like Yale and Harvard, where the idea of self-improvement through eloquence and literary study found a hospitable home in the nineteenth century.

59. Stanley Fish, "How to Recognize a Poem When You See One," in *Is There a Text in This Class?: The Authority of Interpretive Communities* (Cambridge, MA: Harvard University Press, 1980), 327.

60. Stanley Fish, "Interpreting the *Variorum,*" in Fish, *Is There a Text in This Class?,* 167–73. Originally published in *Critical Inquiry* 2, no. 3 (Spring 1976), 465–85.

61. I. A. Richards, *Practical Criticism: A Study of Literary Judgment* (New York: Harcourt Brace & World, 1929).

62. Online syllabus of Professor Anthony Ubelhor, Department of English, University of Kentucky, www.uky.edu.

63. Allan Bloom, *The Closing of the American Mind: How Higher Education Has Failed Democracy and Impoverished the Souls of Today's Students* (New York: Simon & Schuster, 1987), 374.

64. Michel Foucault, "What Is an Author?," in *Language, Counter-Memory, Practice,* ed. Donald F. Bouchard, trans. Donald F. Bouchard and Sherry Simon (Ithaca, NY: Cornell University Press, 1977), 131.

65. Ibid., 132.

66. Ibid., 131.

67. Peter Brooks, *Reading for the Plot: Design and Intention in Narrative* (New York: Alfred A. Knopf, 1984). "Freud's Masterplot" was originally published in *Yale French Studies* 55/56. *Literature and Psychoanalysis. The Question of Reading: Otherwise* (1977), 280–300.

FOUR   *What's Love Got to Do with It?*

1. Andrew Dickson White, *Autobiography* (New York: Century Company, 1907), 1:364, cited in Henry W. Simon, *The Reading of Shakespeare in American Schools and Colleges* (New York: Simon & Schuster, 1932), 47.

2. John Fulton, *Memoirs of Frederick A. P. Barnard, Tenth President of Columbia College in the City of New York* (New York: Macmillan, 1896), 36. Cited in Simon, 47.

3. Charles W. Eliot, *The Man and His Beliefs* (New York: Harper, 1926), 1:212–13. Cited in Simon, *The Reading of Shakespeare,* 48.

4. Simon, *The Reading of Shakespeare in American Schools and Colleges,* 47.

5. Jane Austen, *Mansfield Park* (London and New York: Penguin, 1985), 334–35.

6. Jane Austen, *Persuasion* (London and New York: Penguin, 1985), 192, 178.

7. U.S. Department of Education Statistics; Modern Language Association; Association of Departments of English. I am grateful to David Laurence, the director of the MLA Office of Research and ADE, for helping me to locate this information.

8. R. P. Blackmur, "A Critic's Job of Work," in *Form and Value in Modern Poetry* (Garden City, NY: Doubleday Anchor, 1957), 339.

9. Ibid., 341.

10. Ibid., 367.

11. Ibid., 339.

12. Ibid., 343.

13. Ibid., 353. My emphasis.

14. In Marjorie Garber, *Academic Instincts* (Princeton, NJ: Princeton University Press, 2001), 3–51.

15. Burke never completed college, though he taught in several as a lecturer and visiting professor; Wilson, an influential editor and book reviewer, had a major hand in developing popular appreciation for several important American novelists, and in his own essays and books helped shape twentieth-century literary taste.

16. Edmund Wilson, *The Fruits of the MLA* (New York: New York Review, 1968), 20.

17. Modern Language Association of America, *Professional Standards and American Editions: A Response to Edmund Wilson* (New York: Modern Language Association of America, 1969), book epigraph.

18. Wilson, *Fruits*, 35.

19. Wilson, *Fruits*, 10.

20. Lewis Mumford, "Emerson Behind Barbed Wire," *The New York Review of Books*, January 18, 1968, 3–5, 23.

21. Wilson, *Fruits*, 4, 6–7.

22. Ibid., 7.

23. Ibid., 8.

24. Ibid., 13.

25. Ibid., 20.

26. Ibid., 38.

27. Ibid., 8.

28. Ibid.,17.

29. Ibid., 19.

30. John H. Fisher, "The MLA Editions of Major American Authors," in *Professional Standards*, 25.

31. *The Divine Comedy of Dante Alighieri*, trans. Allen Mandelbaum (Berkeley: University of California Press, 1980), 44.

32. Virginia Woolf, "How Should One Read a Book?," *The Second Common Reader*, ed. Andrew McNeillie (New York: Harcourt, Brace and Company, 1986), 270. Originally published in *The Yale Review*, 1926.

33. Ibid.

34. Andrew McNeillie, introduction to *The Common Reader, First Series*, xi; Woolf, *Diary*, May 23, 1921.

35. Samuel Johnson, "Life of Gray," in *Lives of the English Poets* (New York: Everyman, 1968), 2:388–89.

36. Ibid., 392.

37. Virginia Woolf, "William Hazlitt," in *The Second Common Reader*, 179.

38. Ibid., 182.

39. Ibid., 183. The Hazlitt passage is from "On Old English Writers and Speakers," in *The Complete Works of William Hazlitt,* ed. P. P. Howe (London: Dent, 1930), 2: 292–93.

40. Virginia Woolf, *New York Herald Tribune,* September 7, 1930; *Times Literary Supplement,* September 18, 1930.

41. William Hazlitt, "On the Pleasure of Hating," in *The Plain Speaker: The Key Essays,* ed. Duncan Wu (Oxford: Blackwell, 1998), 102–13.

42. Ibid., 104.

43. Sigmund Freud, *The Interpretation of Dreams,* vol. 4, *The Standard Edition of the Complete Psychological Works of Sigmund Freud,* trans. and ed. James Strachey (London: Hogarth Press and the Institute of Psycho-Analysis, 1955), 264.

44. Freud, "Creative Writers and Day-Dreaming," in *Standard Edition,* vol. 9, 143–53. Delivered as a lecture in the rooms of Hugo Heller, December 6, 107. Reported in *Die Ziet* the following day, full text published in a "newly established Berlin literary periodical" in 1908.

45. Ibid., 152–53.

FIVE   *So You Want to Read a Poem*

1. George Puttenham, *The Art of English Poesy* (1589), ed. Frank Whigham and Wayne A. Rebhorn (Ithaca, NY: Cornell University Press, 2007), 311.

2. Freud, *The Interpretation of Dreams,* vol. 4, *The Standard Edition of the Complete Psychological Works of Sigmund Freud,* trans. and ed. James Strachey (London: Hogarth Press and the Institute of Psycho-Analysis, 1955), 525.

3. Cleanth Brooks, "The Heresy of Paraphrase," in *The Well-Wrought Urn* (New York: Harcourt, Brace, 1947); in *The Norton Anthology of Criticism and Theory,* ed. Vincent Leitch et al. (New York: Norton, 2001), 1,356.

4. Ibid., 1,357.

5. Ibid., 1365.

6. Ibid., 1,362.

7. Cleanth Brooks, "The Formalist Critics," *The Kenyon Review* 13, no. 1 (Winter 1951), 72.

8. Cleanth Brooks, "The Heresy of Paraphrase," 1,368.

9. Ibid., 1,369.

10. Ibid., 1,370.

11. Ibid., 1,371.

12. See Steve Ellis, "The Punctuation of 'In a Station of the Metro,'" in *Paidenma* 17:2–3 (Fall/Winter 1988) for a specific account.

13. For this and other terms within "genetic criticism," see Jed Deppman, Daniel Ferrer, and Michael Grodin, eds., *Genetic Criticism: Texts and Avant-Textes* (Philadelphia: University of Pennsylvania Press, 2004).

14. Ezra Pound, *Gaudier-Brzeka,* 1916 (New York: New Directions, 1974), 89.

15. "Beyond a native poetics, there is something Eastern behind the Western surface . . . Confucius complements Homer . . ." Kenneth Lincoln, *Sing with the Heart of a Bear: Fusions of Native and American Poetry, 1980–1999* (Berkeley: University of California Press, 2000), 57.

16. Rachel Blau Duplessis, *Genders, Races, and Religious Cultures in Modern American Poetry, 1908–1934* (Cambridge, UK: Cambridge University Press, 2001), 35.

17. Samuel Taylor Coleridge, *Table Talk* (London: George Routledge and Sons, 1884), 63.
18. C. S. Lewis, "Hamlet: The Prince or the Poem," *Proceedings of the British Academy* 28 (Oxford University Press). Reprinted in Alvin B. Kernan, *Modern Shakespearean Criticism* (New York: Harcourt, Brace, Jovanovich, 1970), 301–11.
19. Reuben A. Brower, "Reading in Slow Motion," in Brower and Richard Poirier, *In Defense of Reading: A Reader's Approach to Literary Criticism* (New York: E. P. Dutton, 1962), 3–21.
20. Paul de Man, "The Return to Philology," in *The Resistance to Theory* (Minneapolis: University of Minnesota Press, 1986), 23–24.
21. Ibid., 24.
22. For an excellent analysis of this problem, see Jane Gallop, "The Historicization of Literary Studies and the Fate of Close Reading," *Profession* (2007), 181–86.
23. As George Puttenham writes in what his modern editors call "the core fantasy" of his treatise *The Art of English Poesy*, his objective in describing poetry, metrical forms, and "poetical ornament" (that is, figures of speech) was to "have appareled him to our seeming in all his gorgeous habiliments, and pulling him first from the cart to the school, and from thence to the court, and preferring him to your Majesty's service, in that place of great honor and magnificence to give entertainment to princes, ladies of honor, gentlewomen, and gentlemen, and by his many modes of skill to serve the many humors of men . . ." The "Majesty" here being addressed is Queen Elizabeth, at whose court reputations—and fortunes—were indeed made and unmade, depending upon royal favor. George Puttenham, *The Art of English Poesy: A Critical Edition*, eds. Frank Whigham and Wayne A. Rebhorn (Ithaca, NY, and London: Cornell University Press, 2007), 1, 378.
24. John Strype, *Memorials of the Most Reverend Father in God Thomas Cranmer*, 2 vols. (London, 1853), 1:129. Cited in Whigham and Reborn, 1.n.
25. E. de Selincourt, *The Poems of Edmund Spenser* (London: Oxford University Press, 1912), xxi.
26. Edmund Spenser, "A Letter of the Authors," in dc Selincourt, *Poems of Edmund Spenser*, 407.
27. Jonson, "An Expostulation with Inigo Jones," in *Ben Jonson*, vol. 8, ed. C. H. Percey and Evelyn Simpson (Oxford: Clarendon Press, 1947), 403.
28. Robert Bly, *Talking All Morning* (Ann Arbor: University of Michigan Press, 1980), 107–8.
29. Larry Rohter, "Is Slam in Danger of Going Soft?," *The New York Times*, June 3, 2009.

SIX   *Why Literature Is Always Contemporary*

1. Ben Jonson, "To the Memory of My Beloved, the Author, Mr. William Shakespeare, and What He Hath Left Us," in *The Norton Anthology of English Literature*, ed. M. H. Abrams (New York: Norton & Company, 2000), 1,414.
2. Virginia Woolf, "William Hazlitt," in *The Second Common Reader* (1932), ed. Andrew McNeillie (New York: Harcourt Brace, 1986), 180.
3. Francis Meres, *Palladis Tamar, or Wits Treasury* (1598), in *The Bedford Companion to Shakespeare: An Introduction with Documents*, ed. Russ MacDonald (Boston: Bedford Books, 2001), 32.

4. Susan Stewart, "Scandals of the Ballad," in *Crimes of Writing* (Durham, NC: Duke University Press, 1994), 121.

5. Ibid., 122.

6. Jonathan Yardley, "Getting History Right," *The Washington Post*, July 12, 2009.

7. Samuel Taylor Coleridge, *Lectures and Notes on Shakespeare and Other English Poets*, ed. T. Ashe (London: George Bell and Sons, 1897), letter of June 15, 1827.

8. T. S. Eliot, "Shakespeare and the Stoicism of Seneca," in *Selected Essays* (New York: Harcourt, Brace & World, 1932, 1950), 111.

9. It's worth noting "cheering up" is a phrase found at least twice in Shakespeare (2 *Henry IV* 4.4.13; *Macbeth* 4.1.127) and is not in itself a modern idiom.

10. T. S. Eliot, "Hamlet and His Problems," in *Selected Essays*, 121.

11. E. Talbot Donaldson, *Chaucer's Poetry: An Anthology for the Modern Reader* (New York: Ronald Press, 1958, second edition, 1975), 1,044–45.

12. Hugh Grady and Terence Hawkes, eds., *Presentist Shakespeares* (London: Routledge, 2007). Evelyn Gajowski, ed., *Presentism: Gender and Sexuality in Shakespeare* (Basingstoke, UK, and New York: Palgrave Macmillan, 2009).

13. Hugh Grady, "Shakespeare Studies, 2005: A Situated Overview." *Shakespeare: A Journal* 1 (2005), 112.

14. Ewan Fernie, "Shakespeare and the Prospect of Presentism," *Shakespeare Survey* 58 (2005), 8.

15. Roger Fry, letter to Helen Anrep, August 4, 1927. In *Letters of Roger Fry*, ed. Denis Sutton (London: Chatto and Windus, 1972), 2:603.

16. Virginia Woolf, "How Should One Read a Book?," *The Second Common Reader*, 265. Originally published in *The Yale Review*, 1926.

17. Ibid., 266.

18. Ibid., 268–69.

19. Ibid., 270.

20. William Wordsworth, "Essay Supplementary to the Preface" of the 1815 edition of *The Lyrical Ballads*, in Paul D. Sheats, ed., *Poetical Works of William Wordsworth* (Boston: Houghton Mifflin, 1982), 814.

21. Thomas de Quincey, *Murder Considered as One of the Fine Arts: Three Memorable Murders: The Spanish Nun* (New York and London: Putnam, 1889), 5.

22. Jorge Luis Borges, "Kafka and His Precursors" (1951). In *Other Inquisitions 1937–1952*, trans. Ruth L. C. Simms (New York: Simon & Schuster, 1964), 108.

23. Jorge Luis Borges, "Pierre Menard, the Author of *the Quixote*," trans. James E. Irby in *Labyrinths*, eds. Donald A. Yates and James E. Irby (New York: New Directions, 1964), 39.

24. Ibid., 41–42.

25. Ibid., 42.

26. Ibid., 43.

27. Ibid., 42.

28. André Maurois, preface to Borges, *Labyrinths*, xii.

29. Borges, "Pierre Menard," 44.

30. Virginia Woolf, "How It Strikes a Contemporary," in *The Common Reader, First Series* (1925), ed. Andrew McNeillie (New York: Harcourt Brace, 1984), 231. Originally published in the *The Times Literary Supplement*, April 5, 1923.

31. Ibid., 233.

32. Ibid., 240.

33. Ibid., 241.
34. Ralph Waldo Emerson, "Shakespeare; or, the Poet," "Representative Men" (1950). *Ralph Waldo Emerson, Essays and Lectures,* eds. Joel Porte, Harold Bloom, and Paul Kane (New York: Library of America, 1983), 718.
35. Oscar Wilde, preface to *The Picture of Dorian Gray,* in *The Complete Works of Oscar Wilde* (New York: Harper & Row, 1989), 17.
36. Richard Ellmann, *Oscar Wilde* (New York: Alfred A. Knopf, 1988), 319.
37. Wilde, "The Critic as Artist," in *The Complete Works,* 1,026; Ellmann, *Oscar Wilde,* 312.
38. I have elsewhere discussed this scene as evidence of Shakespeare's present and shifting modernity. See Marjorie Garber, *Shakespeare and Modern Culture* (New York: Pantheon, 2008), 272–73.

SEVEN *On Truth and Lie in a Literary Sense*

1. T. S. Eliot, "Burnt Norton," *Four Quartets* in *The Complete Poems and Plays, 1909–1950* (New York: Harcourt, Brace and Company, 1952), 118.
2. Errol Morris, "Play It Again, Sam (Re enactments, Part One)," as cited in Week in Review, Op-Extra, *The New York Times,* April 6, 2008.
3. Sir Philip Sidney, *Defence of Poesie,* ed. Dorothy M. Macardle (London: Macmillan, 1962), 33.
4. Ibid.
5. Ibid., 18. The truth value of "poesie" (by which Sidney means all imaginative writing, whether in verse or in prose) lay in its verisimilitude, not in its verifiability.
6. Motoko Rich and Brian Stelter, "As Another Memoir Is Faked, Trust Suffers," *The New York Times,* December 31, 2008, C1.
7. Gabriel Sherman, "The Greatest Love Story Ever Sold," *The New Republic,* December 25, 2008.
8. Harris Salomon, president of Atlantic Overseas Pictures, which was scheduled to produce a film based on the story *Flower at the Fence.* Quoted in Sherman, "Greatest Love Story." The objects of Salomon's attack included not only Lipstadt but also Kenneth Walzer, director of the Jewish Studies program at Michigan State University.
9. Motoko Rich, "Publisher Cancels Holocaust Memoir," *The New York Times,* December 28, 2008.
10. York House Press, "Publishers' Statement Regarding New Herman Rosenblat Book," January 2, 2009.
11. Jacques Derrida, *Demeure: Fiction and Testimony* (Stanford: Stanford University Press, 2000), 29.
12. Melissa Trujillo, "Writer Admits Holocaust Book Is Not True," Associated Press, February 29, 2008.
13. Daniel Mendelsohn, "Stolen Suffering," Week in Review, Op-Ed, *The New York Times,* March 9, 2008.
14. Mimi Read, "A Refugee from Gangland," *The New York Times,* February 28, 2008.
15. Anne Bernays, letter to the editor, *The New York Times,* March 7, 2008. Others wrote to the same effect, including Corinne Demas, the author of a memoir of her own, as well as books of fiction for children and adults. Demas, who teaches fiction writing at Wellesley College, noted that "readers will dismiss a work of fic-

tion when the character's story doesn't ring true, but call that same work a memoir, and they're gullible," then went on to suggest that "Given the current appetite for sensational memoirs, it's not surprising that young writers eager to be heard will eschew the tradition of fiction—where everything depends upon the power of the prose—for one where they can easily capture an audience through their titillating content." Corinne Demas, letter to the editor, *The New York Times,* March 7, 2008.

16. Perhaps the most dismaying response to the James Frey scandal was the feeling on the part of many readers that, true or false, his book had given them the feel-good, "redemptive" experience they'd hoped for when they bought his "novel—er, memoir." Mendelsohn, "Stolen Suffering."

17. Daniel Defoe, *Fortunes and Misfortunes of the Famous Moll Flanders* (London: printed for and sold by W. Chetwood, at Cato's-Head, in Russel-street, Covent-Garden, and T. Edling, at the Prince's-Arms, over-against-Exeter-Change in the Strand, 1722).

18. Jill Lepore also cites the example of *Robinson Crusoe* in an article on history and fiction, "Just the Facts, Ma'am," *The New Yorker,* March 24, 2008, 79–82.

19. Samuel Richardson, *Pamela; or, Virtue Rewarded,* eds. T. C. Duncan Eaves and Ben D. Kimpel (Boston: Houghton Mifflin, 1971), 7. Prefatory letter attributed to the Reverend William Webster. For Richardson as "editor," see 3, 4, 6, 9, 412.

20. James W. Pennebaker, *Writing to Heal: A Guided Journal for Recovering from Trauma and Emotional Upheaval* (Oakland, CA: New Harbinger Press, 2004), and *Opening Up: The Healing Power of Expressing Emotions* (New York: Guildford Press, 1997).

21. Josef Breuer and Sigmund Freud, *Studies on Hysteria,* vol. 2, *The Standard Edition of the Complete Psychological Works of Sigmund Freud,* trans. and ed. James Strachey (London: Hogarth Press and the Institute of Psycho-Analysis, 1955), 8.

22. Sigmund Freud to Wilhelm Fliess, September 21, 1897, in *The Complete Letters of Sigmund Freud to Wilhelm Fliess, 1887–1904,* trans. and ed. Jeffrey Moussaieff Masson (Cambridge, MA: Harvard University Press, 1985), 264.

23. Paul de Man, "Autobiography as De-Facement," in *The Rhetoric of Romanticism* (New York: Columbia Univresity Press, 1984), 69.

24. "Best-Seller List," *The New York Times Book Review,* March 9, 2008.

25. All published by William Morrow, an imprint of HarperCollins, a trade press.

26. Drake Bennett, "House of Cards." *Boston Globe,* April 6, 2008, C2.

27. Ibid.

28. Ibid.

29. Ibid.

30. Matthew Gilbert, "Blurring in 'Billionaires' Is No Accident," *The Boston Globe,* July 19, 2009, N1.

31. Janet Maslin, "Harvard Pals Grow Rich: Chronicling Facebook Without Face Time," *The New York Times,* July 20, 2009, C4.

32. Motoko Rich, "New CUNY Center to Focus on the Art of the Biography," *The New York Times,* February 23, 2008.

33. Ibid.

34. Ibid.

35. Ibid.

36. Plutarch, *Life of Alexander,* trans. John Dryden (New York: Modern Library, 2004), 3.

37. For example, the "Epistle Dedicatory" to Nicholas Harpsfield's biography of

Thomas More, in which he says that the biographer presents a "lively image" of a human being that compares favorably to the work of a sculptor or a painter, or Izaak Walton's biography of John Donne, where he will present *"the best plain Picture"* of Donne's life and, using the language of drawing, the most accurate that *"my artless Pensil, guided by the hand of truth, could presnt."* Judith H. Anderson, *Biographical Truth: The Representation of Historical Persons in Tudor-Stuart Writing* (New Haven: Yale University Press, 1984), 15.

38. David Hume, "Of the Study of History," in *Essays Moral, Political, Literary* (1777), ed. Eugene F. Miller (Indianapolis: Liberty Fund, 1987). Lepore, "Just the Facts, Ma'am," 81.

39. Anderson, *Biographical Truth*, 2.

40. Ibid., 69.

41. Ibid., 1.

42. Ibid., 69.

43. Julia Blackburn, *The Three of Us: A Family Story* (New York: Pantheon, 2008). "100 Notable Books of 2008," *The New York Times*, December 7, 2008.

44. Elizabeth McCracken, *An Exact Replica of a Figment of My Imagination* (New York: Little, Brown, 2008).

45. For example, chosen at random from a biography sitting on my desk at the moment, p. 340, "I intend no sacrilege . . ." *Variety* article by Azariah Rapoport, December 18, 1963, or—just below it—p. 340, "Unashamed vulgarity . . ." *Boston Globe*, February 1, 1964. Humphrey Burton, *Leonard Bernstein* (New York: Doubleday, 1994), 562.

46. Sometimes, however, the absence of footnotes leads to difficulty for the publisher or the author. See, for example, Laura Secor, "Muse of the Beltway Book," *The New York Times*, June 27, 2004; Timothy Noah, "How to Curb the Plagiarism Epidemic," *Slate*, January 28, 2002.

47. Virginia Woolf, "The New Biography," originally published in the *New York Herald Tribune*, October 30, 1927. Reprinted in Woolf, *Collected Essays* (London: Hogarth Press, 1967), 4, 230.

48. Ibid., 231.

49. Ibid., 229.

50. Ibid.

51. Ibid., 231.

52. Ibid.

53. Ibid., 234.

54. Virginia Woolf, *Flush: A Biography* (New York: Harcourt, Brace and Company, 1933), 82.

55. Ibid., 175.

56. Lytton Strachey, *Queen Victoria*, 1921 (New York: Harcourt, Brace & World), 125–26.

57. *Correspondence of Sarah Spencer Lady Lyttelton, 1787–1870*, ed. Mrs. Hugh Wyndham (New York: Charles Scribners' Sons, 1912), 303.

58. Ibid., 354.

59. Ibid., 402.

60. Virginia Woolf, "The Art of Biography," in Woolf, *Collected Essays* (London: Hogarth Press, 1967), 4, 223.

61. Lytton Strachey, *Eminent Victorians*, 1918 (London and New York: Penguin, 1986), 1–2.

62. Ibid.
63. Woolf, "The Art of Biography," 4, 223.
64. Ibid., 4, 224.
65. Ibid., 4, 226.
66. John Updike, *On Literary Biography* (Columbia: University of South Carolina Press, 1999), 36.
67. N. Janet Malcolm, *The Silent Woman: Sylvia Plath & Ted Hughes* (New York: Knopf, 1994), 154, 24.
68. David McCullough, *John Adams* (New York: Simon & Schuster, 2001), 175.
69. Janet Browne, *Charles Darwin: Voyaging* (New York: Knopf, 1995), 391.
70. Laura Hillenbrand, *Seabiscuit: An American Legend* (New York: Random House, 2001).
71. David Shipman, *Judy Garland: The Secret Life of an American Legend* (New York: Hyperion, 1993), 155.
72. Steven Bach, *Marlene Dietrich: Life and Legend* (New York: William Morrow, 1992), 229.
73. Thomas C. Reeves, *A Question of Character: A Life of John F. Kennedy* (New York: Free Press, 1991), 272.
74. Anne Sewell, *Black Beauty* (London and New York: Puffin, 2008), 2.
75. Hillenbrand, *Seabiscuit*, 41, 58.
76. Ibid., 107.
77. From Jonathan Miles, "All the Difference," a review of Brian Hall, *Fall of Frost* (New York: Viking, 2008), in *The New York Times Book Review*, May 11, 2008, 14.
78. René Wellek and Austin Warren, *Theory of Literature*, 3rd edition (New York: Harcourt, Brace & World, 1956), 80.
79. Ibid., 78.
80. Ibid., 76–77.
81. Ibid., 77. I have made a similar argument in an essay called "Bartlett's Familiar Shakespeare," in Marjorie Garber, *Profiling Shakespeare* (New York: Routledge, 2008), 278.
82. Friedrich Nietzsche, "On Truth and Lie in an Extra-Moral Sense," trans. Walter Kaufmann, *The Portable Nietzsche* (New York: Penguin, 1954), 46.
83. Ibid.
84. Victor Brombert, "Pass the Madeleines," *The New York Times*, November 9, 1997.
85. Michiko Kakutani, Books of the Times, *The New York Times*, August 9, 2002. Her remarks are prefatory to a discussion of a subsequent book by the same author, *The Art of Travel*.
86. Pierre Bayard, *How to Talk About Books You Haven't Read*, trans. Jeffrey Mehlmann (New York: Bloomsbury USA, 2007).
87. Laura Bohannan's "Shakespeare in the Bush," which first appeared in *Natural History* in 1966, and which Bayard cites from the Internet, is a classic account, and appears in the first essay in David Scott Kastan's edited collection of *Critical Essays on Shakespeare's Hamlet*, published in 1995. (London: G. K. Hall; Prentice Hall International).
88. Stuart Kelly, *The Book of Lost Books* (New York: Random House, 2005).

EIGHT   *Mixed Metaphors*

1. Hugh Blair, *Lectures on Rhetoric and Belles Lettres,* eds. Linda Ferreia-Buckley and S. Michael Halloran (Carbondale: Southern Illinois University Press, 2005), 7.
2. John McCain, presidential debate, October 15, 2008, Hofstra University; Brian Ross and Avni Patel, "Buried in Eloquence, Obama Contradictions About Pastor," March 19, 2008, at http://abcnews.go.com; George Will, "Obama's Eloquence Fatigue," *The Washington Post,* August 3, 2008; "Dem Race: Clinton Says Obama Offers Words, Not Actions," *USA Today,* February 20, 2008.
3. For one of many available analyses, see Kelly Nuxoll, "Palin's Sentences Lack Transparency and Accountability," *The Huffington Post,* October 3, 2008.
4. George Lakoff and Mark Johnson, *Metaphors We Live By* (Chicago and London: University of Chicago Press, 1980), 157.
5. Ibid., 3.
6. In *Metaphors We Live By,* all of the headings are capitalized—THEORIES ARE BUILDINGS, LOVE IS MAGIC—I find it somewhere between distracting sign-posting and baby talk and have therefore silently converted all of the capitalization to less distracting quotation marks.
7. Lakoff and Johnson, *Metaphors We Live By,* 245.
8. Ibid., 18.
9. George Lakoff, *Moral Politics: How Liberals and Conservatives Think* (Chicago and London: University of Chicago Press, 1996, 2002), 153.
10. Vladimir Propp, *Morphology of the Folktale,* 1928, trans. Laurence Scott (Philadelphia: American Folklore Society, 1958), and "Boris Eichenbaum," in *Norton Anthology of Theory and Criticism,* ed. Vincent B. Leitch (New York: Norton, 2001), 1,060.
11. Charles E. Reagan, *Paul Ricouer: His Life and His Work* (Chicago: University of Chicago Press, 1996), 54. Stephen J. Gould, *Dinosaur in a Haystack: Reflections in Natural History* (New York: Random House, 1996), 443–45.
12. *The Poetics of Aristotle,* trans. and commentary by Stephen Halliwell (Chapel Hill: University of North Carolina Press, 1987), 55.
13. Aristotle, *Rhetoric: The Complete Works of Aristotle,* vol. 2, ed. Jonathan Barnes (Princeton: Princeton University Press, 1984), 2,240.
14. Donald Davidson, "What Metaphors Mean," in Sheldon Sacks, ed., *On Metaphor* (Chicago and London: University of Chicago Press, 1978), 29.
15. Paul de Man, "The Epistemology of Metaphor," in Sacks, *On Metaphor,* 11, 15.
16. Ibid., 14, 19.
17. Ibid., 19–20.
18. Andrzej Warmniski, *Readings in Interpretation* (Minneapolis: University of Minnesota Press, 1987), lv.
19. Samuel Johnson, "Life of Cowley," in *Lives of the English Poets* (Dutton: New York, 1968), 11, 12.
20. John Dryden, "Discourse of the Original and Progress of Satire," in *Discourses on Satire and Epic Poetry* (1667) (Whitefish, MT: Kessinger Publishing, 2004), 6.
21. Johnson, "Life of Cowley," 12.
22. John Donne, "Obsequies to the Lord Harrington, Brother to the Lady Lucy, Countess of Bedford," in John Donne, *The Complete English Poems,* ed. Albert

James Smith (London: Penguin Classics, 1986), 35–40; Abraham Cowley, *The Mistress* (1656).

23. Johnson, "Life of Cowley," 12–13.
24. T. S. Eliot, "The Metaphysical Poets," *Selected Essays* (New York: Harcourt, Brace, and World, 1932, 1960), 247.
25. Ibid., 248.
26. Ibid., 250.
27. Ibid., 242–43.
28. T. S. Eliot, "Whispers of Immortality," in *Collected Poems 1909–1935* (New York: Harcourt Brace, 1952), 32–33.
29. George Lakoff and Mark Turner, *More Than Cool Reason: A Field Guide to Poetic Metaphor* (Chicago: University of Chicago Press, 1989), xi.
30. Ibid.
31. W. S. Merwin and J. Mouissaieff Masson, trans. *Sanskrit Love Poetry* (New York: Columbia University Press, 1977), reprinted as *The Peacock's Egg* (San Francisco: North Point Press, 1981); Lakoff and Turner, *More Than Cool Reason*, 60, 70, 89, 91, 101, 102; Jerome Rothenberg, ed., *Technicians of the Sacred: A Range of Poetries from Africa, America, Asia, Europe, and Oceania* (Berkeley and Los Angeles: University of California Press, 1985), 40.
32. Lakoff and Turner, *More Than Cool Reason*, 92.
33. Ibid., 90.
34. Ibid., xii.
35. Ibid., 267.
36. To underscore this idea and its importance, we might recall Nietzsche's image of the "mobile army" discussed in chapter 7, a passage that Lakoff and Turner dispute—characterizing it as the "It's All Metaphor Position."
    Paul de Man's reading of this passage is indicative, since he sees it as a reminder of "the figurality of all language":

    > What is being forgotten in this false literalism is precisely the rhetorical, symbolic quality of all language. The degradation of metaphor into literal meaning is not condemned because it is the forgetting of a truth but much rather because it forgets the un-truth, the lie that the metaphor was in the first place. It is a naïve belief in the proper meaning of the metaphor without awareness of the problematic nature of its factual, referential foundation.

    Paul de Man, *Allegories of Reading: Figural Language in Rousseau, Nietzsche, Rilke, and Proust* (New Haven: Yale University Press, 1979), 111.
37. John Keats, letter to Benjamin Bailey, November 22, 1817, in *Selected Letters of John Keats*, ed. Grant F. Scott (Cambridge, MA: Harvard University Press, 2002), 54.
38. De Man's comments on metaphor were written some years prior to the emergence of the cognitive theories popularized by Lakoff and his collaborators, but they nonetheless provide a thoughtful counterpoint, since De Man is concerned chiefly with stressing "the futility of trying to repress the rhetorical structure of texts in the name of uncritically preconceived text models such as transcendental teleologies or, at the other end of the spectrum, mere codes." Contrary to the primacy claimed by cognitive theorists for stories and parables as the building blocks of mind, De Man offers the possibility that "temporal articulations, such as narratives

or histories, are a correlative of rhetoric and not the reverse." Paul de Man, "The Epistemology of Metaphor," 16, 19, 27, 28.

39. Rosalie Colie, *Shakespeare's Living Art* (Princeton, NJ: Princeton University Press, 1974), 11.

40. Thus, King Lear's despairing "In such a night / To shut me out" harks back, in her view, to the lyrical conversation between Jessica and Lorenzo in act 5 of *The Merchant of Venice,* and both are indebted to the classical "O qualis nox?" Colie, 11–12.

41. Harold Bloom, *The Anxiety of Influence* (New York: Oxford University Press, 1973), 94.

42. Ibid., 70.

NINE   *The Impossibility of Closure*

1. *Oxford English Dictionary* draft additions, March 2007.

2. *The Indexer: The Journal of the Society of Indexers* 15:72/2 (1986). *OED, obelisk,* 2.b.

3. Erwin Panofsky, *"Et in Arcadia Ego:* Poussin and the Elegiac Tradition," in *Meaning and the Visual Arts* (Garden City, NY: Doubleday Anchor, 1955), 295–320.

4. Barbara Herrnstein Smith, *Poetic Closure: A Study of How Poems End* (Chicago: University of Chicago Press, 1968), 3–4.

5. Peter Brooks, *Reading for the Plot: Design and Intention in Narrative* (New York: Alfred A. Knopf, 1984), 101–2.

6. For example, Susan Winnett, "Coming Unstrung: Women, Men, Narrative, and Principles of Pleasure," *Publications of the Modern Language Association* 105, no. 3 (May 1990), 505–18, and Teresa de Lauretis, "Desire in Narrative," in *Alice Doesn't* (Bloomington: Indiana University Press, 1984), 103–57.

7. Roland Barthes, *Roland Barthes,* trans. Richard Howard (New York: Farrar, Straus and Giroux, 1977), 174–75.

8. Thomas De Quincey, *Confessions of an Opium Eater* (London: W. Scott, 1886), 92–93.

9. Joel J. Brattin, "Dickens and Serial Publication," PBS, 2003, www.pbs.org.

10. Frank Kermode, *The Sense of an Ending: Studies in the Theory of Fiction* (New York: Oxford University Press, 1966), 7.

11. Ibid., 23–24.

12. Edward. W. Said, *Beginnings: Intention and Method* (New York: Columbia University Press, 1975, 1985), 6.

13. Ibid., xii.

14. Ibid., 380.

15. Ibid., xiii.

16. Jacques Derrida, "Structure, Sign and Play in the Human Sciences," in *Writing and Difference,* trans. Alan Bass (Chicago: University of Chicago Press, 1978), 292–93.

17. William James, *Principles of Psychology* (New York: Henry Holt, 1890), 403–4.

18. Walter Benjamin, "The Work of Art in the Age of Mechanical Reproduction" (1936), in *Illuminations,* ed. Hannah Arendt (New York: Schocken Books, 1969), 241.

19. Sigmund Freud, *The Interpretation of Dreams,* 593.

20. Sigmund Freud, "Analysis Terminable and Interminable," vol. 23, *Standard Edition*, 219.
21. Ibid., 219–20.
22. Ibid., 236.
23. Ibid.
24. George Orwell, *Animal Farm* (1946) (New York: Harcourt Brace, 2003), 18.
25. Ibid., 48.
26. Ibid., 63.
27. Ibid., 75.
28. Ibid., 92.
29. E. B. White, *Charlotte's Web* (1952) (New York: HarperCollins, 1980), 80–81.
30. Orwell, *Animal Farm*, 97.
31. White, *Charlotte's Web*, 183.
32. Jorge Luis Borges, "The Library of Babel," in *Labyrinths: Selected Short Stories and Other Writings*, trans. James E. Irby (New York: New Directions, 1964), 51, 58.
33. André Maurois, preface to Borges, *Labyrinths*, xviii.
34. Borges, *Labyrinths*, 249.

Index

ABOUT THE AUTHOR

Marjorie Garber is the William R. Kenan, Jr., Professor of English and Visual and Environmental Studies at Harvard University, and chair of the Program in Dramatic Arts. She has served as director of the Humanities Center at Harvard, chair of the department of Visual and Environmental Studies, and director of the Carpenter Center for the Visual Arts. A member of the Board of Directors of the American Council of Learned Societies and a trustee of the English Institute, she is the former president of the Consortium of Humanities Centers and Institutes, and a continuing member of its board. She has published fifteen books and edited seven collections of essays on topics from Shakespeare to literary and cultural theory to the arts and intellectual life. *Shakespeare After All* received the 2005 Christian Gauss Award from the Phi Beta Kappa Society.

Newsweek magazine chose *Shakespeare After All* as one of the five best nonfiction books of 2004, and praised it as the "indispensable introduction to an indispensable writer . . . Garber's is the most exhilarating seminar room you'll ever enter."

Her previous book from Pantheon is *Shakespeare and Modern Culture.* She lives in Cambridge, Massachusetts.

A NOTE ON THE TYPE

The text of this book was set in Ehrhardt, a typeface based on the specimens of "Dutch" types found at the Ehrhardt foundry in Leipzig. The original design of the face was the work of Nicholas Kis, a Hungarian punch cutter known to have worked in Amsterdam from 1680 to 1689. The modern version of Ehrhardt was cut by the Monotype Corporation of London in 1937.

Composed by Creative Graphics,
Allentown, Pennsylvania

Printing and binding by Berryville Graphics,
Berryville, Virginia

Designed by M. Kristen Bearse